W9-BLH-724

Philosophy

Reference Sources in the Humanities Series
James Rettig, Series Editor

PHILOSOPHY

A GUIDE TO
THE REFERENCE
LITERATURE

Hans E. Bynagle
Library Director
Whitworth College

LIBRARIES UNLIMITED, INC.
Littleton, Colorado
1986

LIBRARIES UNLIMITED, INC.
P.O. Box 263
Littleton, Colorado 80160-0263

Library of Congress Cataloging-in-Publication Data

Bynagle, Hans E. (Hans Edward), 1946-
   Philosophy : a guide to the reference literature.

   (Reference sources in the humanities series)
   Includes indexes.
   1. Philosophy--Bibliography. I. Title. II. Series.
Z7125.B97 1986   [B72]   016.1   86-2942
ISBN 0-87287-464-8

CONTENTS

PREFACE

This guide to the reference literature of philosophy has been compiled and written with a diversity of users in mind. It is intended for professional philosophers and teachers of philosophy; for students of philosophy at both undergraduate and graduate levels; for librarians, as an aid in reference work and collection development; and, to a lesser extent, for the general reader or inquirer who may come to philosophy with little or no background. Not everyone, needless to say, will be equally well served by every part of this guide, and that is undoubtedly true also of the work as a whole. Nonetheless, I have tried to keep all of these potential audiences in mind throughout, and have tried in particular — though not always successfully, I'm sure — to gear the level of information provided in the annotations to the audience(s) most likely to use the work in question or to derive the greatest benefit from it. That same principle applies to the introduction, which is addressed primarily to those without a close acquaintance with the field of philosophy, though readers who are not in that position may also find in it some things that are helpful.

A number of published sources offer guidance to the reference literature of philosophy, but the present work, in addition to updating significantly the existing older guides, presents a unique combination of comprehensive coverage and extensive annotations. Of the various types of guides listed and described in chapter 2, most are quite dated, and remain only marginally useful except for certain special purposes. Only two, in fact, are recent enough to invite specific comparison with this guide. The latest, Tice and Slavens's *Research Guide to Philosophy* (see entry 10), is only secondarily concerned with reference literature; its section on reference works lists and annotates fewer than fifty sources. Also, its coverage effectively stops three years short of its 1983 publication date. The other work, Richard De George's *Philosopher's Guide* (entry 3), though excellent in its way, is now six years or more out of date. In some respects more comprehensive than this guide, it covers much else besides reference works and also devotes considerable space to research tools outside philosophy proper. On the other hand, for most of the items it lists it provides no more, or little more, than bare citations. Annotations are relatively few, and those it has are minimal, with few exceptions, and exclusively descriptive. The present guide, in contrast, provides very full annotations designed to facilitate preliminary assessments of a work's potential usefulness, to give guidance for its use, or both.

An additional difference between the present guide and De George's is their respective arrangements. This guide is organized primarily by types of reference sources, and thus offers a complement or alternative to the subject arrangement employed by De George. Each of these approaches has something to be said for it. The fact that the one chosen here forces the user to rely mainly on the index for subject access seems to me a virtue in this instance, since it can deal more effectively with the overlapping of subjects within philosophy which makes any subject arrangement somewhat perilous.

The cutoff date for this guide is August 1985, but it is possible that works (particularly foreign works) published close to this temporal limit did not come to my attention in time to be included. As to its scope, this guide is intended to encompass the entire realm of philosophy: works dealing with any period, movement, school, branch, major figure, or geographical-cultural subdivision, non-Western as well as Western, have been candidates for inclusion. This inclusiveness may falter, admittedly, with regard to certain borderline areas. However, important interdisciplinary or multi-disciplinary works (concerned, for instance, with the history of ideas, or with ethics from the perspectives of several disciplines) have also been included, provided they give substantial attention to distinctly philosophical subject matter and do so in ways not paralleled in works that are more exclusively philosophical.

This broad definition of scope is qualified by certain emphases. Because it is aimed primarily at English-speaking (and especially American) users, this guide emphasizes English-language works. It does include important works in European languages, however, particularly if they offer significant content or distinct perspectives not available in English-language sources. There is a further emphasis, in the case of non-English items, on works whose usefulness might occur at a low to medium level of specialization; foreign-language works reserved for very advanced or specialized scholarship are generally omitted. This also explains in large part the exclusion of works that require facility in non-Western languages, though my own lack of any such facility plays some part there as well.

A second emphasis is recency. In general, the older a work, the more stringently it has been judged as to its importance and usefulness. Availability has also been a positive consideration, to the extent that any English-language reference work in print at the time of compilation was almost automatically included. Two points need to be mentioned in this connection. One is that for any work first published before 1945, the chances for inclusion are substantially improved when there has been a subsequent reprinting. Not only does reprinting constitute some evidence (admittedly weak) of importance, but it usually implies a wider availability. The second point is that quality has not been a significant criterion for comparatively recent works. The annotations in many cases are critical and evaluative as well as descriptive, and I have taken the approach that it is more useful to include a work of dubious quality and signal its shortcomings than to omit it. The judgments expressed in the annotations, incidentally, unless explicitly attributed to others, are ultimately mine, whatever help I may have gotten from other sources, and I take responsibility for them.

It has been my goal to examine firsthand as many items as possible, and I was able to realize that goal for about 95 percent of the items eventually included. For the remainder, I have endeavored to corroborate bibliographic and descriptive information by using at least two independent sources, and to draw critical comments, if any, from authoritative sources.

In the introductory chapter, I discuss the factor of *perspective* as an important and sometimes problematic dimension of many reference works in philosophy. I also provide there an overview of five major philosophical traditions which it is helpful to be aware of in this connection. Some comment on the question of perspective as it relates to this guide seems apropos here. A certain element of perspective is undoubtedly entailed by the emphasis on English-language works. In the nature of things, more works in English share the perspective of what is known as the Anglo-American tradition than of any other. However, the perspectives of other traditions are well represented by works both in English and in other languages. In any case, I have not knowingly imposed any particular perspective beyond what I have indicated. But since one is often blind, if not to one's biases, then to their full effect, it is best to identify my own orientation. My philosophical training and, it seems, my intellectual propensities fall largely within the Anglo-American tradition, and within Analytic philosophy, though only in the widest sense distinguished in the introduction. Never completely satisfied with this tradition, I have made modest excursions into others, attracted variously by their mood, their motivations, or the sorts of questions they raised; but I confess I have often found their promise more enticing than their product. If any of this has colored my work on this guide, I am not aware of it.

Another matter that invites comment is the inclusion of two chapters not really concerned with reference works: one dealing with core journals, the other with professional organizations and research centers. Both of these seemed justified by two considerations. The first is their utility in situations in which other sources of information for these areas are not readily or conveniently available. Second, they provide guidance to two avenues by which professionals, students, and others can keep up with developments in the field of philosophy, or perhaps pursue their research or interests beyond the confines of whatever resources are already at hand. The criteria for inclusion in these chapters, which are necessarily selective, deserve some explanation. In the case of core journals, some weight has been given to a journal's potential reference value—that is, whether it includes, besides standard articles, such things as reviews of new books, lists of new publications, notes and news, etc. This is in addition to considerations of which journals are most widely read and most often cited. In the case of organizations, size of membership, where applicable, was one criterion, but as much or more weight was given to whether an organization's activities extend beyond holding meetings and conferences, particularly into publishing, direct support of research, or reference and referral service in its area of interest. Applying these imprecise criteria was not always easy, and I can hardly swear that my judgments have been entirely consistent in marginal cases: perhaps some journals and some organizations that are not included have as good a claim as some that are. I feel confident, however, that the most important journals and organizations are indeed represented. I hope these two chapters will prove useful complements to those focused on reference literature in the usual sense.

I want to acknowledge my indebtedness to a number of individuals and institutions: to Whitworth College, for support and encouragement, and for a congenial environment in which my professional responsibilities as library director are enriched by opportunities to use my academic training and further my interests in philosophy; to Doris Banks, my colleague in the Whitworth College Library, for unstinting generosity in giving me use of her computer, which proved an immense boon; to Forrest Baird, my colleague in philosophy at Whitworth, for helpful comments on the introduction; to my sister Ida, for assistance with transliteration and deciphering of Russian-language entries; to James Rettig, my editor, and to the publisher, for their patience as well as their good advice; to at least a dozen libraries in which I pursued my research, especially those at Gonzaga University, the University of Washington, and the University of Chicago, all of which have been most accommodating; and most of all, to my wife Jan and my children, Maria and Derek: too much of the time and attention I have given to this project was their sacrifice.

1

INTRODUCTION

Anyone familiar with reference literature in general will not be struck immediately by anything exceptional about reference works in philosophy. The types of works listed in this guide are, for the most part, also common in other disciplines: encyclopedias, dictionaries, bibliographies, and indexes to periodical literature, both with and without abstracts. One will also meet up with some types of works that may not exist in every field: concordances, lexicons, or directories, for example. Yet these are certainly not unique to philosophy, and on the whole there is little that distinguishes the field in terms of the sorts of reference tools one will need or encounter. So if there is any special difficulty in using the reference literature of philosophy—apart from the inevitable idiosyncrasies of individual works—the source of such difficulty will probably lie elsewhere.

The most likely sources of difficulty, in my estimation, are two closely related problems: *scope* and *perspective*. Effective and judicious use of many reference works in philosophy requires some understanding of their scope or perspective, or both. On the one hand, one may need to know how much of the philosophical universe, so to speak, a work takes into its purview (i.e., what its scope is). On the other hand, one may need to know from what position or point of view the work regards whatever parts of the philosophical universe are included (its perspective). Yet scope and perspective are often not immediately obvious on coming to a philosophical reference work. For example, chapter 3 of this guide lists seven different English-language works which are titled quite simply either *Dictionary of Philosophy* or *Philosophical Dictionary* (to say nothing of similar titles in other languages). All of these differ significantly with respect to either scope or perspective, or both, yet none bear any obvious signs of such differences. True, there are clues, which professionals and advanced students can usually pick up rather quickly. But the beginner may well feel confused or bewildered, or may be led unwittingly into a situation somewhat akin to exploring a country without knowing what country it is, or seeing part of a country and taking it as representative of the whole, or perhaps getting a description of a country from someone who doesn't live there and wouldn't care to.

The problems of scope I am thinking of are not primarily those having to do with the scope of one or another branch of philosophy, though there are indeed problems in that regard. What one philosopher includes in the branch of philosophy called "ethics" may not coincide with what another subsumes under that label, and the same is true for other branches, say metaphysics or social philosophy or philosophy of history. A set of questions which one thinker considers an important part of a field, another will exclude for any of a variety of reasons: as not properly philosophical, as meaningless, as trivial, or perhaps simply as outside his or her own predilections or expertise. Such divergencies may be more pronounced in the non-reference literature of philosophy — of actual philosophical argumentation, especially — but they can assert themselves even in such seemingly non-polemical works as bibliographies, not to mention philosophical dictionaries and encyclopedias.

Still, to reiterate, the problems of scope to which I wish to call attention are not primarily those just noted, but another sort, though these are sometimes at the root of the former. I refer to problems of scope occasioned by the diversity of philosophical schools, movements, and traditions which characterizes the world of philosophy. These schools, movements, and traditions are differentiated not simply by their answers to philosophical questions, but by particular conceptions of what philosophical problems are, or which are the more important problems, and of how such problems may be resolved or, if not resolved, fruitfully debated and clarified. It is in relation to such differences that problems both of scope and of perspective tend to become acute. A work which presents itself as concerned with philosophy or some branch of philosophy, without any explicit qualification, may limit its scope to the concerns, doctrines, thinkers, or writings of only one movement, or perhaps a few. On the other hand, even if it encompasses several different schools, movements, or traditions, it may and almost inevitably will treat them from the perspective of a particular one. Such a perspective may be deliberate or not; it may be overt or subtle; and it may assert itself in a variety of ways: in explicit critiques of opposing positions, in selection or emphasis, in failures of accuracy or fairness in presentation of competing viewpoints, even in the kind of background knowledge that is presupposed.

It would be pointless to decry in general either restrictions of scope or the manifestations of perspectives. Any author must be granted the right to limit the range of his or her concerns. The effects of perspective are to some extent inevitable, and even where they are not, they may have a legitimate function and positive value. (It is not a fault of an astronomy text to describe the configuration of the heavens from the perspective of earth, that usually being the perspective of interest to its readers.) What one might decry is a tendency of philosophical works, including reference works, not to "wear on their sleeves" any clear indications of either perspective or scope. This leaves the reader or the user to figure it out, or suffer the consequences. There is certainly a case to be made for more "truth in labeling." However, even if philosophical reference works were to become uniformly explicit in this regard, problems would not vanish. To be aware of scope or perspective is one thing, to attach some meaningful content to that awareness is another, and it is still another, no doubt, to act appropriately and effectively on that awareness.

To appreciate adequately the dynamics of scope and perspective in philosophy and its reference literature, and to be somewhat equipped against their hazards, it is helpful, even essential, to have at least a basic orientation to the philosophical landscape. For the uninitiated, this can pose some difficulty. Even to get a sense of the major philosophical traditions, to say nothing of countless lesser schools and movements both within and outside the major traditions, is not altogether easy. It is not difficult to familiarize oneself with the labels that are conventionally attached to them, but this is only minimally useful. One needs to be able to place these labels, metaphorically speaking, on at least a rough philosophical map, a map which represents something of the general character of the major philosophical "regions" and how they relate to one another. It is hard, however, to provide much help in this regard within a brief compass—the compass, for instance, of this introduction. The major philosophical traditions are notoriously difficult to characterize in a nutshell, at least in a way that is meaningful apart from a more detailed antecedent acquaintance with them. Generalizations, especially, are perilous and apt to be misleading.

Fortunately, one can begin to sketch a philosophical map, albeit a *very* rough one, in terms that are largely geographical (a circumstance which makes the metaphor of a "map" somewhat more than just a metaphor). The major divisions of philosophy, while they do not by any means fall neatly along geographical boundaries, do accord to a significant extent with geographical regions, at least in terms of their dominance. So an elementary geographical schema can make a somewhat useful starting point, provided one keeps in mind from the outset that as a philosophical map it is very rudimentary indeed.

The most basic division to begin with is that between Western and non-Western philosophy. With regard to non-Western, one may think particularly of eastern and southern Asia, highlighting perhaps China and India, which have the most substantial philosophical traditions. (The term "Oriental," incidentally, is sometimes used to designate philosophies of far eastern Asia only, and sometimes to encompass those of southern Asia, mainly India, as well. The latter use may be unwise, since "Oriental" ordinarily brings to mind China and Japan and their near neighbors.) Non-Western also takes in parts of western Asia (the Middle East), and we may include other parts of the world not usually considered part of "the West" (a term I take to refer chiefly to Europe and the Americas). A case in point would be Africa, insofar as we are thinking of native philosophies, though rather little is known of these.

The line between Western and non-Western philosophy is one that runs through most of the history of philosophy. The other lines we need to draw, all of them demarcating major areas within Western philosophy, refer to modern developments, dating from the present century or the late nineteenth century. The first region we can demarcate here is Marxist philosophy, which dominates the Soviet Union and the countries of Eastern Europe. This constitutes a large and quite active philosophical domain, but one with which few English-speaking philosophers have extensive contact.

The next line it is useful to draw serves to divide the philosophical tradition which dominates most of the European continent, known accordingly as Continental philosophy, from the dominant philosophical tradition of England, the United States, and certain countries subject to strong British or American influence, such as Canada and Australia, known as Anglo-American philosophy. This line is perhaps less "clean" even than the others, but it does mark a real and well-recognized division.

A final realm of philosophical thought which we need to identify here disturbs the tidiness of our geographical scheme, because it overlaps the two regions we have already labeled Continental and Anglo-American. We can label it Neo-Scholasticism. (The name derives from Scholasticism, referring to various philosophical "schools" of the medieval period, from which this tradition takes its primary inspiration.) It is the reigning but by no means exclusive philosophical orientation among Catholic thinkers, and it has a sufficiently large following both in Europe and in North America to be included among the major extant traditions of Western philosophy.

To sum up, we have identified five very broad philosophical domains: Non-Western, Marxist, Continental, Anglo-American, and Neo-Scholastic. It must be emphasized again that the map we have sketched is a very crude one — cruder, possibly, than even the crudest early maps of the New World. We shall need to introduce at least some of the more important refinements, as well as to characterize these philosophical domains in more substantive terms. We can begin by saying a bit more about non-Western philosophy.

This is a very large area, and one of tremendous diversity. Just a few of the major movements can be listed here: Buddhism; Jainism; Hindu philosophies (at least six distinct systems more or less loosely allied to Hindu religion, including Vedanta, Mimamsa, Yoga, and Vaisesika); Confucianism and Neo-Confucianism; Taoism; the Chinese Yin-Yang School; and Islamic philosophy. These are some of the historically important traditions. Not all of them are active today, and those that are may be caught up in considerable interaction with Western philosophy. Up until the modern period, however, these non-Western philosophies developed in total or near-total isolation from Western philosophy, with one major exception. This exception is Islamic philosophy, which developed under the strong influence of Western, particularly Greek, philosophy, and in fact played a crucial role in the transmission of Greek thought and Greek philosophical texts to medieval Christendom. Thus it straddled from its earliest beginning what was otherwise a fairly clear line between Western and non-Western philosophy.

That this line is much less clear now has already been suggested. In fact, the term non-Western is hardly meaningful any more except with reference to the traditions. Western philosophies have penetrated deeply into the non-Western world, not merely as subjects of study but as adopted positions and modes of philosophizing. Marxism, if not the example likely to come to mind first, may be the most significant. But Continental, Anglo-American, and even Neo-Scholastic philosophies have also drawn much interest and considerable followings in parts of the non-Western world. There is a significant current in the opposite direction, that is, from the non-Western to the Western world, as well. Whether this is *equally* significant is doubtful. There is indeed widespread interest in non-Western thought (often in association with religious interests or motives), but very few philosophers in the West have come to "do philosophy" in a non-Western mode.

The close association between philosophy and religion in much of non-Western thought requires some comment. Most of the philosophical traditions mentioned above are also religious traditions, and probably better known as such. This association of philosophy with religion is so prevalent and in many instances so close that it is often assumed to be universal in the non-Western world. To combat this notion, some scholars have been at pains to emphasize philosophical elements which are largely independent of direct religious concern, notably in the areas of epistemology (or theory of knowledge), logic, philosophy of language, and social philosophy, and to bring to the fore historical movements which were non- or anti-religious, for example the materialistic Carvaka school which sprang up in India about the seventh century A.D. When all is said and done, however, there remains a vast area in which religion and philosophy are not only closely intertwined but where it is virtually impossible to separate them. In addition to the many theoretical questions this raises—what constitutes religion and what constitutes philosophy?—it poses, for a guide such as this, the practical problem of which works to include as pertaining to non-Western philosophy, and which to exclude as being chiefly concerned with religion. The solution I have adopted is a pragmatic one, and largely forced by my comparative ignorance of non-Western thought. If a work presents itself as dealing with non-Western philosophy, it has been considered for inclusion; if it presents itself as concerned with religion, it has generally been left out. The user of this guide is urged to keep in mind, however, that reference works which cover non-Western religion, or some aspect thereof, may contain a great deal that is relevant for philosophy. The problem discussed here is not unique to non-Western philosophy. In a broad sense, it is ubiquitous, while it arises in a more focused way in connection with, for instance, Neo-Scholasticism and other avowedly Christian philosophies. Nevertheless, the problem tends to be less acute in Western thought, partly because a distinction between philosophy and theology has been explicitly addressed, debated, and often embodied in practice as a vocational division of labor, whereas in traditional non-Western thought such a distinction is seldom even contemplated.

Turning to Western philosophies, let us take up Marxist philosophy first. Like other aspects of Marxism, Marxist philosophy derives its impetus and its fundamental ideas from the writings of Karl Marx and his associate, Friedrich Engels, despite the fact (ironically) that Marx himself considered philosophy an activity proper only to the precommunist order. While this is one notion of Marx that clearly has *not* been taken up in Marxist philosophy, there is some continuity between this idea and the prevalent hostility in Marxist philosophy toward other philosophical positions, which are regarded as not simply wrong but as expressions of class interests and instruments of political struggle. Marxist philosophy is not easily summarized, but its two central tenets can be readily designated by their conventional labels: dialectical materialism and historical materialism. The former asserts the primacy of matter as the fundamental reality and attempts to state general principles concerning the organization and development of matter. The latter is a theory about history and attempts to state general principles concerning the development of human thought and society in the historical process. Marx's well-known thesis concerning the primacy of economic factors in history is one ingredient of historical materialism. In most communist countries, Marx's thought has been wedded to that of Lenin and is accordingly known as Marxism-Leninism. The crude map with which we began correctly indicates the dominance of Marxist philosophy in the Iron Curtain countries, but it is really far more widely dispersed than that. We have already noted its presence in the non-Western world, and we need only think of China to recognize the rather formidable "refinement" this requires in our philosophical map. Nor is Marxist philosophy confined to the communist world. Marxist philosophers can be found in many countries, often combining their Marxism with other philosophical orientations. The best-known instance of this may be Jean-Paul Sartre's attempt to wed a somewhat unorthodox Marxism to French Existentialism. Acquaintance with Marxism in the non-communist West, especially in the United States, tends to be more by way of exponents working outside than those working inside the communist sphere.

The terms "Continental" and "Anglo-American" have been in currency for many years to distinguish the main twentieth-century philosophical traditions of the non-communist West, yet they are something less than official names for well-defined movements. Philosophical dictionaries seldom include them. The standard *Encyclopedia of Philosophy* (entry 19), interestingly, does not list either term in its index, though in the introduction to that work the editor gives notice of his personal commitments to what he calls the "Anglo-Saxon" tradition (a variation on "Anglo-American" encountered occasionally). Perhaps the terms are too indeterminate to be accorded the formal recognition of a dictionary or encyclopedia entry, yet they are widely used to designate recognizably distinct philosophical orientations. As noted previously, the traditions they designate are comparatively recent developments, although they do have roots in an older bifurcation between Continental Rationalism and British Empiricism dating back to the seventeenth century.

"Continental philosophy" has frequently been used as practically synonymous with two related movements, Phenomenology and Existentialism. This is less common now than formerly, and in any case the term can be used in a wider sense to encompass other movements that have flourished on the European continent. These include, for instance, an older strain somewhat inadequately labeled Idealism, which has its roots especially in the late eighteenth- and early nineteenth-century philosophies of Immanuel Kant and G. W. F. Hegel, and also a more recent movement which goes by the name of Structuralism. I will not attempt to describe even briefly these other movements, and can offer only the most rudimentary characterizations of Phenomenology, which remains central, and Existentialism, which, while possibly on the wane, has enjoyed exceptional prominence, even popularity, for a philosophical movement, in part because of its literary expressions by writers such as Sartre, Camus, and Marcel.

Phenomenology is primarily a philosophical method, one which focuses on careful inspection and description of phenomena or appearances, defined as any object of conscious experience, i.e., that which we are conscious *of*. The inspection and description are supposed to be effected without any presuppositions, and that includes any presuppositions as to whether or not such objects of consciousness are "real" or correspond to something "external," or as to what their causes or consequences may be. It is believed that by this method the essential structures of experience and its objects can be uncovered. The sorts of experiences and phenomena which Phenomenologists have sought to describe are highly varied, including, for instance, time consciousness, mathematics and logic, perception, experience of the social world, and moral, aesthetic, and religious experience.

To go beyond this admittedly thin characterization seems impossible without delving into specific examples of phenomenological description, and also without running into major divergencies as to the nature of the phenomenological enterprise and what it can accomplish. Even so far as it goes, this characterization applies less clearly to certain later figures ordinarily counted as part of the phenomenological movement, such as the Frenchman Merleau-Ponty, than it does to the uncontested father of Phenomenology, Edmund Husserl, and those who have stayed rather close to his thought.

Existentialism, unlike Phenomenology, is not primarily a philosophical method. Neither is it exactly a set of doctrines (at least not any *one* set) but more an outlook or attitude supported by diverse doctrines centered about certain common themes. These themes include the human condition, or the relation of the individual to the world; the human response to that condition (described often in strongly affective and preponderantly negative terms such as "despair," "dread," "anxiety," "guilt," "bad faith," "nausea"); being, especially the difference between the being of persons (which is "existence") and the being of other kinds of things; human freedom; the significance (and unavoidability) of choice and decision in the absence of certainty; and the concreteness and subjectivity of life as lived, as opposed to abstractions and false objectifications.

Existentialism is often thought to be antireligious (and is, in some of its versions) but there has in fact been a strong current of Christian Existentialism, beginning with the figure often credited with originating Existentialism, the nineteenth-century Danish philosopher Kierkegaard. As for Existentialism's relationship to Phenomenology, this is a matter of some controversy, but at least one can say that many of the more recent existentialist thinkers, Sartre among them, have employed phenomenological methods to arrive at or support their specific variations on existential themes.

Continental philosophy has not been without a following in the Anglo-American sector, particularly in the United States. Though decidedly a minority outlook, it does claim the loyalty of some American philosophers, actually dominates philosophy departments in a few American universities, and in any case is widely studied.

Anglo-American philosophy is sometimes equated with what is called Analytic or Analytical philosophy. It is also used in a broader sense to encompass other movements that have flourished chiefly on British and American soil, for instance Pragmatism, Naturalism, and Process Philosophy. There is much to be said for the wider meaning, which avoids the suggestion that philosophy in England and America is more monolithic than it really is. The equation of Anglo-American with Analytic is also unfortunate from another point of view, in that Analytic philosophy has become the dominant mode of philosophizing in some other areas as well, notably the Scandinavian countries, to say nothing of the inroads it has made in areas where other approaches still dominate the field (e.g., in West Germany). However, given all those qualifications, there is no question that Analytic philosophy is the most important philosophical current within the Anglo-American sphere, and also the one most often contrasted with (and actively opposed to) the Continental movements mentioned above.

What Analytic philosophy is is not so easy to say. I believe it is possible to distinguish at least three variants, though they probably represent points on a spectrum rather than distinct alternatives. In the widest sense and also the loosest, Analytic philosophy is hardly more than a philosophical style, one which takes extreme care with the meanings of words (sometimes with precise definitions of terms and consistency in their use, sometimes with the nuances of ordinary language), which tends to present arguments in meticulous step-by-step fashion (often endeavoring to leave nothing implicit), and which pays close, sometimes minute attention to logical relations (often using logical symbolism or specialized logical terminology to render such relations transparent). In a narrower sense, "Analytic philosophy" designates a philosophical outlook which holds that the primary task or even (in its more extreme version) the only proper task of philosophy — the primary or proper method for attacking philosophical problems — is analysis of one sort or another: of meanings, of concepts, of logical relations, or of all of these. We can call this the methodological version. Finally, one may occasionally encounter the term "Analytic philosophy" in contexts where it is reserved for one or more specific doctrines regarding the outcome of correct philosophical analysis. While the Analytic tradition (in either of the two wider senses) owes a great deal to certain specific doctrinal versions — and to major figures who propounded them, such as Bertrand Russell, G. E. Moore, and Ludwig Wittgenstein — it would be false to say that Analytic philosophy is the dominant orientation among British and American philosophers if one has in mind this narrower meaning. In fact, it is not clear that this is true under any but the widest meaning distinguished above.

Common to those who subscribe to the Analytic approach, whether in the broadest sense or a narrower one, is the conviction that to some significant degree, philosophical problems, puzzles, and errors are rooted in language, and can be solved or avoided, as the case may be, by a sound understanding of language and careful attention to its workings. This conviction has focused much attention on language and on its close relative, logic, as objects of study for their own sake. (The relationship between language and logic is itself a question subjected to considerable inquiry and debate.) Detractors are apt to point to the concern (they might say obsession) with language and logic as one aspect of the trivialization of philosophy with which they charge the Analytic movement. Many who are generally loyal or sympathetic to Analytic philosophy may agree that it has tended to draw philosophy away from "deep" questions. In any case, the last two decades have seen, on the one hand, increased self-searching as to the limitations of the Analytic approach, and on the other, more efforts to apply it to such deeper questions — about the meaning of life, for instance, or the nature of the moral life — in a way that takes them seriously. There has also been more extensive application to "real-life" moral and social issues.

We turn, finally, to Neo-Scholasticism. Like the labels connected with other philosophical traditions we have discussed, the term "Neo-Scholasticism" has a somewhat variable denotation. Not uncommonly, it is used interchangeably with the term "Neo-Thomism," a term derived from the name of St. Thomas Aquinas, a medieval philosopher whose thought was revived in spirit and to a considerable extent in substance by Catholic thinkers in the midnineteenth-century, and given quasi-official status in Catholicism by a papal encyclical in 1879. Insofar as Neo-Thomism (some of its adherents prefer simply Thomism) is the major force within Neo-Scholasticism, the equation is not too far wrong. But in a stricter sense, Neo-Scholastic philosophy harkens back to medieval Christian philosophy more generally, and may draw on and seek to develop the views of other philosophers besides St. Thomas, such as Bonaventure, Duns Scotus, and William of Ockham. Like its medieval ancestor, Neo-Scholasticism owes a great deal to Aristotle (St. Thomas is often credited with achieving a great synthesis of Aristotelian philosophy and Christian theology) and to other classical philosophers. However, it also interacts with contemporary currents in both the Anglo-American and Continental spheres, depending to some extent, as one might expect, on the setting in which it is pursued.

This concludes our brief overview of the main philosophical traditions that characterize the present and recent philosophical landscapes. Dozens, even hundreds of lesser movements within, without, and overlapping the boundaries of these traditions have not been mentioned, let alone described. Nor have I said anything, beyond a bare mention here or there, about historical schools and movements that may have been among the major philosophical alternatives in their time, but have since died out, been absorbed, or been reduced to minor outposts on the philosophical landscape. However, most problems of scope and perspective that crop up in connection with modern reference sources (and many other types of philosophical literature, such as histories, introductory texts, journals, etc.) can be characterized and clarified with reference to the five traditions discussed above. Even how (or whether) a given work deals with philosophies of the past often depends on its perspective in relation to one of the extant traditions.

2

GENERAL BIBLIOGRAPHIC AND RESEARCH GUIDES

1. Bertman, Martin A. **Research Guide in Philosophy.** Morristown, N.J.: General Learning Press, 1974. 252p.

Aimed at the undergraduate student, Bertman's guide is unique in the variety of practical guidance it offers for research and writing (e.g., "On Giving One's Opinion"; "What Is a Philosophical Problem?"; "Taking Notes"; "Marking Up Books: A Shorthand System"), on the mechanics of documentation, and on the use of a college library. For guidance to the philosophical literature, it provides an annotated list of important journals and a chapter of bibliographical lists characterized as "somewhat annotated" — meaning, it turns out, that they are coded with symbols to indicate such evaluations as "excellent," "a classic work," "of questionable worth," "provides especially good bibliography," or "valuable introduction to the topic." Among the lists included are "Reference Works," "Fields of Philosophy," "History of Philosophy," and "Individual Philosophers." A sketch of the history of philosophy and a glossary of philosophical terms round out the offerings.

When it comes to specifics, Bertman's work is in many instances dated; but for purposes of general guidance, it still presents useful material.

2. Borchardt, Dietrich Hans. **How to Find Out in Philosophy and Psychology.** Oxford: Pergamon Press, 1968. 97p.

Though dated, Borchardt's guide remains worthwhile for its chatty but informative historical surveys of the major types of comprehensive reference sources: dictionaries and encyclopedias, general retrospective bibliographies and handbooks, current bibliographies and reviewing journals, and national bibliographies. It is these surveys, with their strong international orientation, rather than any extensive coverage of more specialized works in narrower subdivisions of the field, that constitute the chief focus of Borchardt's work and that are also its special strength. In addition, they belie to a large extent the book's self-description (repeated in several works which cite it, e.g., Tice and Slavens, entry 10), as being intended more for the layperson and the undergraduate than for the advanced student. Laypersons and undergraduates would not be likely to have much interest in an early twentieth-century German dictionary, or wish to consult the *Repertorium der Nederlandse wijsbegeerte!* Even the historical background on many reference works, fascinating as it may be, is more likely to interest the specialist than the beginner.

The combining of philosophy and psychology in a single reference work is supported with the observation that "many standard reference works have done so and there are compelling reasons for this treatment, quite apart from the very sound one that it is impossible to disentangle their common history until the second half of the nineteenth century" (introduction). In actuality, though, the two fields are usually treated separately, i.e., successively, within each chapter or section of a chapter devoted to a particular type of source. Joint treatment occurs only in discussion of older works in which the combination was still to be found. Such works are few, though more often found in this historically oriented guide than in most others.

3. De George, Richard T. **The Philosopher's Guide to Sources, Research Tools, Professional Life, and Related Fields.** Lawrence, Kans.: Regents Press of Kansas, 1980. 261p.

This work succeeds De George's earlier *Guide to Philosophical Bibliography and Research* (1971). Aimed particularly at the professional philosopher and the advanced student, it is a solid, reputable, and broadly useful work. Roughly half the volume is a comprehensive bibliography of research resources in philosophy, including bibliographies, indexes, dictionaries and encyclopedias, standard histories and biographies, collected works, and major series and journals. The first half is divided into three sections: (1) "General"; (2) "History of Philosophy," with chapters for the major periods that include subsections for individual philosophers; and (3) "Systematic Philosophy," with chapters (amply subdivided) for branches, selected schools and movements, and nations and regions. Liberal use is made of cross-references. The second part groups a bibliography of philosophical serials with a chapter covering aids to writing and publishing and a directory of philosophical organizations, research centers, institutes, and other institutions and facilitators of professional life. The final third of the volume comprises divisions devoted to research tools outside philosophy proper, both general and in related fields, which may be of use in philosophical studies. Related fields include most of the standard academic disciplines, though religion is distinguished by a chapter of its own.

While comprehensive, *The Philosopher's Guide* is only selectively annotated; the annotations it provides are minimal, with few exceptions, and exclusively descriptive.

4. Higgins, Charles L. **The Bibliography of Philosophy: A Descriptive Account.** Ann Arbor, Mich.: Campus Publishers, 1965. 29p. (University of Michigan Department of Library Science Studies, 7).

This work is a slim, very selective guide to major bibliographic sources in philosophy plus some useful general sources. Unquestionably dated (it antedates the two most significant sources in English, the *Philosopher's Index* (entry 101) and the *Encyclopedia of Philosophy* (entry 19), it may still be useful on occasion for its very full descriptions of such older standards as Rand's *Bibliography of Philosophy, Psychology and Cognate Subjects* (entry 115), Varet's *Manuel de bibliographie philosophique* (entry 119), and the *Répertoire bibliographique* (entry 107).

5. Jordak, Francis Elliott. **A Bibliographical Survey for a Foundation in Philosophy.** Washington, D.C.: University Press of America, 1978. 435p.

Intended to serve the particular needs of the philosophy program in the two-year colleges of the Wisconsin Center System (some of its subject divisions are actually course titles), this guide also claims a broader usefulness "for small and medium sized libraries . . . both public and private" and "for the people who use these libraries in order to obtain a firm foundation in philosophy" (introduction). Such usefulness is undermined, however, by uneven selection and by lack of consistent focus as to the intended audience. An astonishing instance is the omission of the *Philosopher's Index* (entry 101) from the lists of reference works, while more esoteric foreign-language publications such as the *Répertoire bibliographique* (entry 107) and Totok's *Handbuch der Geschichte der Philosophie* (entry 117) are included. Some other inclusions, too, are hardly suitable for a "foundation" in philosophy. Add to these objections some poorly categorized items, and one is forced to conclude that this cannot be commended as a reliable guide. One feature that may be uniquely useful, however, is its use of lengthy quotations from standard sources such as *Choice,* Sheehy's *Guide to Reference Works,* and Katz's *Magazines for Libraries*; these generally constitute the sole content of its annotations.

6. Koren, Henry J. **Research in Philosophy: A Bibliographical Introduction to Philosophy and a Few Suggestions for Dissertations.** Pittsburgh, Penn.: Duquesne University Press, 1966. 203p.

"The purpose of this little work is to introduce graduate students in philosophy to the bibliographical sources and tools of philosophy" (foreword). Obsolescence, unfortunately, has made too many inroads for it still to be recommended for this function, but it may yet serve some use for graduate students and others in supplementing more recent guides. Among its less readily duplicated and in some cases unique material are coverage of some older and more out-of-the way bibliographies, including historical and national bibliographies and works on individual philosophers; a five-page explanation of the *Répertoire bibliographique de la philosophie* (entry 107), including its history, arrangement, and scope; general information about books and their classification (chapter 1); and "A few suggestions about dissertations" (chapter 6), including choosing a topic, research procedures, tips on writing, etc. More generally, it emphasizes Thomistic and Continental philosophy more than most other guides.

7. Matczak, Sebastian A. **Philosophy: Its Nature, Methods and Basic Sources.** New York: Learned Publications; Louvain: Editions Nauwelaerts; Paris: Beatrice-Nauwelaerts, 1975. 280p. (Philosophical Questions Series, 4).

The goal set by Matczak for this work is "to meet the need of a concise and yet all-embracing work of the essential questions and sources in philosophy" (preface). Part 1, "The Nature of Philosophy," is a short treatise, liberally augmented with bibliographic references, on "the notion of philosophy and its methods . . . as distinguished from the methods of other sciences" (introduction). Some attempt is made to represent differing perspectives, though Matczak's own Christian and Catholic orientation can be discerned. Part 2, "Basic Bibliographical Sources," contains chapters ranging from "General Bibliographies" (not limited to philosophy) to "Individual Philosophers," though the latter is somewhat mistitled, since many items deal with historical periods and philosophical systems or schools. Part 3, "Basic Descriptive Sources," covers encyclopedias, dictionaries, and biographical sources. Part 4 is devoted to periodicals, part 5 to philosophical institutions. The latter includes a chapter on libraries.

As a guide to sources, Matczak competes with De George (entry 3) in terms of generality and comprehensiveness. It lists an even larger and more varied selection of philosophical and general resources. On the other hand, it is older, somewhat less accurate and reliable, and arguably more partisan in its orientation. Annotations are minimal in both, but even more so in Matczak.

8. Matczak, Sebastian A. **Research and Composition in Philosophy.** 2d ed. Louvain: Editions Nauwelaerts, 1971. 88p. (Philosophical Questions Series, 2).

Much of this work could serve as a general introduction to the processes and techniques, including the mechanics, of scholarly research and writing. Its advantage for the philosophy student is its employment of philosophical examples. On the other hand, it is outdated with regard to such matters as footnote and bibliography forms, so that it should at least be used in conjunction with a general guide such as Turabian's *A Manual for Writers of Term Papers, Theses, and Dissertations* or the *MLA Handbook.* Chapter 6, "Bibliographical Sources of Philosophy," is a basic list of bibliographies, encyclopedias, dictionaries, biographical sources, histories, and periodicals, covering materials in the major European languages as well as English. This section, too, is dated, but can still be useful where a more recent source of at least equal comprehensiveness is not available.

The second edition differs very little from the first, published in 1968.

9. **Reader's Guide to Books on Philosophy.** 2d ed. Library Association, County Libraries Group, 1974. 56p.

This is one of a series of subject guides for general readers issued by the County (i.e., Public) Libraries section of Britain's Library Association. The first edition (1957), according to Borchardt (entry 2), contained about 550 references, was systematically arranged, annotated, and dealt "almost exclusively with British and (to a lesser degree) American philosophers after 1900" (p. 21). (No examination copy or additional information could be obtained to compare the second edition.)

10. Tice, Terrence N., and Thomas P. Slavens. **Research Guide to Philosophy.** Chicago: American Library Association, 1983. 608p. (Sources of Information in the Humanities, No. 3).

While the title may suggest similarity to works by De George (entry 3), Borchardt (entry 2), or Koren (entry 6), this guide is unique among those listed in this chapter in being primarily a systematic-*cum*-bibliographical survey of the field. It does include a well-annotated list of reference works (compiled by Slavens), but this is highly selective, including just under fifty works. It is also less up-to-date than the 1983 copyright date would lead one to expect.

The 500-page survey portion, the work of Tice (a member of the University of Michigan philosophy faculty), comprises thirteen chapters on the history of philosophy, including the leading modern schools and movements (Marxism, Existentialism, Analysis, etc.), and seventeen on areas of philosophy. The latter include boundary areas such as philosophy of psychology and psychoanalysis, as well as traditional core areas such as metaphysics. The important area of practical ethics, however, including the burgeoning fields of bioethics and professional ethics, is given surprisingly short shrift. Throughout, there is a focus on "the principal changes since the late 19th century," and treatment of earlier periods concerns itself primarily with later (especially recent) secondary literature, not primary sources. Attention is largely confined to monographic literature; some key journal articles may be mentioned, but are neither cited in full nor indexed. Coverage is through 1982. Well over four thousand works—an estimated thirty-four hundred cited in full and included in the author/title index—are identified, succinctly characterized, and not infrequently accorded critical or evaluative comment, all in the course of systematic profiles of the major periods and divisions of the field. Some inadequacies may be inevitable in such an ambitious undertaking, but on the whole the feat is carried off with remarkable success.

3

GENERAL DICTIONARIES, ENCYCLOPEDIAS, AND HANDBOOKS

11. Abbagnano, Nicola. **Dizionario di filosofia.** 2d ed. Turin: Unione Tipografico-Editrice Torinese, 1971. 930p.

Abbagagno's is the most important and most highly regarded single-volume philosophical dictionary in Italian. It combines short definitions and explanations with lengthy expositions and survey articles. There are entries for terms, concepts, schools, movements, etc., but *not* for individuals.

12. Angeles, Peter A. **Dictionary of Philosophy.** New York: Barnes & Noble, 1981. 326p.

Among the handful of works with identical or similar titles, Angeles's is unusual in sticking rather closely to the narrower meaning of "dictionary" — that is, concentrating on the lexical function and eschewing any tendency to become encyclopedic. Therefore, on the one hand, one finds a preponderance of definitions which tend to be not merely short but formulated as much as possible in single sentences. (Several such definitions, often numbered, may be needed to indicate variant meanings, competing explanations or views on a topic, or major aspects of the idea, school, theory, etc., being defined.) Etymologies are often furnished as well. On the other hand, one finds few topics systematically treated, no bibliographic references, and no entries for persons. There *is* an index of philosophers whose ideas or views are specifically referred to, and certain terms and expressions, because they are peculiar to specific thinkers, are identified and explained as such: "bad faith (Sartre)," "bundle theory of the mind (Hume)," "slave morality (Nietzsche)." Also, some terms are given multiple entries in order to reflect the distinctive conceptions of different thinkers; for instance, there are entries for "knowledge (Aristotle)," "knowledge (Descartes)," "knowledge (Hume)," etc. As the latter strategy shows, the approach cannot always remain *strictly* lexical; in philosophy, that is virtually impossible, and in any case undesirable. But Angeles succeeds in staying about as close as one can or should.

This dictionary is aimed at the non-specialist, with emphasis on "terms most commonly covered in beginning philosophy courses" (preface). This does not preclude usefulness to others, but advanced students will find many definitions quite elementary and sometimes simplistic or superficial. Only terms in Western philosophy are covered, but there is no special emphasis on either Anglo-American or Continental philosophy.

13.   Baldwin, James Mark. **Dictionary of Philosophy and Psychology.** New York: Macmillan, 1901-1905. Reprinted, Gloucester, Mass.: Peter Smith, 1960. 3 vols. in 4.

In addition to the editions cited above, there have been several reprintings of this standard work by Macmillan (e.g., in 1910, 1918, 1928), sometimes labeled "New Edition" but merely containing minor corrections; several previous reprintings by Peter Smith (the earliest, New York, 1940); and a more recent reprinting, at a rather steep price, by Gordon Press (1977). Volume 3 of this work, which is printed in two books, is a major bibliography compiled by Benjamin Rand and is often cited separately (entry 115).

As its title announces, this encyclopedic dictionary covers psychology as well as philosophy. Baldwin himself was a psychologist, and psychological topics constitute a sizeable share of the work's content. One can see this in the first few pages, with entries for "aberration," "abnormal psychology," "aboulia," and "absent-mindedness." Selective attention is also paid to concepts, terms, and individuals in the fields of anthropology, biology, economics, education, philology, physiology, and physical science, primarily as they relate to philosophy and psychology. Articles are generally short, and many are devoted to definitions or explanations of fairly narrow concepts and to biographical data on minor figures.

A strong recommendation for Baldwin's work at the time of its original publication, and an important factor in its continuing historical significance, was the collaboration of a number of illustrious figures as contributors or editorial advisors. Among the best-known were Bernard Bosanquet, John Dewey, William James, G. E. Moore, Charles Sanders Peirce, Josiah Royce, and Henry Sidgwick. All articles, even very short ones, are signed. Some, such as those by Peirce and Dewey, have been duly recorded in standard bibliographies on their respective authors.

It is conventional to ascribe any enduring value of Baldwin's work exclusively to its historical interest; for other purposes, it has presumably been superseded by more current works, notably the *Encyclopedia of Philosophy* (entry 19). Perhaps, though, this judgment fails to do justice to a great deal of material (biographical entries being only the most obvious example) which is as valid now as it was in 1901, some of it not readily found elsewhere, or not in the convenient combination represented here. It is true, of course, that the work's usefulness in this regard is contingent on the user's caution and some ability to judge what has or has not been vitiated by time.

14. Briggs, Michael H. **Handbook of Philosophy.** New York: Philosophical Library, 1959. 214p.

This is actually a dictionary, and no more than a dictionary, although the term does not appear in its title. The choice of the label "handbook" is presumably due to its aim of serving primarily the student new to philosophy who needs quick mastery of a new vocabulary, and might use this work with an introductory text. In this respect, it bears closest resemblance to the much more recent dictionary by Angeles (entry 12), though its definitions tend to be longer. Terms include those from the usual range of philosophical topics, and also some from "frequently mentioned subjects and sciences such as psychical research and physics" (preface). There are very few foreign terms; when one is used, its English equivalent is supplied. There are no biographical entries, though there are terms derived from names: Augustinism [*sic*], Socratic Method, Marxism, etc. The goal of simplicity and non-technicality is not invariably achieved, and sometimes it is achieved at the cost of oversimplification. On the whole, though, this "handbook" succeeds in what it sets out to do.

15. Brugger, Walter, and Kenneth Baker. **Philosophical Dictionary.** Spokane, Wash.: Gonzaga University Press, 1972. 460p.

Brugger is the editor of the German original, the *Philosophisches Wörterbuch*, thirteenth edition (Freiburg, 1967), of which this American edition, conceived and edited by Baker, is in part a translation and in part an adaptation. The bibliographies of the German work have been omitted, along with an outline of the history of philosophy and a number of articles "not suitable for an American readership" (preface). On the other hand, new articles "dealing with contemporary Anglo-American concerns," written by American contributors, have been added. These include, e.g., articles on Behaviorism, Lonerganism, and Process Philosophy. Baker has also added an introduction titled "The Future of Christian Philosophy," in which the work's already transparent Catholic and Neo-Scholastic viewpoint is made even more explicit.

Entries are provided in this dictionary for concepts only (which *do* include schools and movements, such as Platonism and Neo-Platonism, Thomism, and Existential Philsophy), not for individuals. It eschews an "atomizing" approach which "devotes a separate article to every expression," opting for medium-length articles on relatively broad topics. Partly for this reason, and partly because of a greater selectivity engendered by its editors' conception of what is most vital in past and present philosophy, it features fewer entries than most other English-language dictionaries of recent vintage. Even so, it offers some four hundred articles on topics from Absolute to yoga.

16. **Dictionary of Philosophy.** 2d ed. Antony Flew, editorial consultant. Edited by Jennifer Speake. New York: St. Martin's Press, 1984. 380p.

This concise, easy-to-use dictionary provides explanations of terms as well as brief articles on key individuals, movements, and ideas, and on branches of philosophy. While some articles are more technical or presuppose more background than others, the book can generally serve both students and professionals. The emphasis is on Anglo-American philosophy, but some coverage is given both to Continental and to non-Western philosophy. This dictionary, the second edition of which is only marginally revised from the original published in 1979, has more entries than its competitor of roughly the same vintage, Lacey's (entry 30), and more substantial biographical articles. It also includes many helpful abbreviations, nicknames, and shorthand designations for concepts, theories, and arguments, seldom found in other dictionaries: "boo-hooray theory," "Buridan's ass," "Hume's fork," "veil of appearance," "wff," etc. However, Flew, unlike Lacey, offers no bibliographies. In terms of general usefulness for an Anglo-American audience, Flew and Lacey can be ranked together as the two prime dictionaries; and I would grant Flew at least a slight edge in the comparison.

While Flew's name, well-known in British philosophy, is prominently identified with this work (it appears alone on the cover), the extent of his responsibility for it is not clear. His name also appears in a list of thirty-three contributors.

17. Eisler, Rudolf. **Wörterbuch der philosophischen Begriffe.** 4. Aufl. Berlin: E. S. Mittler, 1927-1930. 3 vols.

This three-volume fourth edition evolved from a single-volume work which appeared in 1899, and has prevailed for many years as the preeminent encyclopedic dictionary of philosophy in German. It is in the process, however, of being superseded by a thoroughgoing revision under the editorship of Joachim Ritter (entry 35). Though this edition was actually completed after Eisler's death (under the supervision of K. Roretz), it enjoyed the cooperation and consequent imprimatur of the respected Kant-Gesellschaft. It treats terms and concepts only, but tends to follow a historical approach which systematically canvasses the definitions, views, and arguments of major thinkers on a topic.

Eisler also produced a briefer dictionary, the *Handwörterbuch der Philosophie* (2. Aufl. Berlin: E. S. Mittler, 1922, 785p.), aimed more at the non-specialist and closer to the scope of his original *Wörterbuch*. This has also been very successful, and was reprinted as late as 1949.

18. **Enciclopedia filosofica.** 2d ed. interamente rielaborata. Florence: G. C. Sansoni, 1967-1969. 6 vols.

The six-volume second edition of this Italian encyclopedia succeeds a four-volume edition, published in 1957, which was considered a landmark in its time. This was the largest and most comprehensive encyclopedia of philosophy in any language prior to the *Encyclopedia of Philosophy* edited by Paul Edwards (entry 19); and in this extensively revised edition, it is the only work even close to the latter in size and scope. Both editions were produced under the *aegis* of the Centro di studi filosofici di Gallarate (identified on the title page) and are the work primarily of Italian scholars, with some international collaboration. Reflecting Italian philosophical penchants, the *Enciclopedia* shows some bias toward idealistic and religious philosophy, and understandably affords more space to Italian thinkers, including obscure ones, than to those of other countries. Nonetheless, it is justly admired for the sweep of its coverage and its truly international scope. Eastern thought receives some attention, though much less than Western; there are, for example, articles on Buddhism and Hinduism, and survey articles on India and China. The first edition reputedly contained some twelve thousand articles; an estimate for the second is not available, but the number is undoubtedly even larger. Articles range from very short—mainly definitional and biographical—to very lengthy. Longer articles are signed, and usually include bibliographies. Most items cited in the latter are in the major European languages, i.e., French, Spanish, and German, as well as Italian, but English-language works are cited as well. (A possible use of this encyclopedia for the student with no facility in Italian might be to trace important sources in other languages, including perhaps non-English works on English-speaking philosophers.)

A handsome set physically, the *Enciclopedia filosofica* features a modest number of high-quality plates, mostly portraits but also some other types of illustrations. Columns, rather than pages, are numbered, and each volume has about sixteen hundred columns. Volume 6 has a classified list of articles as well as an index of terms and names not used as entries.

19. **Encyclopedia of Philosophy.** Ed. by Paul Edwards. New York: Macmillan and Free Press; London: Collier Macmillan, 1967. 8 vols. Reprinted, 1972. 8 vols. in 4.

The aim of this monumental reference work is succinctly stated in Edwards's introduction: "to cover the whole of philosophy as well as many of the points of contact between philosophy and other disciplines." Accordingly, it "treats Eastern and Western philosophy; it deals with ancient, medieval, and modern philosophy; and it discusses the theories of mathematicians, physicists, biologists, sociologists, psychologists, moral reformers, and religious thinkers where these have had an impact on philosophy." The realization of this ambitious undertaking involved the efforts of an international editorial board of 153 distinguished scholars, and an equally international cast of more than five hundred contributors.

Notwithstanding its comprehensiveness and its aim of universality, the *Encyclopedia* does have some degree of bias toward Anglo-American philosophy and its concerns with logic, language, and analysis. This manifests itself most readily in the choice of topics and the allocation of space. The careful user is well-advised to read the introduction, which acknowledges the bias but also describes measures taken to counteract it (e.g., the use as much as possible of authors with some sympathy for their topics) and rightly warns against hasty judgments based on superficial comparisons of relative space allotments, comparisons that may fail to reckon with differences in the distribution of relevant material over a number of articles. This warning, alas, has not always been heeded by reviewers and annotators.

The *Encyclopedia* is organized on the supposition that most users benefit more "from a smaller number of long and integrated articles than from a multitude of shorter entries." Few if any of its fifteen hundred articles occupy less than half a page, and some, as the editor suggests, with good reason, are in effect small books. (The article on the history of logic occupies fifty-eight pages; the twin articles on the history of ethics and problems of ethics together take up fifty-three pages.)

Among the *Encyclopedia*'s more unusual offerings are articles on philosophy in specific countries; a glossary of logical terms (under "Logical Terms, Glossary of"); excellent survey articles titled "Philosophical Bibliographies," "Philosophical Dictionaries and Encyclopedias," and "Philosophical Journals"; and a number of unconventional but valuable entries, e.g., "All and Any," "German Philosophy and National Socialism," and "Newtonian Mechanics and Mechanical Explanation."

Useful to both the specialist and the non-specialist (though not uniformly for each), the *Encyclopedia of Philosophy* achieves, on the whole, a remarkable combination of informativeness, incisiveness, balance, and readability. These qualities have been abetted by editorial policies which encouraged authors to deal freely with controversial material, to take stands if they wished, to break new ground if they could, and, not least, to feel no compulsion to be "serious and solemn at all costs."

20. Ferrater Mora, José. **Diccionario de filosofía.** 5th ed. Buenos Aires: Editorial Sudamericana, 1965. 2 vols.

Since its first edition, published in 1941, this has been a highly regarded work. Borchardt (entry 2), calling it "the only Spanish dictionary of philosophy of any significance," praises the comprehensiveness of its coverage and the "catholicity" of its bibliographies. Gerber, in the *Encyclopedia of Philosophy*, calls it "one of the most useful dictionaries published in the twentieth century" and "a monumental one-man contribution." The latter is an apt characterization of its size and scope, if nothing else. Its two volumes run to more than one thousand pages each. Articles tend to be short and seldom run more than a few pages, even on major topics; the typical article is one or two columns of a three-column page. Entries cover the usual range of an encyclopedic dictionary, but there is a heavy emphasis on individuals. The latter include many Iberian and Latin-American thinkers little known outside their own linguistic and cultural domain. Bibliographies cite materials in many languages, though Spanish sources are emphasized. There are no illustrations.

21. **Filosofskaia entsiklopediia.** Glavnyj redaktor F. V. Konstantinov. Moscow: "Sovetskaia entsiklopediia," 1960-1970. 5 vols.

This comprehensive Russian encyclopedia exhibits predictable Marxist-Leninst emphasis and viewpoint. Published under the auspices of the Institute of Philosophy of the Academy of Science (Akademii Nauk) of the USSR, it is part of a more comprehensive publishing project, the *Entsiklopedii slovari spravochniki.* The major articles include substantial bibliographies. "Especially valuable for its detailed coverage of the theoretical bases of Communist doctrine" (R. Neiswender, *Guide to Russian Reference and Language Aids* in A. J. Walford, *Guide to Reference Material,* 4th ed., 1982).

22. Foulquié, Paul, and Raymond Saint-Jean. **Dictionnaire de la langue philosophique.** 2e ed. revue et augmentee. Paris: Presses Universitaires de France, 1969. 778p.

A work which acknowledges its indebtedness to the standard French dictionary by Lalande (entry 31), this is, like Lalande's, a dictionary of terms and concepts. It has no entries for persons, or even for schools or viewpoints such as Aristotelianism or Thomism. Its fifteen hundred or so terms are generally treated in alphabetical sequence, but in some cases related terms are grouped together. Thus, "essence" and "exister" (to cite an example of some importance in the context of French philosophy) are grouped with other related terms under "être." Similarly, "indéterminisme" is found under "déterminisme." Cross-references are of course provided in these instances.

The chief distinguishing feature of Foulquié's work, a feature highlighted by a judicious employment of distinct typefaces, is its use of quotations from significant philosophical writings to illustrate the use or uses of a term, somewhat in the manner of the *Oxford English Dictionary*. Sources are identified by author, title, and even page numbers, but no dates or publishing data are given.

23. Frolov, Ivan Timofeevich, ed. **Dictionary of Philosophy.** Transl. from the Russian. Ed. by Murad Saifulin and Richard P. Dixon. Moscow: Progress Publishers; New York: International Publishing Co., 1985. 464p.

A translation of the fourth edition of a standard Soviet work, *Filosofskiĭ slovar'*, this encyclopedic dictionary is universal in scope, covering both Western and (much more spottily) Eastern philosophy; but it wears its Marxist character like the red insignia on a Soviet military uniform. Thus, an article titled "Criterion of Truth," striking a typically Marxist note, declares dogmatically that "social practice is the Criterion of Truth." The article on agnosticism announces that it was Lenin who "laid bare the epistemological roots of Agnosticism." And the article on Utilitarianism begins: "a bourgeois ethical theory. . . ." There are also numerous articles on specifically Marxist topics, e.g., "Criticism and Self-Criticism," "Internationalism," "Marxism-Leninism," "State of the Whole People," and biographical entries for Russian philosophical figures.

An earlier version of this dictionary (Moscow: Progress Publishers, 1967) was based on the second edition of *Filosofskiĭ slovar'*, edited by Mark M. Rozental' and Pavel F. IUdin (in many citations transliterated as M. Rosenthal and P. Yudin). *Filosofskiĭ slovar'* is the successor to an earlier work by Rozental' and IUdin, *Kratikiĭ filosofskiĭ slovar'*, an English version of which, adapted and edited by Howard Selsam, was published in 1949. The various editions and printings since 1939 of these successive dictionaries provide an interesting reflection of the ups and downs of Soviet politics. Whereas in early editions Stalin was cast in the role of a major philosophical authority, neither the present work nor its immediate predecessor even has an article on him.

The main editor of the present work, Ivan T. Frolov, is a key figure in officially sanctioned Soviet philosophy.

24. Grooten, J., and G. Jo Steenbergen. **New Encyclopedia of Philosophy.** Transl. from the Dutch, ed., and rev. by Edmond van den Bossche. New York: Philosophical Library, 1972. 468p.

This one-volume encyclopedic dictionary is a translation, with some adaptation, of a Dutch work, *Filosofisch Lexicon,* originally published in 1958. Over two dozen contributors are listed on its title page; their specific contributions are identified only in the case of longer articles. The work can be recommended chiefly for its Continental perspective and emphasis, in contrast to the Anglo-American emphasis of more-or-less comparable works by Flew, Lacey, Reese, Runes, and Urmson. Illustrative of this emphasis are substantial entries (half a column or more) on such Continental figures as Rudolf Stammler, Désiré-Joseph Mercier, and Alphonse Gratry, who are given no entries or at most a sentence or two in the works previously mentioned. (A startling omission, on the other hand, is Maurice Merleau-Ponty.)

For general purposes, the best to be said for this work is that it can supplement but certainly not substitute for any of the mentioned single-volume dictionaries or encyclopedias. Detracting from its value are the absence of some important terms (e.g., Emotivism, Cosmological Argument) and the presence of a number of articles that are either too obscure or barely informative (cf. those on ethics, goods, ontology, and Nicholas of Cusa). Translation and editorial matters, also, are less than expertly handled. Clumsy translation has produced many quirks of expression or syntax, including some unnecessary carryovers of Dutch-language conventions into English. Examples of the latter are the use of "the" before abstract nouns (*the* idealism, *the* morality, *the* anthroposophy, etc.) and non-capitalization of derivatives of proper nouns (*a*ristotelian, *k*antian, *t*homism), the latter style not consistently followed. The cross-referencing system, which employs asterisks to signal terms that have their own entries, occasionally fails, and there are instances of cross-references referring to non-existent entries (dropped, one conjectures, from the English edition).

25. Gutmann, James, et al., eds. **Philosophy A to Z.** Based on the work of Alwin Diemer, Ivo Frenzel, and others. Transl. by Salvatore Attanasio. New York: Grosset & Dunlap, 1963. 343p. (Universal Reference Library).

The material in this volume is in large part a translation, with some revision and amplification, of the *Philosophie* volume by Diemer, Frenzel, and others, in a popular German series, the *Fischer Lexikon* (Frankfurt-Main: Fischer Bücherei, K. G., 1958). Entirely new articles were added on Idealism (Abraham Edel), Christian Philosophy (Arthur Holmes), Jewish Philosophy (Alexander Altmann), Islamic Philosophy (Richard Walzer), and Pragmatism (H. Standish Thayer). More like an introductory overview than a typical dictionary or encyclopedia, the work features a relatively small number of articles on broad topics—chapters, more or less, on the main areas and branches of philosophy, Eastern included. A brief, very selective bibliography is provided at the end.

26. Julia, Didier. **Dictionnaire de la philosophie.** Paris: Librairie Larousse, 1964. 320p.

In some ways, Julia's is a standard sort of encyclopedic dictionary, featuring articles on individuals, concepts, schools of thought, etc., and also some on philosophical classics such as Descartes's *Discourse on Method* and Kant's *Critique of Pure Reason.* What is fairly unusual, however, is that it is addressed to the layperson and intends specifically to show the applicability of philosophy to daily life. In the service of this cause it deploys many illustrations, going well beyond routine portraits of philosophers to include paintings, current events photos, and other kinds of illustrations seemingly calculated to arouse curiosity as to what their connection might be with philosophy. Most of these illustrate topics of popular interest, sometimes borderline or semiphilosophical, which also abound: euthanasia, fanaticism, feminism, hysteria, racism, socialist realism, sublimation, xenism, and others of like nature. Something of the work's orientation is suggested by William Gerber's observation, in his *Encyclopedia of Philosophy* article, that "Marx gets more space than anyone else, and Trotsky gets more than Aristotle." Whether it succeeds in its goals or not, Julia's dictionary represents an interesting concept which one would like to see tried more often, and in English.

27. Klauder, Francis J. **The Wonder of Philosophy: A Review of Philosophers and Philosophic Thought.** New York: Philosophical Library, 1973. 75p.

Thomistic in its perspective and purpose, this brief guide offers thumbnail sketches of selected branches of philosophy (those, one surmises, which have been the chief preoccupation of Thomistic thought) and of the main periods and figures of Western philosophy generally. There is also a three-page summary of Oriental philosophy. Granting the legitimate limits set by its perspective and purpose, this may still be judged a work of highly idiosyncratic selectivity (one suspects the author's choices reflect mainly his personal teaching interests in specific courses) as well as recurrent superficiality. In addition, it is marked by oddities of organization. The section on the modern period, for instance, consists entirely of brief notes on six philosophers who, for unexplained reasons, are not included in the alphabetical dictionary of Western philosophers which forms part 3 of the book. Altogether, a work of very limited utility.

28. Klaus, Georg, and Manfred Buhr. **Philosophisches Wörterbuch.** 8., berichtigte Aufl. Berlin: Das europäische Buch, 1972. 2 vols.

The *Ausgangspunkt,* or point of departure, for this East German dictionary, says its foreword, is the works of Marx, Engels, and Lenin as well as the fundamental documents of the German Socialist Party and the international workers movement, in particular the Communist Party of the Soviet Union. Central to its aims, avowedly, is the presentation of Marxist-Leninist philosophy per se. However, it is also a general dictionary in the sense that it provides general coverage of philosophical and logical terminology, the history of philosophy, and aspects of other disciplines relevant to philosophy. Even there, of course, the Marxist perspective is operative. And in fact, it is an avowed part of the work's strategy to further understanding of Marxism-Leninism by contrasting it with "bourgeois philosophy and imperialist ideology."

Some eighteen hundred entries include terms, concepts, schools, movements, etc., but not names of individuals.

A West German edition of the previous edition of this work was issued under the title *Marxistisch-leninistisches Wörterbuch der Philosophie* (Reinbek: Rowolt, 1972, 3 vols.).

29. Krings, Hermann, Hans Michael Baumgartner, and Christoph Wild, eds. **Handbuch philosophischer Grundbegriffe.** Munich: Kosel-Verlag, 1973-1974. 3 vols.

Far from attempting to be a general encyclopedia, this German reference work takes seriously the focus on *Grundbegriffe,* i.e., fundamental or "foundational" concepts, signaled in its title. It features no more than about 150 articles on concepts which, in the editors' view, are pivotal for philosophical thought. Examples include such varied concepts as the Absolute, Consciousness (*Bewusstsein*), Evil (*das Böse*), Finiteness (*Endlichkeit*), Progress (*Fortschritt*), and Society (*Gesellschaft*). Each of these is subjected to a substantial conceptual analysis with extensive reference to its history in philosophical thought. Excluded in this approach are concepts which can be explicated with a brief definition. Likewise excluded are terms which have a purely "designative" character, such as those designating the various philosophical disciplines (logic, philosophy of language) or philosophical movements (Idealism, Utilitarianism). Needless to say, there are no entries for names of individuals.

Nearly all the contributors to this work are German. Historically German philosophical tendencies, particularly Idealism, are much in evidence, but do not exclude other perspectives. The extensive bibliographies, while emphasizing German sources, also cite numerous works in other languages, chiefly English and French.

30. Lacey, A. R. **Dictionary of Philosophy.** New York: Scribner's, 1976. London: Routledge and Kegan Paul, 1976. Pbk. ed., New York: Scribner's, 1977. 239p.

When published in 1976, Lacey's dictionary was, for general purposes, the first serious competitor to D. D. Runes's long-lived but oft-maligned dictionary of 1942 (entry 36). It was soon joined, however, by roughly similar works by Flew and Reese (entries 16 and 34) and a somewhat less similar work by Angeles (entry 12), not to mention a dubiously "revised" edition of Runes. It stands, however, as both a worthy competitor and a useful complement to any or all of these works. Its special strength is its bibliographies, which are sometimes surprisingly extensive for a work of this type. It has a decidedly Anglo-American cast, and emphasizes particularly epistemological and logical topics, but it does cover all periods, branches, and major movements and figures within Western philosophy. It gives no coverage to non-Western philosophies. Intended for the student and the layperson, it may occasionally aim a little high; in any case, it has much to offer the professional philosopher and philosophy teacher as well.

31. Lalande, André, ed. **Vocabulaire technique et critique de la philosophie.** 10e ed., rev. et augm. Paris: Presses Universitaires, 1967. 1323p.

This work is published under the aegis of the Société Française de Philosophie, in whose *Bulletin* the first edition of this work appeared in twenty-one parts (1902-1923). Its focus is the clarification of terms and concepts; there are no biographical entries, nor is there historical or systematic treatment of topics per se. In addition to definitions, there are examples of use by philosophers (translations for those in Latin and Greek are provided in two appendices at the back), and usually also etymologies and equivalents of the term in German, English, and Italian. A highly unusual feature is the inclusion, in the form of footnotes, of comments on the definitions, written by members of the Société Française de Philosophie.

32. Mittelstrass, Jürgen, et al. **Enzyklopädie Philosophie und Wissenschaftstheorie.** Mannheim: Bibliographisches Institut-Wissenschaftsverlag, 1980- . Vols. 1- .

Still in progress, this German encyclopedia has been issued through volume 2 (H-O) as of this writing. While taking into its purview most of the traditional range of philosophy, it concentrates deliberately on developments, concepts, and figures in logic and philosophy of science, and on connections—historical, conceptual, logical, methodological—between philosophy and the natural sciences and mathematics. Articles, mostly of short to medium length, include both brief explanations of concepts and biographical entries.

33. Peterson, Russell A. **Dictionary of Philosophical Concepts.** Lake Mills, Iowa: Graphic Publishing Co., 1977. 120p.

The preface explains that this work is "not to be looked upon as a dictionary in the usual sense of the term," which is somewhat of a relief when one studies its definitions. The following, though among the shortest, are typical: "*Learn.* To learn is to condition the mind to teleologically define the part of the material of knowledge." "*Variables.* Inherent within every variable is the value condition." Such definitions are meant, as the preface has it, "to be looked upon as a tool enabling the mind to conceptualize for potentiality," and as "grist for the inquiring mind." Whatever the value of Peterson's "dictionary" for some such function, the inquirer who needs to pin down the standard use (or uses) of a philosophical term, or to find a summary of the more prominent interpretations and applications of a concept, will have to look elsewhere.

34. Reese, William L. **Dictionary of Philosophy and Religion: Eastern and Western Thought.** Atlantic Highlands, N.J.: Humanities Press, 1980; Hassocks, Sussex, England: Harvester Press, 1980. 644p.

The combination of philosophy and religion in this single-volume dictionary is unique, at least among modern dictionaries. It offers a genuine advantage wherever there is frequent need for reference to both, or from one area to the other. This advantage might be even greater but for two shortcomings. First, Reese's work is much more adequate as a dictionary of philosophy (in which category it compares favorably with roughly contemporaneous works by Flew and Lacey; entries 16 and 30) than as a dictionary of religion (in which category it does not compare favorably with any other standard work). This is due partly to its understandable focus on concepts and ideas in its coverage of religion, rather than, say, religious history or religious institutions. It is also due partly to its relative neglect of any but the most prominent religious thinkers, as compared with fairly good coverage of second-rank figures in philosophy. And finally, it is due to its relatively perfunctory treatment of religious perspectives on such topics as ethics, immortality, and the soul. This, in fact, touches directly on its second major shortcoming: it often fails to make the connections between philosophical and religious thought in just those areas where the connections are most important. Still, such coverage of religion as it offers may be accepted as a bonus, along with its fairly good coverage of Eastern philosophy (compared, that is, with such competitors as Flew and Lacey). Topical articles in this dictionary tend to emphasize nutshell summaries of the views of individual thinkers, at some expense, frequently, to systematic development. Cross-references are extensive and often refer to a specific numbered point within an article.

35. Ritter, Joachim, et al., eds. **Historisches Wörterbuch der Philosophie.** Basel/Stuttgart: Schwabe, 1971- .

Billed as a thoroughgoing revision of the standard *Wörterbuch* of Rudolf Eisler (entry 17), this work is still in progress as of this writing (September 1985); the latest volume, volume 5, published in 1980, takes its coverage through "Mn" in the alphabet. Ritter himself, now deceased, saw this project through the publication of volume 3 (G-H); his name still appears on the title pages of volumes 4 and 5, but is joined by that of Karlfried Gründer as coeditor. The more than 700 contributing authorities listed on the title page of volume 1 have by now increased to more than 950.

What this revision carries over from Eisler's work may be more a conception, approach, and set of emphases than its actual content. Ritter's *Vorwort* to volume 1 explains at some length the growth of the project beyond originally modest intentions and the need, soon realized, to rebuild "from the ground up." Articles which have been carried forward with relatively little revision by the editorial staff (a small minority) are signed "Eisler (red.).."

Each volume of the *Historisches Wörterbuch* runs from twelve hundred to fifteen hundred columns (with columns numbered rather than pages). Articles tend to be long, at least half of a double column, with a few, but very few, shorter definitions. They cover a mixture of concepts, terms, schools, movements, etc., but there are no entries for individual philosophers. Extensive bibliographies are provided. There is some coverage of Oriental philosophy, though it is not detailed.

36. Runes, Dagobert D., ed. **Dictionary of Philosophy.** Rev. ed. New York: Philosophical Library, 1982. 360p.

From the time of its original appearance in 1942, this work has been castigated frequently for its sins. Yet it has remained for over forty years in wide use, and in print, partly because of the incorrigibility of its several publishers (it has seen many paperback versions by Littlefield, Adams), partly because it long served a need not met by anything better, and partly because of its genuine merits.

The seventy-two contributors to the original edition included many noted figures in American (and in a few cases European) philosophy: Alonzo Church on logic, William Frankena on ethics, Paul Kristeller on Renaissance philosophy, to name a few. But thirteen of them, including E. S. Brightman, Rudolph Carnap, Alonzo Church, C. J. Ducasse, and Irwin Edman, felt obliged to publish in several philosophical journals "a public disavowal of any editorial responsibility," prompted, as they explained, by unheeded objections to its publication "in its present form" and Runes's substantial tampering with their articles without their consent (see, e.g., *Mind* 51:296).

As if determined to perpetuate this initial tarnish on its reputation, various publishers have reissued the dictionary in numerous "editions" (at least through a sixteenth) which in fact have been no more than reprintings with only the most minute corrections and additions. The present "revised and enlarged edition" does go beyond that—but not enough to redeem its reputation. Few articles have been updated, not even major ones (e.g., ethics, philosophy of religion, philosophy of science); new articles are confined largely to entries for a few prominent figures (and here the selection is not always the best); and recent developments indicated in one place go unacknowledged in another (e.g., the prominence gained by Karl Popper since 1942 is recognized by a new biographical entry, but not by any revision in the article on philosophy of science, where Popper's influence has been dramatic).

Still, when all is said and done, Runes's work has had, and continues to have, its uses. It did, after all, benefit from the distinction and scholarship of its original contributors. Many of its entries do contain useful definitions or offer materials or perspectives which can at least supplement or complement other sources. Runes also provides better coverage of certain areas, notably Oriental philosophy, than such current competitors as Flew (entry 16) and Lacey (entry 30). And finally, its age can become a genuine virtue when one needs coverage of individuals, ideas, and sources once prominent but now sunk into relative obscurity.

37. Schmidt, Heinrich. **Philosophisches Wörterbuch.** 21. Aufl., neu bearb. von Georgi Schischkoff. Stuttgart: Alfred Kröner, 1982. 787p.

If one counts all of its twenty-one editions, stretching from 1912 to 1982, this German dictionary is possibly the most widely used philosophical dictionary ever, in any language. More than half of its editions have been published under the supervision of a variety of editors since Schmidt's death in 1935. It has survived and overcome a serious smirch on its reputation created by the intrusion of pro-Nazi and anti-Jewish elements in editions published during the Nazi era.

In content, Schmidt is most nearly comparable to the works of Flew and Runes in English, though it is somewhat longer and more comprehensive than either of these. It does have articles on individuals, and these include, as one would expect, many German philosophers, and more generally European philosophers, not commonly found in English-language dictionaries. Coverage of Eastern philosophy is very spotty, but there are articles on, e.g., Chinese philosophy, Indian philosophy, Buddhism, and Buddhist logic. Brief bibliographical references are provided.

38. Urmson, James Opie, ed. **Concise Encyclopedia of Western Philosophy and Philosophers.** London: Hutchinson, 1960. New York: Hawthorn Books, 1960. 431p. (Some printings, without illustrations, 319p.).

The list of this encyclopedia's forty-nine contributors would make a good start for a "Who's Who" of mid-twentieth-century Anglo-American philosophy. It includes A. J. Ayer, Isaiah Berlin, R. M. Hare, H. L. A. Hart, Walter Kaufmann, Alasdair MacIntyre, Ernest Nagel, Gilbert Ryle, Ruth Saw, P. F. Strawson, B. A. O. Williams, and Urmson himself. Individual articles are not signed, though the authorship of some has been no secret (e.g., "Epistemology" is by Ryle, "Heidegger" by Kaufmann).

Urmson favors longer articles on broad subjects rather than short entries for narrower ones (which makes the "encyclopedia" label appropriate), and explains in his introduction that "the total number of articles included has been restricted on the principle that it is better to have a fair number of useful articles than to have a large number of useless ones." Among the principles of selection is a fairly narrow interpretation of what constitutes philosophy, namely, a definition "conforming to the usage of *professional* philosophers in the *western* tradition" (italics added); but at the same time the encyclopedia is aimed primarily at non-specialists. Beyond this, Urmson concedes that some of his selection decisions may "have inevitably been marginal and arbitrary," an admission which has not spared him criticism for a variety of omissions, imbalances, or departures from his announced criteria. On the whole, nonetheless, it seems to be agreed that the material he did include is useful and reliable, as well as of considerable interest due simply to the prominence of its authors. There is an emphasis on philosophers and their work, particularly British and American philosophers, which is complemented by a similar emphasis in the more than one hundred plates (in most printings). These plates, incidentally, together with attractive typography, make this an uncommonly handsome work in its genre. There are no bibliographies with the articles (though there are references to key works in the text), but there is a list of suggestions for further reading at the back.

39. Voltaire, Marie François Arrouet de. **Philosophical Dictionary.** Transl., with an introduction and glossary, by Peter Gay. New York: Basic Books, 1962. 2 vols.

Among the many dictionaries and encyclopedias from past centuries which are generally *not* included in this guide, this one (which saw its first French edition in 1764) deserves to be excepted. This is not because it is the only one to have been reprinted in modern times (there are others which have seen small-run reprintings for specialized scholarly purposes); it is rather that, having seen several modern translations and editions (of which the one cited here is the latest), it is more prevalent and more widely available in libraries than any other.

De George (entry 3) observes, largely correctly, that Voltaire's work "is now only of historical interest." One should at least add "and literary interest," however, for it is chiefly Voltaire's style, wit, and irreverent opinions that have kept this classic alive. Even in its time, it could hardly serve as a dictionary of technical philosophy, Voltaire being concerned mainly with matters of popular philosophy and religious controversy. Among the few technical topics he did deal with are soul, beauty, certainty, chain of events, great chain of being, fate, and necessary.

40. Ward, Keith. **Fifty Key Words in Philosophy.** London: Lutterworth Press, 1968. 85p. (Fifty Key Word Books).

This brief and handy reference guide offers a judicious selection of the most significant terms in philosophy, excluding ethics. Some are the names of schools and movements (e.g., Behaviorism, Pragmatism), others are keywords for particular philosophical problems (determinism, mind, sense-data, truth). Cross-references are furnished liberally. Explanations average about a page and a half in length and generally should satisfy the author's hope that, among other things, this work "may be useful . . . as a modest introduction to philosophy for the general reader" (introduction). There is an index of forty-four terms not treated in separate articles and also a list of philosophers mentioned in the text, in chronological order.

41. Wiener, Philip P., editor-in-chief. **Dictionary of the History of Ideas: Studies of Selected Pivotal Ideas.** New York: Scribner's, 1973-1974. 4 vols. plus index vol.

This outstanding reference work stands squarely within the "history of ideas" tradition associated with Arthur O. Lovejoy (*The Great Chain of Being*) and with the *Journal of the History of Ideas,* edited for many years by Wiener. As such, it is certainly not confined to philosophical subject matter, but is multidisciplinary and, still more significantly, interdisciplinary in content and orientation. Nonetheless, philosophical ideas proper are prominent among the topics it covers; it has, for example, articles titled "Antinomy of Pure Reason," "Design Argument," "Free Will and Determinism," "Necessity," "Perennial Philosophy," "Relativism in Ethics," "Time," and "Utilitarianism." Other articles deal with topics which at least straddle the boundaries of philosophy, including "Alienation in Hegel and Marx," "Causation," "Determinism in History," "Equality," "God," "Progress," and "Taste in the History of Aesthetics from the Renaissance to 1770." In addition, even when the subject is not primarily or explicitly philosophical, there are apt to be philosophical aspects, implications, and connections. This is true, for instance, for articles titled "Behaviorism," "Game Theory," "Relativity," "Sense of the Tragic," and "Utility and Value in Economic Thought."

Collectively, the foregoing examples should suggest the tremendously rich variety represented in this unique resource. A very helpful "Analytical Table of Contents" at the front of volume 1 lists the individual articles under seven broad headings, such as "the history of ideas about the external order of nature studied by the physical and biological sciences . . . ," "the historical development of economic, legal, and political ideas and institutions, ideologies, and movements," and "the history of religious and philosophical ideas." The editor's preface also identifies three broad types of studies offered by this "dictionary" (a misleading title in view of the typical length of such studies and the absence of any brief entries): "cross-cultural studies limited to a given century or period, studies that trace an idea from antiquity to later periods, and studies that explicate the meaning of a pervasive idea and its development in the minds of its leading proponents." What it does *not* offer, it should be noted, is articles on the ideas of individual thinkers. One would look in vain for an article on Plato's ideas, or Kant's. A very thorough index does allow one to trace references to the contributions of Plato, Kant, or others to specific topics.

A galaxy of distinguished contributors from many fields, ranging from art history to physics and from economics to literary criticism, includes stellar authorities on the history of philosophical ideas such as Monroe Beardsley, Isaiah Berlin, George Boas, Sidney Hook, John Passmore, and Richard Popkin. All articles are signed.

4

SPECIALIZED DICTIONARIES, ENCYCLOPEDIAS, AND HANDBOOKS

42. Ballestrem, Karl G. **Russian Philosophical Terminology.** Dordrecht, Netherlands: D. Reidel, 1964. 117p.

Designed to facilitate the study of Soviet philosophy, this glossary contains about one thousand Russian philosophical terms arranged in cyrillic alphabetical order and followed by English, German, and French equivalents. No attempt is made to expand upon the meaning or significance of any term. Terms selected include any that appear regularly in Russian philosophical texts, but those that are central or that have a specific meaning in Soviet philosophy (e.g., *zakony dialektiky*) are marked with an asterisk. The latter device is intended to help the student identify first the most basic vocabulary. Indexes for English, German, and French terms permit reference from these to the corresponding Russian expressions, which are numbered.

This is a publication of the Institute of East European Studies, University of Fribourg, Switzerland.

43. Bottomore, Tom, et al., eds. **A Dictionary of Marxist Thought.** Cambridge, Mass.: Harvard University Press, 1983. 587p.

Though by no means confined to Marxist *philosophy,* this dictionary does provide extensive coverage of philosophical concepts (alienation, dialectics, historical materialism, praxis, truth), Marxist treatments of specific areas of philosophy (aesthestics, ethics, theory of knowledge), the philosophical background of Marxism (Feuerbach, Hegel, "Young Hegelians"), philosophical schools and movements within Marxism (Frankfurt School, legal Marxism, revisionism, Western Marxism), and individual Marxist philosophers (Althusser, Lukács, Marcuse, Plekhanov). Without a doubt it is the best source that is both in English and in dictionary form and that is not itself a work of Marxist partisanship.

44. Buhr, Manfred, and Alfred Kosing. **Kleines Wörterbuch der marxistisch-leninistischen Philosophie.** Berlin: Dietz, 1974. West Berlin: Das europäische Buch, 1974. 334p.

This compact dictionary does not restrict itself to specifically Marxist-Leninist topics and thinkers; it takes in, as its foreword explains, any philosophical concepts and names important for study of the works of Marx, Engels, Lenin, and contemporary Marxist-Leninist philosophers, and for understanding the "ideological class-struggle between socialism and imperialism." Consequently, it is close to, but not quite, a general philosophical dictionary with a Marxist perspective. Separate indexes are provided for keywords (entries for concepts, philosophical schools and branches, etc.) and for personal names.

45. Burr, John R., ed. **Handbook of World Philosophy: Contemporary Developments since 1945.** Westport, Conn.: Greenwood Press, 1980. 643p.

Twenty-eight essays survey philosophical thought and activity, from 1945 to roughly 1977, in individual countries or in some cases larger geographical/cultural regions (Africa, Islamic countries, Latin America). Each is written by a specialist, generally an "insider," but in a few instances not (e.g., those on France and the Soviet Union). A selective but substantial bibliography is provided with each article. Good indexes add to the work's value, as do two appendices: a directory of philosophical associations by region and country, and a list of congresses and meetings that take place on a more or less regular basis.

The chief fault of this *Handbook* is the unevenness of its coverage, if only in terms of space allotted. France, with sixty-five pages, gets twice as much space as *any* other country. Australia gets twenty-six pages, permitting the luxury of a six-page discussion of a single philosophical topic, while a nine-page article on Italy and a fifteen-page article on Britain allow only the briefest treatment of major trends and thinkers. Nonetheless, Burr's *Handbook* performs a useful service not matched by any other reference work.

46. Bynum, William F., E. J. Browne, and Roy Porter, eds. **Dictionary of the History of Science.** Princeton: Princeton University Press, 1981. 494p.

Topics in the philosophy of science are a minority, but a very significant minority, among those covered by this excellent reference work. In the absence of a dictionary devoted specifically to philosophy of science, this is at minimum a welcome substitute, and arguably more effective for its combination of philosophical and historical material. An analytical table of contents in the front helpfully identifies 130 entries relating specifically to philosophy of science. Thirty-three of these are indicated to have bibliographies. Topics are as diverse as causality in quantum physics, Mill's canons, paradox of the ravens, and theory-laden terms. Other philosophical (or philosophically infused) topics are listed under the heading "Human Sciences"; entries in this section include "Chain of being," "Man-machine," "Mind-body relation," and "Social Darwinism."

There are no biographical entries as such, but a biographical index at the back gives basic biographical data as well as references to pertinent articles. It includes numerous philosophers, both classical (Bacon, Descartes, Leibniz, Mach, Spencer) and recent or contemporary (Carnap, Nagel, Popper).

47. Cairns, Dorion. **Guide for Translating Husserl.** The Hague: Martinus Nijhoff, 1973. 145p. (Phaenomenologica, 55).

For translators aiming at publication, this is an essential tool; anyone endeavoring to read Husserl in the original German may find it equally useful. Essentially a glossary of key terms and expressions, Cairns's guide gives translations in standard English editions of Husserl's works, cites general German-English dictionaries, and indicates preferred translations where options exist. In numerous instances, French renderings are also cited as an additional aid.

48. Chapman, Colin. **An Eerdman's Handbook: The Case for Christianity.** Grand Rapids, Mich.: William B. Eerdmans, 1981. 313p.

This handbook of Christian apologetics—the endeavor to make a reasonable case for Christianity and to defend it against philosophical and other objections—is designed for a popular, non-scholarly audience. While much of its material is theological or historical rather than philosophical, a number of philosophical topics are addressed: the traditional theistic proofs, the problem of evil, verification in philosophy and in science, the meaning of life, the relation between reason and faith, and others. Particularly pertinent is the section "Understanding and Testing the Alternatives," which offers short sketches of ten key thinkers (Aquinas, Descartes, Locke, Hume, Rousseau, Kant, Hegel, Kierkegaard, Marx, Freud) and ten -isms (Catholic Scholasticism, Deism, Rationalism, Atheism, Agnosticism, Mysticism, Pantheism, Marxism, Existentialism, Humanism). Though intentionally elementary and at times shallow, the work is well done on the whole, taking into consideration its undisguised bias and the intended audience. A special asset is the wealth of pithy quotes selected to illustrate or characterize specific arguments, positions, or trends of thought. As with other *Eerdmans Handbooks* (. . . *to the Bible, to the World's Religions, to the History of Christianity,* etc.), numerous illustrations and creative design add life as well as visual interest.

49. Cranston, Maurice W., and Sanford A. Lakoff, eds. **A Glossary of Political Ideas.** New York: Basic Books, 1968. 180p. British edition, **A Glossary of Political Terms,** by Maurice W. Cranston. London: Bodley Head, 1966. 110p. (A Background Book).

This dictionary offers an excellent introduction to central concepts of political philosophy (and political theory more generally) which, while ubiquitous in political argument and discussion, are problematic in that they carry evaluative meanings, or heavy loads of philosophical freight, or both. Definitions are provided where possible, ambiguities are exposed where not. Among the fifty-one terms included are: common good, communism, conservatism, democracy, equality, human rights, justice, law, liberalism, progress, reactionary, state, utility/utilitarianism, utopia/utopian. A brief bibliography, citing mainly standard and classic sources, is included with each article.

Fifteen scholars, mostly British, contributed to this work. The American edition has been somewhat altered from the British original so as to better serve an American audience.

50. Deferrari, Roy Joseph. **A Latin-English Dictionary of St. Thomas Aquinas, Based on the "Summa Theologica" and Selected Passages of His Other Works.** Boston: St. Paul Editions, 1960. 1115p.

This is an abridgement of the *Lexicon of St. Thomas Aquinas* (entry 51). "It contains all the words and meanings given in the *Lexicon* and most of the research value, but the omission of examples more easily allows a choice of wrong meanings from among the many definitions given" (McLean, *Philosophy in the 20th Century: Catholic and Christian,* vol. 1, p. 5).

51. Deferrari, Roy Joseph, Sister M. Inviolata Barry, and Ignatius McGuiness. **A Lexicon of St. Thomas Aquinas Based on the "Summa Theologica" and Selected Passages of His Other Works.** Washington, D.C.: Catholic University of America Press, 1948-1953. 5 fascicles in 2 vols.

Designed to facilitate understanding of Aquinas's language generally "and not its philosophical and theological aspects exclusively," this lexicon "includes all the words in the *Summa Theologica* and such other words from the remaining works as seem in the judgment of the authors to be of great importance" (foreword). For each word, one or several differing English meanings are given, followed by illustrations of its use in each meaning. If a definition of a term is supplied by Aquinas himself, this precedes any other examples. The text used is that of the Leonine edition (Rome, 1888-1906) for the *Summa,* that of Vives (Paris, 1871-1880) for his other works.

52. Dennon, Lester E., ed. **Bertrand Russell's Dictionary of Mind, Matter, and Morals.** New York: Philosophical Library, 1952. 290p.

Like a number of other "dictionaries" published by Philosophical Library (see entry 85 for a general comment), this is strictly a compilation of quotes: "more than 1,000 selections from over 100 of Lord Russell's books and articles." In addition to being a source for Russell's views, asserts the preface, this can be used as a dictionary of terms related to the topics indicated in the title. This may be true to some extent; for instance, entries for "mind," "justice," or "proposition," or the well-known identification of "number" from the *Introduction to Mathematical Philosophy* bear this out. But the majority of entries are not (nor do they include) even attempts at definition, for example, "deduction," "democracy," and "freedom." Besides relatively pedestrian terms like the examples just cited, there are also intriguing and characteristically Russellian entries such as "America and tyranny of the herd," "Beliefs, harmful," "Democracy, future of," and "Induction and sacred books." Sources of quotes are identified by title with page numbers.

This work is at least among the best of its breed. Since it is the only one whose subject enjoyed the opportunity to provide a preface (a characteristic statement of his approach to philosophy), it is worth noting that he apparently approved of the project.

53. Devine, Elizabeth, et al., eds. **Thinkers of the Twentieth Century: A Biographical, Bibliographical and Critical Dictionary.** London: Macmillan, 1983; Detroit: Gale, 1983. 643p.

Of the four hundred thinkers treated in this reference work on intellectual history, close to a fourth are (or were) philosophers in a fairly strict sense. They include some whose names are (or were) nearly household words (Dewey, Sartre), a few relatively unknown except to specialists (P. W. Bridgman, H.-G. Gadamer, H. P. Grice, G. H. Mead), and a larger group "in between" who, if not necessarily familiar to every educated individual, have had a well-recognized and often wide-ranging influence in twentieth-century thought (Buber, Collingwood, Foucault, Husserl, Jaspers, Ortega y Gasset, Popper, Teilhard de Chardin, Whitehead, Wittgenstein). Among the other figures included, many had a philosophical side or produced work which has been of interest to philosophers, for example, Kenneth Arrow, Karl Barth, Jacob Bronowski, Durkheim, Einstein, Freud, Roger Fry, Buckminster Fuller, Galbraith, Gandhi, Heisenberg, Thomas Kuhn, Lenin, C. S. Lewis, Lewis Mumford, Poincaré, Schweitzer, Toynbee, Von Neumann, and Max Weber.

Each entry includes a brief biographical sketch, a list of the individual's books (articles only rarely, which in some cases constitutes an unfortunate omission), a list of critical studies, and an interpretive essay, usually about a page in length. Lack of any kind of subject access—a classification of thinkers by fields of activity or influence, for instance—is a drawback.

54. **Dictionary of Logic as Applied in the Study of Language: Concepts/Methods/ Theories.** Ed. by Witold Marciszewski. The Hague: Martinus Nijhoff, 1981. 436p. (Nijhoff International Philosophy Series, vol. 9).

While the main theme of this dictionary is the application of logic in the study of language, many of its articles should be of more general interest to logicians, philosophers of science and mathematics, information scientists, and others. It does presuppose an advanced level of knowledge of the general field of logic. The seventy-two articles (there are no short definitions) treat topics as diverse as analyticity, the method of counterexample, decidability, definition, Gödel's theorem, many-valued logic, Polish notation, quantifiers, questions, logical syntax, trees, truth, and the theory of types. Each article includes bibliographic references, and there is a general bibliography at the back (dominated by English-language writings, perhaps surprising in view of the fact that the editor and thirteen of fifteen contributors are Polish scholars). Also at the back are an index of symbols and a subject index and glossary, the glossary serving mainly to correlate synonymous terms and expressions.

55. Eisler, Rudolf. **Kant-Lexikon: Nachschlagewerk zu Kants sämtlichen Schriften, Briefen und handschriftlichem Nachlass.** Berlin: Mittler, 1930. Reprinted, Hildesheim, Germany: Georg Olms, 1961; pbk., 1964. Reprinted, New York: Burt Franklin, 1971. 642p.

Partly a dictionary and partly an index to Kant's works (though far from exhaustive), this reference work strives to let Kant speak for himself as much as possible while at the same time offering something more than a hodgepodge of quotations. Eisler provides explanations of the (German) terms and such comment as he deemed necessary to show or clarify connections. There are numerous cross-references. Sources of quotations from Kant's works, including letters and manuscripts, are carefully identified.

56. **Encyclopaedia of Religion and Ethics.** Ed. by James Hastings with the assistance of John A. Selbie . . . and other scholars. New York: Scribner's; Edinburg: T. & T. Clark, 1908-1922. 12 vols. plus index.

Despite its age, this remains the most comprehensive religious encyclopedia in English, and also the one with the most extensive coverage of philosophical matters. These include especially topics in Eastern philosophy, philosophy of religion, and religious apologetics (e.g., arguments for the existence of God, theodicy, the relation between faith and reason); metaphysical issues of significance for religious thinking (immortality, the mind-body problem, naturalism, libertarianism and necessitarianism); and topics in philosophical ethics (ethical idealism, natural law, Utilitarianism). Recent developments, and current debates, of course, are not represented. On the other hand, this can be an exceptionally valuable guide to the thought and literature of the late nineteenth and twentieth centuries. Because topics are often not under the most obvious headings (or those most familiar to contemporary students), consultation of the very thorough index volume is strongly advised.

57. **Encyclopedia of Bioethics.** Warren T. Reich, editor-in-chief. New York: Free Press; London: Collier Macmillan, 1978. 4 vols.

For purposes of this encyclopedia, "bioethics" encompasses a vast range of ethical issues and value-related problems in the life sciences and health care. That its opening article deals with probably the most prominent of these, abortion, seems somehow appropriate. But succeeding articles deal with issues as diverse as advertising by medical professionals, behavior control, environmental ethics, gene therapy, informed consent in human research, population ethics, sexual ethics, truth-telling, and warfare as it relates to medicine and biomedical science. Other articles cover essential background for intelligent discussion and assessment of specific bioethical issues: basic concepts and principles, general ethical theories, religious traditions, historical perspectives, and surveys of disciplines bearing on bioethics. Many of these background articles can serve a general use beyond their application to bioethics. For instance, the lengthy survey under "ethics" (with twelve individually authored articles on, e.g., deontological theories, naturalism, situation ethics, and Utilitarianism) may profitably be used to supplement and even substitute for material in the *Encyclopedia of Philosophy* (entry 19), since it covers later developments and cites more recent literature.

This is an interdisciplinary (as well as international) work, covering historical, theological, scientific, legal, and social scientific aspects as well as philosophical. The philosophical perspective is heavily represented, however, and of the 285 contributors, 50 are identified as philosophers.

Datedness is a problem in this rapidly developing field, and one would be well advised to augment information from this encyclopedia with some investigation of the literature published since about 1976 (the effective closing date for its coverage). This remains, however, a fundamental reference work, and for most bioethical topics still the best point of departure. Articles are directed "to the educated person who may or may not be a specialist on the topic" (introduction).

58. **Encyclopedia of Indian Philosophies.** Ed. by Karl H. Potter. Delhi: Motilal Banarsidas, 1970- . Princeton: Princeton University Press, 1978-

Potter (professor of philosophy, University of Washington) serves as general editor for this ambitiously conceived reference work, which little resembles an "encyclopedia" in the ordinary sense. Apart from volume 1, the *Bibliography,* each volume covers a particular system or phase in Indian philosophy via a two-pronged approach: first, an extended analytical essay, and second, summaries of as many as possible of the extant philosophical texts. In the volumes issued to date, the summaries comprise the major portion; this appears to be the pattern expected for future volumes as well. The summaries are intended "to make available the substance of the thought contained in these works" for philosophers unable to read the original languages (mainly Sanskrit) or any of the available translations, or who for other reasons "find difficulty in understanding and finding their way about" in these translations.

A list of the individual volumes follows. Those available, which are presumably representative, are described briefly. A late-1983 announcement from the Indian publisher indicated that volumes 4 through 7 were "in progress" and "due to be published shortly," while another eight, not yet numbered, were listed as "under preparation."

59. Volume 1: Karl H. Potter, ed. **Bibliography.** Delhi: 1970. 811p. Rev. ed., Delhi: 1982; Princeton: 1984. 1023p.

See separate listing and description, entry 198.

60. Volume 2. Karl H. Potter, ed. **Metaphysics and Epistemology: The Tradition of Nyaya-Vaisesika up to Gangesa.** Part 1. Delhi: 1977; Princeton: 1978. 752p.

Covers the literature of the classical system of Nyaya-Vaisesika in its earlier stages, i.e., from its inception in the *sutras* (the basic Hindu texts, ca. 400 B.C. to A.D. 600) to the time of Gangesa (about A.D. 1350). Following a "Historical Resume," an analytical essay covers the following topics: theory of value; nature of a philosophical system; relations; substance; qualities and motions; universals, individuators, and absences; meanings and truth; logical theory. Works summarized include the *sutras* of Gautama, the *bhasya* of Vatsyayana, and writings of Udayana.

61. Volume 3. Karl H. Potter, ed. **Advaita Vedanta up to Samkara and His Pupils.** Delhi: 1981; Princeton: 1982. 635p.

Deals with only one (but probably the foremost) of several Vedanta systems, based on the Vedic literature known as the *Upanishads,* "the springs of classical Hinduism." Covers only the earliest segment of the literature of this system, i.e., the *Advaita Vedanta,* up to its most famous figure, Samkara. All of this is explained in the "Historical Resume" (nineteen pages). Following the resume are surveys of major topics addressed in the *Advaita Vedanta* literature: theory of value, philosophy of language, theory of relations, metaphysics, and epistemology. Pages 115 through 346 are devoted to summaries of Samkara's works, the remainder to works by Gaudapada and others. Notes are collected at the end.

62. Volume 4. Larson, Gerald James, and Ram Shankar Bhattacharya, eds. **Samkhya Philosophy.** Forthcoming.

63. Volume 5. Bhattacharya, Sibajiban, and Karl H. Potter, eds. **Navya Nyaya from Gangesa to Raghunatha.** Forthcoming.

64. Volume 6. Larson, Gerald James, and Ram Shankar Bhattacharya, eds. **Yoga Philosophy.** Forthcoming.

65. Volume 7. Coward, Harold G., ed. **Grammarian Philosophy.** Forthcoming.

Under preparation, volume numbers not yet announced:

Malvania, Dalsukh, ed. **Jaina Philosophy.**

Misra, Vidya Niwas, ed. **Kashmir Saiva Philosophy.**

Sundaram, P. K., ed. **Advaita Vedanta** (Part 2).

Krishnamurti Sharma, B. N., ed. **Dvaita Vedanta.**

Jaini, P. S., ed. **Abhidharma Philosophy.**

Ruegg, David Seyfort, ed. **Madhyamika Philosophy.**

Wayman, Alex, ed. **Yogacara Philosophy.**

Nagatomi, Masatoshi, ed. **Buddhist Logicians.**

66. Ferm, Virgilius Ture Anselm, ed. **Encyclopedia of Morals.** New York: Philosophical Library, 1956. Reprinted, New York: Greenwood Press, 1969. 682p.

Among dictionaries or encyclopedias in the field of ethics, Ferm's is, so far, unique. While philosophical concerns dominate, there is also considerable attention to religious views and perspectives and, what is more unusual, to empirical description of moral systems observed in practice. For the latter, Ferm selected, with the advice of a group of anthropologists including Melville Herskovits, "a fairly generous slice of interesting examples of social behavior among societies quite unfamiliar to most readers" (preface). These examples include groups as diverse as the Rio Grande Pueblo Indians, the Aztecs, the Aboriginals of Yirkalla (Australia), and the Riffians (Moroccan Berbers). They certainly do not exhaust the world's variety, but they are representative and offer food for philosophical reflection as well as engrossing social science. This material complements the more standard kinds of articles on religious systems (e.g., Christian, Jewish, Hindu) or subsystems (Quaker, Puritan, Jesuit) and on philosophical topics. There are lengthy articles on individual thinkers (e.g., Aquinas, Sidgwick, Schlick) and on specific ethical theories or schools (e.g., Utilitarianism). Not included are short definitions of terms. Instead, a multitude of cross-references serves as a kind of "index" to direct one to broader topics where such terms are treated in context.

Contributors to this encyclopedia include such distinguished scholars as Lewis White Beck, Howard Brinton, William Frankena, Walter Kaufmann, and Frederick Sontag.

67. Feys, Robert, and Frederic B. Fitch. **Dictionary of Symbols of Mathematical Logic.** Amsterdam: North Holland, 1969. 171p. (Studies in Logic and the Foundations of Mathematics).

That the term "dictionary" may not entirely fit this work is suggested both in the preface by Feys, the original editor, and in the foreword by Fitch, who completed the project. Its purpose is "to enable the reader to find with some ease the meaning and interpretation of symbols currently used in mathematical logic," particularly in a handful of classic and standard texts (identified in the front) and in the *Journal of Symbolic Logic.* It is "intended for readers not having previous knowledge of mathematical logic as well as for logicians who want an explanation of a notation outside their ususal fields" (preface), but it would be difficult for a beginning student to use. The order of presentation is *systematic,* partly for the reason that "the language of mathematical logic is . . . the language of a *formalized* theory," the exact meanings of whose symbols may not be grasped intuitively or given direct verbal translations, but must be understood in the context of the corresponding formalized system, with its axioms, rules, and definitions.

Apart from preliminaries, there are nine chapters covering the following areas of logic: (1) "Propositional Calculus"; (2) "First-Order Functional Calculus"; (3) "Functional Calculus of Higher Orders, and the Theory of Types"; (4) "Combinatory Logic"; (5) "Calculus of Classes"; (6) "Calculus of Relations"; (7) "Arithmetic Formalized as an Independent Discipline"; (8) "Numbers as Defined within Systems of Logic"; and (9) "Metamathematics." Indexes of names, subjects, and symbols follow.

68. Giancotti Boscherini, Emilia. **Lexicon Spinozanum.** The Hague: Martinus Nijhoff, 1970. 2 vols. (International Archives of the History of Ideas, 28).

To serve the Spinoza scholar who "asks from a lexicon not only rapid and easy orientation in the field of Spinozistic concepts, but also the means for terminological and conceptual analysis which is necessarily tied to the original language," this lexicon "sets for itself the following goals: the clarification of the meaning of terms and of concepts, the determination of their reciprocal connections and implications, the bringing out of the semantic ambiguity of some terms, on the one hand, and of the synonymity of other terms, on the other hand, and also the recognition of those elements which are needed for an historical reconstruction of the cultural and environmental milieu of Spinoza" (introduction). The lexicon encompasses all of Spinoza's works—the main part covering the terminology of his Latin texts; an appendix, his Dutch-language writings. There is also a Latin-Dutch glossary. Preface and introduction are in both English and Italian.

69. Goodman, Florence Jeanne. **A Young Person's Philosophical Dictionary.** Los Angeles: Gee Tee Bee, 1978. [55p.]

This slim volume presents what the title page describes, perhaps with tongue in cheek, as "26 nouns which must be known by all who would be wise and virtuous." A short preface suggests, more modestly, that these are "some of the words you might want to have in your philosophical vocabulary." There's one for each letter of the alphabet, from "amiability" to "zest"; among those in between are "beauty," "freedom," "integrity," "matter," "passivity," "utility," and "xenodochy." For each, the author offers a short comment, often designed more to inspire (and to promote, though gently, the author's opinions) than to inform. Attractive black-and-white reproductions of old line drawings or prints illustrate every term. On each facing page, there is another word, starting with the same letter, for which the reader is invited to supply his or her own definition and comment, plus a space to enter a personally chosen word.

While the content often has little connection with "technical" or "scholarly" philosophy, some of it does provide an entry to the sorts of things discussed by professional philosophers. The level of the appropriate audience is somewhat difficult to gauge: the format appears geared for the middle to upper elementary grades, but much of the content would hardly seem comprehensible before the junior high or even high school level.

70. Greenstein, Carol Horn. **Dictionary of Logical Terms and Symbols.** New York: Van Nostrand Reinhold, 1978. 188p.

"The primary objective . . . is to present compactly, concisely, and side by side a variety of notational systems currently used by logicians, computer scientists, and engineers" (preface). That objective, and the considerable success with which it is achieved, should be appreciated by anyone who has ever contended with the differences among notational systems. Familiar, and less familiar, logical expressions, from simple connectives to basic argument forms, are shown not only in such notational systems as Boolean, Polish, Peano-Russell, Hilbert, and set-theory, but even in such modes of representation as logical gates, truth tables, Euler and Venn diagrams, and squares of opposition. In addition to coverage of the more conventional areas of logic—sentential, quantificational, syllogistic, and modal—there are separate sections for notation in epistemic, doxastic, deontic, and tense logics. Greenstein has also gone beyond her stated primary objective by providing two additional and highly useful features: a list of abbreviations and acronyms prevalent in logical and computer literature, and a seventy-seven-page glossary of logical terms.

71. **Handbook of Philosophical Logic.** Ed. by D. M. Gabbay and F. Guenthner. Dordrecht, Netherlands: D. Reidel, 1983- .

A systematic survey of the key areas of philosophical logic (rather than, say, an alphabetically arranged encyclopedia), this may be considered borderline as a reference work. However, in its comprehensiveness, and as the product of a collaborative effort by an international team of authorities, it does perform an encyclopedic function, or something close to it. As such, it should be useful not just to logicians but, as the publisher's advertisements promise, to general philosophers, linguists, mathematicians, and computer scientists as well. The four volumes, as projected, cover the following areas: (1) *Elements of Classical Logic,* (2) *Extensions of Classical Logic,* (3) *Alternatives to Classical Logic,* and (4) *Topics in the Philosophy of Language.* As of this writing, only volume 1 has been published.

72. Kiernan, Thomas P. **Aristotle Dictionary.** New York: Philosophical Library; London: Peter Owen, 1962. 524p.

See entry 85 for a general comment on the series to which this dictionary belongs. As is the case with others of its genre, its "definitions" and articles are confined to quotations from the philosopher's works. It departs from the general pattern, however, by also including a 162-page introductory overview of Aristotle's works (by Theodore E. James). It is also somewhat better than average in two respects. First, its selection of terms and concepts and of pertinent quotations is more judicious than most. Second, it gives the specific source of each quote—in this case, by means of references to the standard Bekker edition of the Greek text of Aristotle's works, published in 1831.

73. Kondakov, Nikolaĭ Ivanovich. **Logicheskiĭ slovar'-spravochnik.** 2d ed. Moscow: Nauka, 1975. 720p. German translation, **Wörterbuch der Logik.** Ed. by Erhard Albrecht and Günter Asser. Leipzig: Bibliografisches Institut, 1978. 554p.

This Russian work (note the German version) is probably the most comprehensive encyclopedic dictionary of logic in existence. Among other dictionaries and handbooks of logic listed in this guide, Gabbay's and Guenthner's (entry 71) may be more extensive when complete; but this is in any case the only one built on an alphabetical arrangement throughout and also centrally concerned with definitions.

An earlier Russian edition was published in 1971 under the title *Logicheskiĭ slovar'*.

74. **Kratkii slovar' po èstetike.** Ed. by Mikhail Fedotovich Ovsiannikov and V. A. Razumnii. Moscow: Izdvesto Politicheskoi Literatury, 1963. 542p. 2d ed., Moscow: Prosveshchenie, 1983. 223p.

"Covers about 250 terms and concepts of Marxist-Leninist aesthetics" (De George, *The Philosopher's Guide,* p. 90, referring to 1st ed.). Ovsiannikov is a major Soviet theoretician in this field, with numerous other publications on aesthetics to his credit.

75. Macquarrie, John. **Dictionary of Christian Ethics.** Philadelphia: Westminster Press, 1967. 366p.

Though theological ethics is its foremost concern, this dictionary also affords substantial coverage of philosophical perspectives, concepts, issues, and thinkers. Illustrative of philosophically oriented entries are "categorical imperative," "choice," "Cynics," "emotivism," "ethical language," "Kant and Kantian ethics," "natural law," "right and wrong," and articles on philosophers such as F. H. Bradley, T. H. Green, Hegel, Mill, and Socrates. Such entries are generally authored by contributors with solid reputations in philosophy, including V. J. Bourke, A. C. Ewing, R. M. Hare, T. E. Jessop, D. M. MacKinnon, and Ninian Smart. Given the attention to both philosophical and theological concerns, there is, disappointingly, less effort to build bridges between them than one would hope.

76. Morris, John, ed. and transl. **Descartes Dictionary.** New York: Philosophical Library, 1971. 274p.

This work is one of a series of dictionaries on individual philosophers issued by the publisher (see entry 85 for a general comment). This one is better than some others: more scholarly, more focused in purpose, and more balanced in its selection of terms. It remains, however, a compilation of quotes only. There are no systematic treatments of Descartes's use of a term or of his views on a subject, nor do the quotes necessarily allow one to form a coherent picture. The most one may expect is some salient or perhaps merely interesting statements on a given topic. Entries relating to Descartes's central concerns include body, demonstration, God, and mind, but there are also selections reflecting his opinions on topics as varied as America, blushing, humility, and rats. Sources are identified with reference to the standard Adam and Tannery edition of Descartes's works. Most of the translations were especially prepared for this volume.

77. Mourre, Michel, ed. **Dictionnaire des idées contemporaines.** New ed. Paris: Editions universitaires, 1966. 720p.

Something close to a handbook of twentieth-century intellectual history (its nearest counterpart in English is Devine's *Thinkers of the Twentieth Century,* entry 53), this *dictionnaire* is dominated but definitely not exhausted by philosophical thinkers and developments. Part 1 consists of nine essays on intellectual trends since 1900. Part 2, titled "Dictionnaire des philosophes et essayists," features articles on key thinkers as various, and often divergent, as Barth, Carnap, Freud, Gandhi, Heidegger, Toynbee, Weber, and Wittgenstein. (Literary figures and theoreticians of science, however, are not included, being covered by companion volumes.) This section also notes major nineteenth-century influences: Comte, Hegel, Marx, Nietzsche, and others.

78. Nauman, St. Elmo, Jr. **Dictionary of American Philosophy.** New York: Philosophical Library, 1973. Pbk. ed., Totowa, N.J.: Littlefield, Adams, 1974. 273p.

A balanced work this is not. Two lists at the front identify, respectively, nineteen "major" philosophers and a smaller group of ten who are "the most outstanding" or "have had the greatest influence." Yet a figure on neither list, William Ames, who "never reached America (he died en route)," gets eleven pages, while two in the "top ten," Peirce and Whitehead, get two pages each. There are also imbalances between biographical and topical entries (only fifteen pages of the latter); in the choice of topics (an entry for conscience but none for science or philosophy of science); within the topical articles (the one on social philosophy discusses John Adams exclusively!); in the choice of individuals counted as philosophers (Ambrose Beirce but not Edward Bellamy); and between biographical matters and discussion of an individual's ideas (C. S. Peirce's thought occupies barely half a page of the two pages under his name, and another page under Pragmatism). The examples could easily be multiplied. Look to this dictionary for informative bits and pieces, and for interesting anecdotes, but not for balanced treatment or even, with any degree of reliability, the most essential information.

79. Nauman, St. Elmo, Jr. **Dictionary of Asian Philosophies.** New York: Philosophical Library, 1978. 372p.

The "Asian Philosophies" of the title refers to Middle Eastern as well as Far Eastern philosophies. Major thinkers, schools of thought, philosophical texts, terms, and concepts are covered in this dictionary, which is really a concise encyclopedia. Survey articles are provided as well, e.g., on Indian philosophy, and Jewish philosophy, but not, curiously, Islamic philosophy. The latter omission represents but one of several seeming disparities in Nauman's work. Another instance is the absence of any mention of Fung Yu-lan in the survey article on Chinese philosophy, though the entry for him runs to four pages and describes him as "one of the most important philosophers in contemporary China." Add to these faults an occasional omission of basic information (the article on the Hare Krishna movement neglects to identify it as a form of Hinduism) and the lack of an index for topics located under other headings (e.g., Krishna under Bhagavad-Gita). The upshot is that this work is useful but not as useful as it could be. There is no competing dictionary devoted specifically to Asian philosophy, but one might look to a good dictionary covering Eastern religions and to more general works such as the *Encyclopedia of Philosophy* (entry 19) for supplementary coverage.

80. Nauman, St. Elmo, Jr. **New Dictionary of Existentialism.** New York: Philosophical Library, 1971. 166p.

Largely supersedes Winn's *Concise Dictionary of Existentialism* (entry 94). It improves on its predecessor in several respects: (1) it covers a wider range of thinkers, now including Nietzsche, Berdyaev, Tillich, and several Existential psychologists; (2) it identifies quotes more precisely; (3) it is *not* restricted to quotes, but augments them with explanatory material by Nauman; and (4) it provides biographical entries for key figures. The selection of entries is somewhat better, with some of Winn's omissions corrected (e.g., absurd, bad faith), though some entries included by Winn have been dropped (e.g., time), and some key concepts are still missing (e.g., authenticity, intentionality). Conspicuously absent are being-for-itself and being-for-others—conspicuously because they have dead-end cross-references under in-itself.

81. **New Catholic Encyclopedia.** Prepared by an Editorial Staff at the Catholic University of America, Washington, D.C. New York: McGraw-Hill, 1967. 15 vols. **Supplement 1967-1974,** vol. 16, 1974. **Supplement: Change in the Church,** vol. 17, 1979.

Though not primarily a philosophical work, the *New Catholic* is simply too rich a resource to overlook or to omit here. "The treatment of philosophy in this encyclopedia is extensive, since an attempt is made to treat all of the subject as this relates to Catholics or Catholicism. . . . Primary emphasis is on Catholic systems and philosophers, but detailed consideration is given to non-Catholic thought that has significantly influenced, either positively or negatively, that of Catholics" (volume 11, p. 292). This self-description introduces the entry titled "Philosophy, Articles on," which provides the best overview of the encyclopedia's philosophical content and which complements, with its systematic approach, the alphabetical access afforded by the index in volume 15. Several hundred entries relating to philosophy are identified.

The *Supplement 1967-1974* has useful updates under "philosophy, contemporary" and "philosophy, recent developments in." Other philosophical topics in both supplements may be traced through their respective indexes.

82. Peters, Francis Edward. **Greek Philosophical Terms: A Historical Lexicon.** New York: New York University Press; London: University of London Press, 1967. 234p.

Peters's dictionary is aimed at neither the scholarly specialist nor the beginner, but at the intermediate student. A useful, authoritative tool for the study of Greek philosophers "on their own terms" (preface), it seeks to strip away as much as possible of the historical baggage accrued through later developments or carried by the common English translations. As a whole, it documents and clarifies the gradual development of philosophical language from its roots in daily life, in myth, and in epic, to an increasingly specialized and technical vocabulary, the latter stage represented particularly by Aristotle. Plato and Aristotle, predictably, dominate this dictionary, but there is also extensive attention given to the terminology of both the Pre-Socratics and the "Post-Aristotelians" (e.g., Stoics, Epicureans, and Neoplatonists).

Entries are arranged alphabetically according to the English transliteration of the Greek terms. Knowledge of Greek or the Greek alphabet is not required, though it is likely that the most common use of this dictionary begins with an awareness of a particular Greek term: perhaps *arete, dike,* or *eidos* (for a student of Plato), or *pathos, psyche,* or *telos* (for a student of Aristotle). However, there is an English-Greek index which permits reference from an English term to its Greek original. Peters describes the index as complete, but at least one omission should make one wonder: the term *eidos* (possibly the most prominent and even notorious term in Plato) is various translated as "idea" or "form," but only the latter appears in the index. Yet that oversight, striking as it may be, should not detract unduly from a high estimation of Peters's work.

83. **La philosophie.** Ed. by André Noiray. Paris: Centre d'étude et de promotion de la lecture, 1969. 545p.

This encyclopedic dictionary of *la philosophie* is actually restricted to contemporary philosophy and its nineteenth- and early twentieth-century antecedents. Besides short entries (a paragraph to two pages) for some four hundred terms, it features what it calls "nine essential articles" of more substantial length. Five of these deal with major modern movements, several especially influential in France: Existentialism, Marxism, Phenomenology, Psychoanalysis, and Structuralism. Another discusses "the idea of philosophy since Hegel," and the remainder consider three significant concerns of modern thought: the nature and theory of science, of technology, and of political society. Throughout, this work seems to strive for greater mass appeal than is typical of philosophical dictionaries. Not only the breadth of subject coverage and the level of treatment, but even some of its physical characteristics contribute to this aim: contemporary design and typefaces; a distinctive treatment for the "nine essential articles," complete with thumb-indexing and contributors' photos; instructions, with diagrams, for "how to use this encyclopedia with maximum profit"; and an unusual placement of notes, including bibliographic references, in the margins.

For those who can handle French, *La philosophie* can be an unusually inviting window on modern European thought.

84. Riedl, John Orth, et al. **A Catalogue of Renaissance Philosophers (1350-1650).** Milwaukee: Marquette University Press, 1940. Reprint, Hildesheim, Germany: Georg Olms, 1973. 179p.

"Catalogue" is an apt term for this work which categorizes Renaissance thinkers into 102 different schools and movements, arranged in rough chronological sequence from early Italian Humanists to Occasionalism. The concept "philosopher" is interpreted liberally, so that "many scientists, ascetics, theologians and rhetoricians have been included . . . partly because some of their writings either were philosophical or had an influence on philosophy, and partly because their inclusion aids materially in the reconstruction of the comprehensive body of knowledge which the first philosophers of modern times received as their inheritance . . ." (foreword). Each entry consists of basic biographical data followed by a list of writings (with minimal bibliographic apparatus). "The biographical details selected were usually those that designated the education, teachers, university connections and pupils of a thinker, and such other details as might help to place him in some one or two of the maelstrom of conflicting tendencies in his lifetime." At the back are a table of universities, bibliography of basic secondary sources, and index of names.

85. Runes, Dagobert D. **Spinoza Dictionary.** New York: Philosophical Library, 1951. Reprinted, Westport, Conn.: Greenwood Press, 1976. 309p.

This is the first of a number of similar "dictionaries" issued over several decades by Philosophical Library. Though never formally designated a series, they are similar enough to warrant a general comment here. Each is confined strictly to quotations from the philosopher or (in one case) group of philosophers which is its subject. The quotations relate to specific terms or concepts, and are accordingly arranged alphabetically, but they are not necessarily definitional or even explanatory. Often, they merely exemplify some of a philosopher's views or pronouncements on a topic.

To call a compilation of quotations a dictionary is neither unprecedented nor entirely inappropriate. Still, it may mislead by creating the expectation that it will yield definitions or systematic explanations. In the case of this series, that expectation is often unjustifiably encouraged by exaggerated claims included in prefaces or cover blurbs. Furthermore, while there is considerable variation in quality in the series, many of the volumes do badly even what they really set out to do: by neglecting topics that are significant, even central, in a philosopher's thought (while sometimes including peripheral topics); by making poor or inadequate selections of quotes; or by failing to identify sources of quotes with any useful precision. Where the last-named deficiency exists, one possible use of a quotations dictionary—namely, as an index to locate specific passages and if desired to trace their context—is effectively frustrated.

Runes's dictionary on Spinoza is not only the first but also one of the better efforts in the series. It offers a selection of quotes on matters most likely to be of interest to, and within the grasp of, the non-specialist wishing to dip into Spinoza's thought—a selection which dodges most of the terminological and stylistic difficulties tending to make that thought so notoriously forbidding. The majority of quotes are drawn from the *Ethics,* but other works and Spinoza's voluminous correspondence are tapped as well (though not the *Principia Philosophiae* or the *Cogitata Metaphysica*). The average length of the quotes significantly exceeds that for the series as a whole, which generally speaking must be counted a virtue. Translations are mainly those by R. H. M. Elwes in *The Chief Works of Benedict de Spinoza*, 3d ed. (1889). Sources of quotes are identified with at least a moderate degree of precision (specific parts or sections of works, or numbered letters in the case of correspondence).

86. Saisselin, Rémy G. **The Rule of Reason and the Ruses of the Heart: A Philosophical Dictionary of Classical French Criticism, Critics, and Aesthetic Issues.** Cleveland: Case Western Reserve University Press, 1970. 308p.

Saisselin's work has two parts. The first is arranged alphabetically by key terms in aesthetics and criticism from the period of French classicism, roughly the 1630s to the late 1700s. An expository and interpretive essay is provided for each term. The second part deals with specific writers, e.g., Corneille, Diderot, Montesquieu, Rousseau, Voltaire. Numerous cross-references connect the various articles. "On the whole, . . . a worthwhile effort to show both the theoretical background and the practice of French classicists" (*Modern Language Journal* 52 [April 1972]:651).

87. Sass, Hans-Martin. **Martin Heidegger: Bibliography and Glossary.** Bowling Green, Ohio: Philosophy Documentation Center, Bowling Green State University, 1982. (Bibliographies of Famous Philosophers).

See entry 236. The glossary, which occupies sixty-four pages, "presents the English, Chinese, French, Italian, Japanese and Spanish translations of just one hundred (100) words, fundamental to Heidegger's thinking" (p. 450). It is preceded by an appropriately Heideggerian rumination on questions about language.

88. **Slovar' po ētike.** Ed. by I. S. Kona. 5th ed. Moscow: Izd-vo Politicheskoi Literatury, 1983. 445p.

For anyone who can read Russian, or who has access to a translator, this Dictionary of Ethics can be an excellent source on Marxist-Leninist ethics and officially sanctioned Soviet perspectives on morality. It covers the history of ethical thought as well as specific topics in moral and social philosophy.

New editions of this work have been appearing with remarkable frequency: the first edition was published in 1965 (under the title *Kratkii slovar' po ētike*), the second (with the present title) in 1970, the third in 1975, and the fourth in 1981.

89. Stewart, David and Algis Mickunas. **Exploring Phenomenology: A Guide to the Field and Its Literature.** Chicago: American Library Association, 1974. 165p.

"[W]ritten for the non-specialist and for the generally educated reader who wants to know more about phenomenology" (preface), this work's seven succinct chapters survey the field, specifically the following topics: general themes; the foundational work of Husserl; its later development; Existential Phenomenology; treatment of traditional problems (e.g., free will, perception, values); application to other disciplines (e.g., psychology, religion); and "ongoing tasks." Complementing each chapter is a selective yet substantial bibliography. Books and articles in English are emphasized, but some foreign-language works are also represented. A total of 426 items are listed, the majority with brief descriptive annotations. Bibliographies on individual thinkers other than Husserl (e.g., Heidegger, Jaspers, and Sartre) are relegated to an appendix.

A complementary work for Anglo-American Analytic philosophy, Michael Corrado's *The Analytic Tradition in Philosophy* (American Library Association, 1975), is a more conventional survey with a much less pronounced bibliographic orientation.

90. Stockhammer, Morris, comp. **Kant Dictionary.** New York: Philosophical Library, 1972. 241p.

This is one of a series of "dictionaries" on individual philosophers issued by the publisher; for a general comment, see entry 85. This one exemplifies most of the worst faults of the genre. Some of its quotes do scant justice to the concepts they deal with, e.g., those for categories and antinomy of pure reason. Others are nearly meaningless without explanation or context; consider, for instance, "Manifold, The": "The manifold is given us in a sensuous intuition." Or see the three quotes under categorical imperative: two are variant formulations of the principle so named, but nothing explains what it *is,* or why it has variant formulations. Since sources of quotes are identified by title only, it is well-nigh impossible to trace them back to their context. This may even frustrate one's appreciation of some of the more tantalizing quotes on non-technical subjects: bible, bigotry, "Kant's thirst," rape, sex education, tobacco, etc. Neither the scholar, the student in need of help, nor the curious layperson ends up well served.

91. Stockhammer, Morris. **Karl Marx Dictionary.** New York: Philosophical Library, 1965. 273p.

See entry 90 and the general comment on the series in entry 85. Like the *Kant Dictionary*, this cites sources of quotes by title only. The presentation of quotes without context or explanation may work somewhat better with Marx than with Kant, since Marx tends (though by no means invariably) to be somewhat less technical and less abstruse. The selection of quotes is fairly good and covers economic and political as well as philosophical topics. The *Communist Manifesto* and *Das Kapital* are especially heavily mined, as one might expect, but seventeen other works are drawn on as well. Translations, based on the *Gesamtausgabe* (Berlin and Moscow, 1927-1935), are by Moore and Aveling.

92. Stockhammer, Morris. **Plato Dictionary.** New York: Philosophical Library, 1963. Pbk. ed., Totowa, N.J.: Littlefield, Adams, 1965. 287p.

See entry 85 for a general comment. Of Stockhammer's several efforts in this vein (cf. entries 90, 91, and 93), this is probably the best. Given a body of writings as large and varied as Plato's, one can inevitably turn up passages that cry out to be included but haven't been (e.g., under the term "Opinion," some of the discussion on the difference between knowledge and opinion in the *Meno*). On balance, though, Stockhammer has managed an interesting and representative selection of quotes. No more than that, however: the pretentious declaration in the introduction that "a new look at Plato's ethics of moral ideas has occasioned this book which is written in a non-technical language" perhaps epitomizes the penchant of works in this series to masquerade as more (or at least as other) than what they are.

Sources of quotes are specifically identified with reference to the standard pagination of the Stephanus edition. The text comes mainly from the archaic translations by Jowett (1871).

93. Stockhammer, Morris. **Thomas Aquinas Dictionary.** New York: Philosophical Library, 1965. 219p.

See entry 85 for a general comment on the series. The vast majority of quotes in this compilation are very short, usually a single sentence. Some entries seem to serve an indexing function rather than to present anything of substance insofar as the entry term itself is concerned. A case in point is this quote under horse and donkey: "Horse and donkey are different beings, but both are animals." No entries are included which do not correspond to a word or words used in the quotations. Thus, there are no entries for the terms "Cosmological Proof," "the Five Ways," "ontology," "*via negativa*," or other such terms likely to come up in discussions of Aquinas's philosophy. The editor states that "only entries that are of interest to the modern reader were included, whereas items of merely medieval concern were omitted" (preface), but offers no further explanation. Most quotes are drawn from the *Summa Theologica,* a few from the *Summa Contra Gentiles.* Citations refer to the standard divisions of these works, including the numbered questions and answers characteristic of Aquinas's philosophical style.

94. Winn, Ralph Bubrich. **A Concise Dictionary of Existentialism.** New York: Philosophical Library, 1960. 122p.

Largely (but not completely) superseded by entry 80, this work resembles other dictionaries in a Philosophical Library series covered by a general comment under entry 85, except that it features quotations from the works of several philosophers: Kierkegaard, Jaspers, Marcel, Heidegger, Sartre, and De Beauvoir. As a distillation of Existentialism it is thin at best; most of its 122 pages are not even very full. Some key concepts are neglected: the absurd, authenticity, bad faith, boundary situations (Jaspers), intentionality, and paradox (Kierkegaard). Others are but scantily covered: e.g., the quotes under the word "Time" include none from Heidegger's *Being and Time.* Sources of quotes are identified by title only.

95. Winn, Ralph Bubrich, ed. **John Dewey: Dictionary of Education.** New York: Philosophical Library, 1959. 150p.

Like some other dictionaries issued by its publisher (see entry 85 for a general comment), this is entirely a compilation of quotations from a major philosopher. The difference in this case is a more limited subject matter. It covers Dewey's thought on education (mostly of a philosophical cast) and also some of the larger philosophical context for that thought. Thus, besides entries for educational topics such as discipline, learning, methods of instruction, reading, and teaching, it features quotes on broader but related Deweyan themes such as art, democracy, experience, happiness, society, and value. Sources of quotes are identified by title only.

96. Wood, Ernest. **Vedanta Dictionary.** New York: Philosophical Library, 1964. 225p.

Like other traditional schools of Indian thought, the Vedanta—a Hindu system based on the *Vedanta Sutras* (also known as the *Brahma Sutras*)—represents an inseparable mixture of religious and philosophical elements. It is, however, not only among the most philosophical systems, but also one that (particularly in the form known as Advaita) has continued to undergo considerable development in the modern period. Entries in this dictionary that have some familiarity for a Western philosophical orientation include the absolute, cause and causation, ethics and morals, materialism, space and time, and freedom of the will. There are also many Sanskrit terms, most of which designate philosophical, religious, and psychological concepts with no direct English equivalent, and entries for major Vedanta thinkers.

Wood, an intimate but not notably scholarly student of Indian and other Eastern religious thought, has also produced a *Yoga Dictionary* (1956) and *Zen Dictionary* (1962), issued by the same publisher. Both of these, however, are very thin on philosophical content.

97.   Wuellner, Bernard, S. J. **Dictionary of Scholastic Philosophy.** 2d ed. Milwaukee: Bruce, 1966. 339p.

"This dictionary, covering most of the technical language used in all branches of scholastic philosophy, is meant chiefly for undergraduate students" (preface). Many others, nonetheless, should find it at least equally useful. Preference is given to terms found in or defined by Aristotle or Aquinas, the twin springs of Scholasticism, but ample heed is given also to the concepts of later thinkers such as Duns Scotus and Suarez and prominent Neo-Scholastics such as Gilson and Maritain. Particular attention is given to compound terms and phrases, which are usually placed under the entry for the principal term. For example, under the entry for cause are located such expressions as "cause of being (*causa in esse*)," "dependent (subordinate) cause," and "false cause, fallacy of." A weakness, perhaps unavoidable, is that many definitions are quite abstract and employ other Scholastic terms that may be as unfamiliar as the term being defined. Some backtracking will usually overcome the problem.

Twenty tables and diagrams bring together many of the most significant classifications and distinctions that are characteristic of Scholastic thought: categories of being, divisions of efficient causes, divisions of the good, types of law and their relations, figures of the syllogism, and others.

5

GENERAL INDEXES, ABSTRACTS, REVIEWING JOURNALS, AND SERIAL BIBLIOGRAPHIES

I. PRINTED SOURCES

98. **Bibliographie de la philosophie,** 1937-1953. Vols. 1-10. Paris: Libraire Philosophique J. Vrin, 1937-1958.

Compiled by the staff of the Institut Internationale de Philosophie, this serial bibliography and index attempts to cover exhaustively philosophical publications, books as well as journal literature, in most Western languages. It did not appear for several years during World War II (1940-1945); the gap is filled by De Brie's *Bibliographia philosophica* (entry 110).

The two major sections of each issue are (1) an integrated, alphabetical author listing of books and journal articles and (2) a systematic subject index subdivided into a chronological/geographical section, an index of philosophers, and an index of concepts and terms. In addition, there are a directory of publishers by country and a directory of periodicals.

Volume 10 of this series, not published until 1958, is a "hybrid" bridging the transition of the *Bibliographie* to a radically revised scope and format. (See entry 99.)

99. **Bibliographie de la philosophie/Bibliography of Philosophy,** 1954- . Paris: Libraire Philosophique J. Vrin, 1954- . Vol. 1- .

The adoption of joint English and French titles accompanied this publication's transition from a bibliography listing both books and periodical articles to one covering books only. A new volume numbering was also begun with this change. However, a transitional volume, covering the years 1952-1953, was published belatedly (1958) as the final volume (number 10) of the original series; this covered only books and carried the dual-language title, but followed the old format and lacked the abstracts that are a major virtue of the new series.

The present publication is not only international in scope but also polylingual, providing abstracts in the language of origin for books in English, French, German, Italian, and Spanish, and in either English or French for books in other languages. In a typical year, well over a thousand books are covered in the *Bibliographie*. The abstracts, which are signed, are intended to be factual and not critical. They vary in length from a few to sometimes more than thirty lines. Entries and abstracts are contributed via "centers of philosophical bibliography" in the individual countries represented in the Institut Internationale de Philosophie, the Paris-based organization responsible for the *Bibliographie* and one of several international bodies (UNESCO is another) associated with its publication.

The *Bibliographie* employs a systematic arrangement with ten broad and rather standard divisions (philosophy in general; logic and philosophy of science; ethics and values; etc.). Indexes are not provided in each quarterly issue — only cumulated annual indexes in the final issue of each volume. One of these indexes combines authors, titles, and title catchwords. Another, labeled "Index of Names," combines publishers, writers of prefaces, translators, and individuals referred to in titles or in abstracts. This system of indexing, which can be cumbersome to use, is perhaps the least satisfactory feature of the *Bibliographie*.

100. **Bulletin signalétique 519: Philosophie,** 1970- . Vol. 23- . Paris: Centre de Documentation du C.N.R.S., 1970- .

Covering worldwide serial literature and aspiring, with at least fair success, to do so exhaustively, this publication is part of the immense indexing and abstracting program carried on by the French Centre National de la Recherche Scientifique (C.N.R.S.) under the umbrella title *Bulletin signalétique*. This particular part has a complex bibliographic history, having appeared first under the title *Bulletin analytique: Philosophie* (1947-1955, volumes 1-9), and subsequently as the *Bulletin signalétique*, in varying combinations of subject coverage with varying subtitles:

> 1956-1960, volumes 10-14: *Philosophie, Sciences humaines.*
>
> 1961-1968, volumes 15-21: *Sciences humaines* (Section 19: Philosophie, Sciences religieuses).
>
> 1969, volume 22: *Philosophie, sciences religieuses.*
>
> 1970- , volumes 23- . As cited above.

Throughout these changes, it has surprisingly maintained a single sequence of volume numbers and has also remained a quarterly. The *tables annuelles,* or annual indexes, presently appear separately as a fifth issue in each volume.

The *Bulletin* employs a classified arrangement, with the *plan de classement* printed in the front of each issue. Abstracts, usually brief, are in French, regardless of the language of the article or the country of origin of the journal in which it is published. Book reviews, but *not* books themselves, are cited, and are often summarized in a short abstract as well. An index of journals covered in each issue is provided, as well as separate author and subject indexes. All three indexes are cumulated in the *tables annuelles.*

101. **The Philosopher's Index**, 1967- . Vol. 1- . Bowling Green, Ohio: Philosophy Documentation Center, Bowling Green State University, 1967- .

Launched in 1967, *The Philosopher's Index* quickly established itself as the preeminent indexing and abstracting service for philosophers and students in the Anglo-American orbit, and for many beyond it as well. All major philosophy journals in English, French, German, Spanish, and Italian are indexed, along with selected journals in other languages and related interdisciplinary publications. Coverage has been extended to books only since 1980, and only to books in English. The subtitle, *An International Index to Philosophical Periodicals,* was not changed to reflect its widened scope until 1982, when the words "*and Books*" were added.

After some initial variation, the *Index* settled into its present pattern of organization, a highly satisfactory one which deserves wider emulation. The basic division is into subject and author listings, with full bibliographic information and abstract (always in English) furnished in the author section. The subject index refers to the full entries in the author section; but since it gives the full title of the cited article or book plus the author's name (instead of, say, a meaningless entry number), the user can often assess the likely relevance of an item from the information in the subject index alone, thus reducing laborious flipping between subject and author indexes. Subject descriptors, while mostly narrow and specific, sometimes cast so wide that they net vast numbers of entries (especially in the annual cumulation) which are unmanageable for most purposes. But there is usually compensation in that items may be listed under several, even many, descriptors.

A separate section of the *Index* covers book reviews. Every issue also has a section explaining the *Philosophy Research Archives*, a microfilm journal also geared to "on-demand" publication. Articles accepted into the *Archives* are covered in the main sections of the *Index.*

For retrospective coverage of materials published prior to 1967, see entries 102 and 103.

102. **The Philosopher's Index: A Retrospective Index to U.S. Publications from 1940.** Bowling Green, Ohio: Philosophy Documentation Center, Bowling Green State University, 1978. 3 vols.

This retrospective index includes articles published in American philosophy journals between 1940 and 1966, and original philosophy books (i.e., not including new editions, reprintings, etc.) published in the United States between 1940 and 1976. The difference between dates of coverage for journal literature and those for books is presumably due to the fact that books began to be included in the regular *Philosopher's Index* series only in 1980 (though this seems still to leave a small gap: some, though certainly not all, books published in 1976 and 1977 appear to have fallen through the "crack").

Arrangement is identical to that used in the current series, with volumes 1 and 2 containing the subject index, and volume 3 the author index with abstracts. Many of the abstracts are reprinted from other sources, including the *Bibliographie de la philosophie, Philosophic Abstracts,* and journals such as the *Review of Metaphysics.*

103. **The Philosopher's Index: A Retrospective Index to Non-U.S. English Language Publications from 1940.** Bowling Green, Ohio: Philosophy Documentation Center, Bowling Green State University, 1980. 3 vols.

This work is similar to entry 102 but covers books and journal literature published outside the United States. While international in scope and encompassing material published in countries which are not English-speaking, it does include only material written in English, differing in that respect from the current *Philosopher's Index.*

104. **Philosophic Abstracts.** 1939-1954. Vols. 1-16. New York: Philosophical Library, 1939-1946 (vols. 1-6). New York: Russell F. Moore, 1947-1954 (vols. 7-16).

Evidently conceived more as a current awareness and reviewing publication than as a comprehensive bibliographic tool, *Philosophic Abstracts* typically covered fifty to one hundred books in each of its quarterly issues. While selective, it did provide international coverage, including non-English as well as English-language books, and employed a geographical arrangement by country of publication. Until 1950, it also carried lists of periodical literature, i.e., journal articles; but these, too, were highly selective, and they did *not* include abstracts.

Many of the abstracts for books were quite lengthy and would more accurately be called reviews, especially those that contained critical and evaluative comment as well as factual information. No doubt this explains why, especially in its early years, so many of its abstracts, which were signed, could be contributed by distinguished figures such as George Boas, Rudolf Carnap, Paul O. Kristeller, Richard McKeon, Ernest Nagel, I. M. Bochenski, and Vernon J. Bourke.

For its first half decade, *Philosophic Abstracts* was edited by Dagobert Runes. Later editors were Ralph Winn and the publisher, Russell F. Moore. Moore also brought out a cumulated index under the title *Decennial Index to Philosophical Literature, 1939-1950* (n.d., 115p.).

105. **Philosophical Books,** 1960- . Vol. 1- . Leicester, England: Leicester University Press, 1960-1978. Oxford: Basil Blackwell, 1978- .

Philosophical Books is a quarterly journal which "aims to provide prompt, scholarly reviews of new professional books and journals in philosophy and the history of philosophy" (from a statement printed at the back of each issue). Founded in 1960 by the editorial committee of the journal *Analysis,* it is very selective and emphasizes books which reflect the concerns of Anglo-American Analytic philosophy. That emphasis, however, while dominant, is not exclusive. A typical issue contains two dozen or more substantial review articles which normally are critical as well as descriptive. A regular discussion feature allows authors of selected titles an opportunity to respond to reviewers. Special issues may be devoted to a single theme.

A *Cumulative Index to Philosophical Books: Volumes 1-15 (1960-1974),* compiled by Julius F. Ariail, has been published separately (Statesboro, Ga.: Sweet Bay Press, 1980, 40p.).

106. **Philosophischer Literaturanzeiger: Ein Referateorgan für die Neuerscheinungen der Philosophie und ihrer gesamten Grenzgebiete**, 1949- . Meisenheim am Glan: Anton Hain, 1949- . Vol. 1- .

Each bimonthly issue of this review journal, which is published in conjunction with the *Zeitschrift für philosophische Forschung,* carries reviews of around twenty new books. If the majority of these are German, or at least German translations, some significant non-German titles are also reviewed in most issues. The board of editors includes philosophers from several countries.

107. **Répertoire bibliographique de la philosophie**, 1949- . Vol. 1- . Louvain: Institut superieur de Philosophie, 1949- .

Writing before the advent of the *Philosopher's Index,* H. J. Koren (see entry 6) called this "perhaps the *most important* tool for assembling a bibliography on a particular subject." While the importance of the *Répertoire* has unquestionably diminished since then, at least for the typical English-speaking scholar or student, it remains for some an alternative and for others a significant supplement to the *Philosopher's Index.* It coves a number of non-English journals not included in the *Index,* and also non-English books, which the *Index* excludes as a matter of policy. Unlike the *Index,* however, the *Répertoire* does not provide abstracts.

The *Répertoire*'s scope and arrangement are thoroughly explained – in French, English, German, Spanish, and Italian – in the introduction to the first issue of each annual volume. As it has since 1949, it focuses its attention on materials in these languages: Catalan, Dutch, English, French, German, Italian, Latin, Portuguese, and Spanish. Works in other languages *may* be included, but the exhaustiveness claimed for the languages mentioned is specifically disclaimed for any others. Entries for books and journal articles are intermingled in the *Répertoire*'s classified arrangement, but those for books are distinguished by an asterisk. The classification scheme divides broadly into a historical section, with both chronological and geographical subdivisions, and a systematic section, subdivided for major branches of philosophic thought. No indexes are provided in the three regular issues which appear in February, May, and August, but the November issue, reserved for book reviews, contains a cumulated general name index (*table onomastique*) for authors, translators, and reviewers, and also, in a feeble gesture toward subject indexing, philosophers mentioned in the titles of works cited.

The present *Répertoire,* an independent publication, succeeds an earlier one which appeared, from 1934 to 1948, as a supplement to the *Revue néo-scholastique de philosophie,* later the *Revue philosophique de Louvain,* and also, for part of the same period, as a supplement to the Dutch *Tijdschrift voor Philosophie* under the title *Bibliographisch Repertorium.* (Most of this period has since been more thoroughly covered by De Brie's *Bibliographia philosophica,* entry 110). Both the *Répertoire*'s origins and its present sponsorship suggest, and explain, a Neo-Scholastic orientation. However, any bias is noticeable in the inclusion of material others might conisder marginal rather than in the exclusion of anything generally considered central to philosophy.

II. COMPUTERIZED DATABASES

108. **Philosopher's Index.** Bowling Green, Ohio: Philosophy Documentation Center, Bowling Green State University.

The *Philosopher's Index* database corresponds to the printed indexes, both current and retrospective, of the same name (see entries 101, 102, and 103), except that it does not include book reviews. It provides coverage from 1940 to the present. In addition to affording the same access by author and subject descriptors available with the printed versions, it permits computer searching by keywords in other fields of the bibliographic record, such as titles and abstracts, and permits rapid execution of complex search strategies involving multiple search terms combined with Boolean operators.

As of September 1985, the *Philosopher's Index* database was available through the DIALOG system (file 57), which can be accessed at most academic and many of the larger public libraries. A guide to the database is available from Dialog Information Services, Inc., 3460 Hillview Avenue, Palo Alto, Calif. 94304. The *Philosopher's Index Thesaurus,* edited by Richard H. Lineback (Bowling Green, Ohio: Philosophy Documentation Center, 1979, 65p.), is intended particularly to facilitate searching of the database.

Those interested in more selective online searching of journal literature citations in philosophy might consider the *Humanities Index* database, available through the H. W. Wilson Company's WILSONLINE. Though not limited to philosophy, the *Humanities Index* covers many of the core philosophy journals listed in chapter 13, plus a few others.

6
GENERAL BIBLIOGRAPHIES

109. Bochenski, Innocentius M., ed. **Bibliographische Einführungen in das Studium der Philosophie.** Berne: Francke, 1948-1953. Nos. 1-23.

This is a series of brief, selective bibliographies featuring mainly twentieth-century materials. All are decidedly out-of-date. However, the annotations (in German) provided in most issues may still be of some interest or utility. In addition, some issues may have continuing value because similar — and updated — coverage is not widely available, at least not in as convenient a form, or because they include references to German materials not readily identifiable otherwise. Following is a list of the individual numbers.

1. I. M. Bochenski and F. Montelone, *Allgemeine philosophische Bibliographie.* 1948. 42p.

2. Ralph B. Winn, *Amerikanische Philosophie.* 1948. 32p.

3. E. W. Beth, *Symbolische Logik und Grundlegung der exakten Wissenschaften.* 1948. 28p.

4. Régis Jolivet, *Kierkegaard.* 1948. 33p.

5. Olaf Gigon, *Antike Philosophie.* 1948. 52p.

6. P. J. de Menasce, *Arabische Philosophie.* 1948. 49p.

7. Michele F. Sciacca, *Italienische Philosophie der Gegenwart.* 1948. 36p.

8. M.-D. Phillippe, *Aristoteles.* 1948. 48p.

9. Régis Jolivet, *Französische Existenzphilosophie.* 1948. 36p.

10. Michele F. Sciacca, *Augustinus.* 1948. 32p.

11. Karl Dürr, *Der logische Positivismus.* 1948. 24p.

12. Olaf Gigon, *Platon.* 1950. 30p.

13/14. Paul Wyser, *Thomas von Aquin.* 1950. 78p.

15/16. Paul Wyser, *Der Thomismus.* 1951. 120p.

17. Fernand van Steenberghen, *Philosophie des Mittelalters.* 1950. 52p.

18. Othmar Perler, *Patristische Philosophie.* 1950. 44p.

19. Georges Vajda, *Jüdische Philosophie.* 1950. 40p.

20/21. C. Régamey, *Buddhistische Philosophie.* 1950. 86p.

22. Odulf Schäfer, *Johannes Duns Scotus.* 1953. 34p.

23. Otto Friedrich Bollnow, *Deutsche Existenzphilosophie.* 1953. 40p.

110. Brie, G. A., de. **Bibliographia Philosophica, 1934-1945.** Vol. I: Bibliographia Historiae Philosophiae. Brussels: Ed. Spectrum, 1950. 644p. Vol. II: Bibliographia Philosophiae. Antwerp: Ed. Spectrum, 1954. 798p.

De Brie's outstanding accomplishment was to fill the gap left by the discontinuation or debilitation of the major serial bibliographies during the war years 1939-1945, when "European scholars were unable to get in touch with the bibliographical literature of Great Britain and the American continent, whereas overseas [i.e., British and American] students lost contact with continental philosophers" (introduction). In particular, his work supplements, as well as cumulates and revises, the *Répertoire bibliographique de la philosophie* (entry 107), which during that period was being published as a supplement to two Neo-Thomist journals.

De Brie's first volume deals with the history of philosophy and is arranged generally in chronological order. Volume II covers philosophy systematically; its arrangement, by branches, virtually duplicates that of the *Répertoire bibliographique.* Between the two volumes, there are over 48,000 entries representing books and articles in a dozen languages: Danish, Dutch, English, French, German, Italian, Latin, Norwegian, Portuguese, Spanish and Catalan, and Swedish. Entries for books, marked with an asterisk, also have citations to reviews appended to them. An unusual feature is the use of Latin for headings and sub-headings: *theoria cognitionis, cosmologia,* etc. This can present difficulties for the user who does not know Latin, but most of the terms are readily decipherable. The introduction is in English as well as five other European languages.

The editor's intention to continue this work with five-year supplements, announced in the introduction and reported by other writers even in fairly recent citations, has never been carried out.

111. **Catalog of the Hoose Library of Philosophy, University of Southern California.** Boston: G. K. Hall, 1968. 6 vols.

Reproduced in these volumes, by means of photolithography, are catalog cards representing some 37,000 volumes in the Hoose Library. According to the introduction, "all titles of significance for the study of Western philosophy" are within the library's scope, but it also offers a number of areas of special strength. These include the classical philosophers, German philosophy, Personalism, Phenomenology, and Latin American philosophy; for at least two historical periods, the Enlightenment and Romanticism, it offers something approaching "the bibliographical ideal of comprehensiveness." The library owns numerous first editions of philosophical texts, as well as incunabula and manuscripts, all reflected here.

The catalog reproduced here is a dictionary catalog, incorporating author, title, and subject entries in a single alphabetical sequence. More than an access tool for a particular library, it can also do duty as a philosophical bibliography of extremely broad scope.

112. Guerry, Herbert, ed. **A Bibliography of Philosophical Bibliographies.** Westport, Conn.: Greenwood Press, 1977. 332p.

Covering philosophical bibliographies in all countries from 1450 to 1974, this comprehensive work is divided into two lists. The first is labeled "Bibliographies of Individual Philosophers" and is arranged alphabetically by names (it includes some coverage of schools designated by individuals' names: Thomism, Hegelianism, etc.). The second list, labeled "Subject Bibliographies," is arranged alphabetically by topic. Coverage is confined, with a few exceptions, to bibliographies published separately, either as monographs or in journals. Annotations, which are few, are usually limited to indicating the number of items cited. Cross-referencing is provided, but is not always thorough. An index of editors/compilers is at the back of the volume.

113. Harvard University Library. **Philosophy and Psychology.** Cambridge, Mass.: Harvard University Library, distributed by Harvard University Press, 1973. 2 vols. (Widener Library Shelflist, 42-43).

Some 59,000 books, periodicals, and pamphlets are included in these two volumes, part of a massive series, begun in 1965, documenting the rich resources of Harvard's Widener Library. Subjects covered, according to the preface, include "metaphysics in general, cosmology, ontology, epistemology, logic, aesthetics, and psychology." Philosophy of religion is encompassed, but not the philosophies of other disciplines (science, history, law, etc.).

The series title, Widener Library Shelflist, may be misleading, since only a portion of volume 1 corresponds to what librarians understand by a shelflist, that is, a listing in classification order, or by call number. Also in volume 1 is a chronological listing by date of publication—an unusual and occasionally valuable aid to historical research. Volume 2 contains a listing by author and title (interfiled). Thus, not only is this in effect a very comprehensive bibliography of philosophy, but one that affords a unique variety of access points.

114. Plott, John C., and Paul D. Mays. **Sarva-Darsana-Sangraha: A Bibliographical Guide to the Global History of Philosophy.** Leiden: E. J. Brill, 1969. 305p.

The authors aspire to promote the "globalization" of the history of philosophy by integrating coverage of Western and non-Western philosophies. This is a laudable aim, though pursued here with rather too much breastbeating about European enthnocentrism and hyperbolical gestures of obeisance to the goal of "the development of WORLD COMMUNITY" (see especially page xii of the introduction). All the more ironic, therefore, that Plott and Mays organize much of "global history" on a scheme of periodization appropriate mainly for Western history. Thus, in chapters labeled with period names such as "Classical," "Medieval," "Renaissance," and "Modern," references on Western philosophers alternate, in simple alphabetical sequence, with references on roughly contemporaneous non-Western philosophers. Disclaimers about the bugbear of periodization (page xvii), quotation marks surrounding such period labels, or even a footnote proclaiming that a label such as "Renaissance" is "only for convenience" and "means nothing in the global context" (page 112), cannot adequately mitigate this ill-advised arrangement. The impression it leaves is that there really is no meaningful way to relate Western and non-Western philosophy.

Despite its faults, this volume does have value as a guide to useful European-language materials, some of them obscure, others easy to overlook. It is the only annotated guide that covers a wide range of non-Western philosophies (Chinese, Japanese, Indian, Arabic, etc.). Though quite dated by now, it can still be a help to those for whom it was primarily designed: undergraduate or early graduate students and philosophy faculty with no specialized knowledge of non-Western thought.

A "synchronological chart" is housed in a pocket inside the back cover.

115. Rand, Benjamin, comp. **Bibliography of Philosophy, Psychology and Cognate Subjects.** New York: Macmillan, 1905. 1 vol. in 2. Reprinted: New York: Peter Smith, 1949.

Rand's bibliography constitutes volume 3 (in two parts) of J. M. Baldwin's *Dictionary of Philosophy and Psychology* (entry 13). It is often, as here, cited separately. Among the most ambitious bibliographical efforts in philosophy by a single individual, it aimed to be "though not exhaustive, . . . comprehensive in its scope" (preface). Some 60,000 titles are listed, journal articles and reviews as well as books. One limitation on its scope was set by Rand's decision to concentrate mainly on philosophical literature available at the time. There are no annotations.

Rand's work is divded into two major sections. The first, labeled "Bibliography A, History of Philosophy," occupies most of part 1. Though it begins with the main historical and geographical divisions, the bulk of it is devoted to individual philosophers, in alphabetical, *not* chronological sequence. Bibliographies B through G, occupying part 2, deal systematically with the major branches of philosophy and with psychology.

Rand has been criticized, in his own time and since, for omitting certain topics (e.g., philosophy of history and philosophy of language) and for other shortcomings. However, the magnitude of his effort is generally acknowledged and acclaimed, and its product remains even now of some value, particularly for its nearly exhaustive coverage of nineteenth-century authors. Furthermore, its conjunction with Baldwin's encyclopedia gave it an unusually wide distribution, so that it is available, even now, in many libraries that do not have in-depth philosophy collections.

116. Tobey, Jeremy L. **The History of Ideas: A Bibliographical Introduction.** Santa Barbara, Calif., and Oxford: American Bibliographical Center/Clio Press, 1975- . Vol. 1, Classical Antiquity, 1975, 211p. Vol. 2, Medieval and Early Modern Europe, 1977, 320p.

Though on the one hand this work limits itself to the period up to about 1727 (the death of Newton), and on the other hand ranges beyond philosophy, it deserves to be included in this chapter as a rich and very useful resource covering a substantial segment of philosophy's long history. Over a third of each volume is devoted to specifically philosophical materials. Other areas covered are the history of science, religious thought, and "aesthetics" (a term Tobey employs beyond its narrow meaning in philosophy to embrace a wide range of criticism, historical scholarship, theorizing, and opinionizing about the arts). All three areas, of course, encompass much that borders on philosophy or is of interest for philosophical thought.

Tobey's mode of presentation is the bibliographic essay. References are embedded in a succinct but highly readable narrative which describes the topography of the subject area, including the important issues and controversies, and relates the cited work to this in terms of its scope or thesis, and often its specific strength, weakness, or bias. In the process, Tobey's personal judgments and opinions frequently come into play; but, when expressed, these represent recognized alternatives, and cannot be considered idiosyncratic. They are also the apparent product of deep immersion in the intellectual history of the periods covered. Works in English are stressed, but important non-English works are also cited.

Citations are handled well. References in the essays are adequate to identify the work in question, but full bibliographic details are reserved for the "index" (more accurately, an alphabetical bibliography by author) at the end of each volume.

117. Totok, Wilhelm, et al. **Handbuch der Geschichte der Philosophie.** Frankfurt am Main: Vittorio Klostermann, 1964- . Vol. I, **Das Altertum,** 1964. 400p. Vol. II, **Mittelalter,** 1974. 676p. Vol. III, **Renaissance,** 1980. 658p. Vol. IV, Part 1, **Frühe Neuzeit: 17. Jahrhundert,** 1982. 612p.

Whatever the connotation of *Handbuch,* this is actually a massive bibliography of the history of philosophy. Tobey (see entry 116) cites this work frequently and extols its thoroughness. He also calls its second volume "the best detailed guide to the literature" of the medieval period, and he mentions a number of specific topics for which Totok is an exceptionally good resource (e.g., Aquinas, mysticism); "the best general guide" (for Aristotle); or even "indispensable" (for Ockham). It should be borne in mind, however, that Totok's work is conceived as supplementing Ueberweg's (entry 118) and as such concentrates on literature of the period from 1920 to the editorial cutoff dates for the individual volumes. Earlier publications are listed only if they are textual editions or other works which still have unusual scholarly significance. Also, despite its monumental coverage, the *Handbuch* does not pretend to be exhaustive, and in fact it gives ample warning to the contrary (see volume I, *Vorwort*).

Materials in Western languages predominate. Periodical articles and essays in collections are listed as well as books. Arrangement is generally chronological, excepting areas outside the mainstream of Western philosophical development (e.g., Oriental, Islamic, and Jewish philosophy). Each volume has an author and a subject index.

Two physical characteristics make this work somewhat forbidding. One is a heavy use of abbreviations. The second is the presentation of bibliographic lists (in alphabetical author arrangement under subject headings and subheadings) set solid, i.e., as if ordinary text in paragraph form. Embedded in this dense arrangement are occasional brief annotations, in italics, which indicate basic works, works still in progress, and sometimes the thesis or theme of a work.

118. Ueberweg, Friedrich. **Grundriss der Geschichte der Philosophie.** 11. & 12. Aufl. Berlin: E. S. Mittler, 1923-28. Reprinted, Basel: Benno Schwabe, 1951-1957 and 1960- . Reprinted, Darmstadt: Wissenschaftliche Buchgesellschaft, 1967- . 5 vols.

Essentially a history of philosophy, this work is so rich in bibliography (though more in its eleventh and twelfth editions than in earlier ones) that it is often listed among the major philosophical bibliographies. Its scope is international, though German scholarship may be emphasized, and it encompasses both monographic and periodical literature. Coverage extends to roughly 1920.

Listed below are the five volumes, each with an individual editor responsible for the latest revision (the twelfth edition in all cases except volume 2, which did not go beyond an eleventh edition).

1. *Die Philosophie des Altertums.* Karl Praechter.

2. *Die patristische und scholastische Philosophie.* Bernhard Geyer.

3. *Die Philosophie der Neuzeit bis zum Ende des 18. Jahrhunderts.* Max Frischeisen-Kohler and Willy Mog.

4. *Die deutsche Philosophie des neunzehnten Jahrhunderts und der Gegenwart.* Traugott K. Oesterreich.

5. *Die Philosophie des Auslands vom Beginn des 19. Jahrhunderts bis auf die Gegenwart.* Traugott K. Oesterreich.

In each volume, bibliographies of primary sources are incorporated in the sections (long or short) concerned with their authors. Bibliographies of secondary sources are gathered at the end, except in volume 5, where they follow individual chapters. The bibliographies can be rather intimidating, not simply for their size but for their typographical density and extensive use of abbreviations — problems similar to those noted for the Totok work (entry 117) which supplements the Ueberweg bibliographies and seems to be modeled on them as well.

The reprint edition by Schwabe listed above (apparently published with other dates as well) is dubbed 13. *Auflage* (thirteenth edition), but clearly states it is an "unaltered photomechanical reprinting" of the eleventh and twelfth editions. An actual new edition, edited by Paul W. Wilpert, has been reputed in progress for some years (cf. De George, entry 3, page 6), but has not appeared so far. A two-volume English translation of Ueberweg (1887 and subsequent) is based on the fourth German edition and omits the bibliographies.

119. Varet, Gilbert. **Manuel de bibliographie philosophique.** Paris: Presses Universitaires de France, 1956. 2 vols. (Logos: Introduction aux etudes philosophiques).

Varet's is a selective bibliography ranging over the entire field of philosophy, and often beyond. Tobey (entry 116) characterizes it, in fact, as "close to being the only bibliographical survey of the entire history of ideas"—alluding, presumably, to the pervasive inclusion of literature on theology, the history of science, and the history and criticism of the arts. Its overall arrangement falls into two parts. Volume 1, *Les philosophies classiques,* covers the history of philosophy more or less chronologically through Kant and neo-Kantian schools. Volume 2, *Les sciences philosophiques,* treats systematically the major areas of philosophical thought, grouped under three headings: "Philosophy of history and culture" (including the philosophies of religion and art), "Philosophies of sciences" (including logic and general epistemology), and "Philosophies of man" (comprising moral, social, political, and educational philosophy, and also philosophy of being, existence, and value). This grouping, and likewise the arrangement within groups, reflects specific conceptions held by Varet regarding the nature and structure of philosophy, and the bibliographer's task of exhibiting and elucidating the same. The working out of these sometimes idiosyncratic conceptions in their finer details may pose obstacles for the unwary user (who will probably not expect, for example, to find sensation and perception covered in a chapter on the philosophy of physics). Varet's peculiarities are more fully described by Jasenas, entry 328, pages 107-11.

Despite the idiosyncrasies, this is, with some twenty- to twenty-five-thousand entries, a rich and very comprehensive resource. Coverage is especially strong for the period 1914-1934, making up to some extent the gap between Ueberweg (entry 118) and De Brie (entry 110). Headings, occasional notes, and prefatory matter are all in French.

7

SPECIALIZED BIBLIOGRAPHIES: BRANCHES, SCHOOLS, AND PERIODS

I. PRINTED WORKS

120. Albert, Ethel M., and Clyde Kluckhohn. **A Selected Bibliography on Values, Ethics and Esthetics in the Behavioral Sciences and Philosophy, 1920-1958.** Glencoe, Ill.: Free Press, 1959. 342p.

Prepared under the auspices of Harvard's Laboratory of Social Relations and Stanford's Center for Advanced Study in the Behavioral Sciences, this bibliography covers literature on values from many perspectives. Only pages 225-299 are devoted to philosophy per se, but sections devoted to other disciplines — anthropology, psychology, sociology, political science, economics, and others — also offer much grist for philosophical mills. While arrangement is by disciplines, there is a guide to the bibliography and an associated numerical guide which give access to topics without regard to disciplinary boundaries or perspectives. An author index is also provided. Many entries include a brief, usually single-sentence summary of content or thesis.

121. Ashworth, E. J. **The Tradition of Medieval Logic and Speculative Grammar from Anselm to the End of the Seventeenth Century: A Bibliography from 1836 Onwards.** Toronto: Pontifical Institute of Medieval Studies, 1978. 111p.

This is a bibliography of secondary works (books, articles, some lengthy book reviews, and a few dissertations) and of modern editions of texts concerned with formal logic from the period indicated in the main title. Its scope is conceived "as including such topics as consequences, syllogistic, supposition theory, and speculative grammar, but as excluding such topics as the categories, the struggle between nominalism and realism, and pure grammar" (preface). A total of 879 items are listed in two parts covering respectively the period up to Paul of Venice and the period after. Four indexes are supplied, covering names, texts, translations, and subjects.

122. Baatz, Charles Albert. **The Philosophy of Education: A Guide to Information Sources.** Detroit: Gale Research, 1980. 344p. (Gale Information Guide Library; Education Information Guide Series, vol. 6).

Baatz builds on an earlier bibliography by Broudy (entry 131) in two ways: (1) by concentrating on the literature published since Broudy's work, i.e., from 1967 to 1978, although a scattering of older works is also included; (2) by employing a modification of the organizational scheme devised by Broudy, diagrammed and explained with some care in the first chapter. The number of books and articles listed, and in most cases briefly annotated, is estimated in the neighborhood of two thousand. Chapter 12 is a very selective bibliography for general philosophical background. Indexes by author, subject, and (for books only) title are included.

123. Bastide, Georges. **Ethics and Political Philosophy.** New York: Cultural Center of the French Embassy, 1961. 96p. (French Bibliographical Digest, no. 34).

Lists 711 French books and journal articles; all appear to be from the period 1946-1958. Among the authors included are Raymond Aron, Simone de Beauvoir, Julien Benda, Jaques Maritain, Pierre Teilhard de Chardin, and Simone Weil. Many entries, especially those for books, have brief annotations.

Also published in French as *Bibliographie Française: Morale et philosophie politique* (Paris: 1961).

124. Baxandall, Lee. **Marxism and Aesthetics: A Selective Annotated Bibliography: Books and Articles in the English Language.** New York: Humanities Press, 1968, 1973. 261p.

Baxandall's aim in this volume is to "afford a guide to the chief Marxist theoretical contributions, practical studies and controversies" represented in English-language works (including translations) up to early 1967. A vast miscellany of sources, beginning with the foundational works of Marx, Engels, Plekhanov, Mehring, Lenin, and Lukács, are cited and annotated, with "descriptive rather than judgmental" annotations. "Decisions as to whether some writings 'really' were Marxist had no place. . . . When in doubt the compiler opted to include rather than exclude" (introduction).

A reviewer of this work in *American Reference Books Annual* (1970, volume 2, page 42) complained that the compiler "is not familiar with the basic principles of bibliographical organization, nor is he accurate and there are many errors." The first of those criticisms perhaps applies to the unusual arrangement by authors' nationality or language-grouping. While there is some justification for that approach in this instance, it should nonetheless have been supplemented with adequate subject access. There are indeed topic indexes for each of the thirty-six geographical and linguistic divisions, but only a very limited general topic index.

125. **Bibliographia Patristica: Internationale patristische Bibliographie.** Berlin: Walter de Gruyter, 1959- . Vol. 1- .

Lists books and periodical literature relating to the early Church Fathers. Theological subject matter predominates: the *philosophica* section is generally brief. However, additional philosophical material is listed in sections on individual authors, notably Augustine, Origen, Tertullian. The *Auctores* sections include both works by (i.e., new editions and translations) and works about an author. Entries are not annotated. Prefatory material is in German; subject headings are in Latin.

Volume 1, published in 1959, covers the year 1956. Published in annual volumes through volume 11; after that, each volume consolidates two years and carries double volume numbers, beginning with volume 12/13, published in 1975 and covering 1967-1968. The latest issue as of this writing is volume 24/25, covering 1979-1980, published in 1984.

126. **Bibliographie der Sozialethik: Grundsatzfragen des öffentlichen Lebens/Bases for Social Living,** 1961/63- . Ed. by Arthur F. Utz, et al. Freiburg im Breslau: Herder, 1963- . Vol. 3- .

Volumes 1 and 2 of this series, covering 1956 to 1961, were published with the subtitle (also given in French and Spanish) as main title; see entry 142.

Books and articles in the four major European languages, and some in others, are listed according to a classification scheme which is outlined in the front of each issue. (Headings in the outline are in German, French, and English). The headings for the five major divisions are given below, together with a sampling of subheadings indicative of the strongly philosophical bent of this bibliographic resource:

    I. Principles of Social Doctrine

         4.3 Social philosophy

         4.4 Social ethics

         7.   Social justice and social security

   II. Philosophy of Law

  III. The Social Order

        13.2 Nature and aim of the State . . .

  IV. The Economic Order

        1.7 Philosophy of economics

        1.8 Ethics of social economy

        7.   The fundamental ethico-economic principles of economic society

        7.2 Private property

        8.   The just price

V. The Political Order
1. History of political philosophy
4.2 Ethical fundamentals, politics and ethics
5.2 Civil rights and liberties; duties

There is only an author index, but this includes authors mentioned in the titles of works cited.

127. **Bibliography of Bioethics.** Ed. by LeRoy Walters. Detroit: Gale Research, 1975-1980. Vol. 1-6. New York: Free Press; London: Collier Macmillan, 1981-1983. Vol. 7-9. Washington, D.C.: Kennedy Institute of Ethics, 1984- . Vol. 10- .

Sponsored and compiled by the Kennedy Institute of Ethics, Georgetown University, this annual bibliography encompasses bioethics as a cross-disciplinary and multidimensional field. Three broad dimensions are identified in the introduction (printed with minor variations in all volumes): (1) "health care ethics . . . the rights and duties of health professionals and their patients"; (2) "research ethics . . . value problems in biomedical and behavioral research"; and (3) "the quest to develop reasonable public-policy guidelines for both the delivery of health care and the conduct of biomedical and behavioral research." The bibliography aims at comprehensive coverage of all English-language materials, and incorporates a variety of print and non-print materials, including, e.g., films and other audiovisual media, court decisions, bills, and unpublished documents, as well as books and articles. (Volume 9 reports that 63.5 percent of its entries are journal articles.)

Entries in the subject index (the main body of the bibliography) include lists of applicable descriptors but, until recently, no abstracts. Beginning with volume 9, some abstracts are being included, but only for articles from fifteen key journals in the field of bioethics. Separate author and title indexes are provided. Other useful features included in each volume are a bioethics thesaurus and lists of bibliographic sources, journals, and newspapers systematically monitored by the research staff of the Kennedy Institute.

An online version, BIOETHICSLINE, is available through the National Library of Medicine network; see entry 174.

128. **Bibliography of Society, Ethics and the Life Sciences.** Hastings-on-Hudson, N.Y.: Institute of Society, Ethics and the Life Sciences; The Hastings Center. 1973-1979/80.

During the years it appeared, this publication offered excellent selective coverage for the wide range of ethical issues relating to medicine, health care, and biological science. From 1975 on, however, it duplicated to a large extent the *Bibliography of Bioethics* (entry 127), although it did offer as an advantage over the latter annotations for selected items. Arrangement is topical, with broad problem areas (behavior control; death and dying; genetics, fertilization, and birth; health care delivery; etc.) subdivided in most cases into more specific issues. The successive volumes are *partly* cumulative; that is, they incorprate selectively the more important items listed in earlier volumes.

While this bibliography is no longer published under the above title, nor on a regular basis, it is continued with modifications in the *Hastings Center's Bibliography of Ethics, Biomedicine, and Professional Responsibility* (entry 146).

129. Blackwell, Richard J. **Bibliography of the Philosophy of Science, 1945-81.** Westport, Conn.: Greenwood Press, 1983. 585p.

This work offers comprehensive coverage of the vast contemporary literature on the philosophy of science, a field which, as Blackwell's introduction notes, has emerged during the years covered as "not only a separate and distinctive branch of philosophy but more significantly as a role model which has had considerable impact on the more traditional parts of philosophy" (and often beyond philosophy, as in "one preeminent case, Kuhn's notion of cognitive paradigms"). The bibliography comprehends both issues concerning the methodology, epistemology, and conceptual framework of science, and issues raised by specific scientific concepts, doctrines and theories, such as quantum mechanics and relativity theory in the physical sciences, biological species and evolution in the biological sciences. Excluded are cognate areas such as philosophy of logic and mathematics, philosophy of technology, philosophy of social sciences, and value issues raised by the natural sciences.

Items cited include books, articles in journals and collections, and book reviews, but not dissertations. Arrangement is topical, and there is an author index. Appendices list volumes in three major series in the philosophy of science, which are also frequently referenced in the bibliography.

130. Bochenski, Joseph M., et al., eds. **Guide to Marxist Philosophy: An Introductory Bibliography.** Chicago: Swallow Press, 1972. 81p.

"This book is a guide to readings . . . written for English-speaking students . . . . [O]nly the minimum has been said about the [Marxist] doctrines, in order to indicate the nature of the books recommended" (introduction).

Following an initial chapter on the philosophical background of Marx (Hegel and Feuerbach) are individual chapters devoted to six basic varieties of Marxism: (1) the thought of Marx himself; (2) German Classical Marxism, originating with Engels; (3) Soviet Marxism-Leninism; (4) Neo-Marxism, including interaction and dialogue with Existentialism, Freudianism, and Christianity; (5) Chinese Marxism; and (6) the New Left. (This last chapter, dominated by Marcuse, reflects the political atmosphere of the late sixties and early seventies.) Quite selective, the guide lists somewhat over 150 sources, primarily books. The selection has been judged rather biased by some reviewers, but the editors would probably defend their choices with reference to criteria spelled out in the introduction, notably the intent to avoid secondary literature by those "whose desire is not to instruct but to gain partisans."

131. Broudy, Harry S., et al. **Philosophy of Education: An Organization of Topics and Selected Sources.** Urbana, Ill.: University of Illinois Press, 1967. 287p. **Supplement.** 1969. 139p.

A much-emphasized dimension of this work, signaled in the subtitle, is its endeavor to develop a structure for the field of philosophy of education and, derivatively, its bibliography. The resulting scheme is diagrammed in the form of a grid, each cell of which represents the intersection of one of four broad problem areas (nature and aims of education; curriculum design and validation; organization and policy; and teaching and learning) with one of eight areas of philosophical inquiry (epistemology; metaphysics; ethics and value theory; aesthetics; logic, semantics, language; philosophy of science; man and society; philosophy of religion). Each division of the bibliography corresponds to a cell in the grid, except for a substantial philosophical background section and two others which fall outside the scheme: one on educational research and the science of education, the other on the nature and status of philosophy of education. A vast number of books and articles, mostly published during the middle third of this century, are listed and briefly described.

The *Supplement* lists an additional 526 items.

132. Brown, Marshall G., and Gordon Stein. **Freethought in the United States: A Descriptive Bibliography.** Westport, Conn.: Greenwood, 1978. 146p.

"Freethought may be defined as thought which is free of dogmatic assumptions (usually those of religious dogma) and which seeks to answer all questions through rational inquiry. As such, it includes atheism, rationalism, and secular humanism" (preface). Philosophical thought is but one element in freethought thus broadly defined, and judging by this bibliographic guide, not necessarily the most important. Nonetheless, significant philosophical positions within and philosophical influences upon American freethought are among the matters covered here, and covered in a way not likely to be paralleled elsewhere.

133. **The Classical World Bibliography of Philosophy, Religion, and Rhetoric.** New York: Garland, 1978. 396p. (The Classical World Bibliographies; Garland Reference Library of the Humanities, vol. 95).

This volume is one of a series of five which reprints bibliographic surveys published originally in the journal *Classical World* and "directed towards the particular requirements of research and pedagogy in the United States and Canada" (introduction). It includes nineteen separately authored bibliographies, each devoted to a special topic and offering "a comprehensive, though not exhaustive, listing, summary, and analysis of major books and articles covering a discrete period of time." Those most centrally concerned with philosophy include surveys of works on the Pre-Socratics from 1945 to 1966; on Plato, 1945-1955; on Aristotle (three separate surveys, including one on Aristotle's psychology, one on the *Poetics,* and a general survey for 1945-1955); on Epicurus and Epicureanism, 1937-1957; on Hellenistic philosophy, 1937-1957; and on Lucretius, 1945-1972. Five surveys are concerned with Cicero, two with Seneca, two with ancient rhetoric, and one with Roman religion. Each bibliography is briefly described in the introduction.

134. Douglas, Kenneth. **A Critical Bibliography of Existentialism (The Paris School).** Yale French Studies, Special Monograph no. 1 (1950). Reprinted, New York: Kraus Reprint, 1966, 1974. [32p.]

Concerned exclusively with three figures of the Paris school, Sartre, DeBeauvoir, and Merleau-Ponty, this work lists publications by them in chronological order, and publications about them under specific topics. Extensive annotations contribute to some continuing usefulness despite the fact that it covers only the early period of its subject.

135. Draper, John William. **Eighteenth Century English Aesthetics: A Bibliography.** Heidelberg: Carl Winters Universitätsbuchhandlung, 1931. (Anglistische Forschungen, Heft 71). Reprinted, New York: Octagon Books, 1968. 140p.

Covering one of the liveliest periods of thought about aesthetics, this bibliography lists contributions by artists and critics as well as philosophers. Works relating to specific art forms (parts 2 through 5) far outnumber the general works on aesthetics in part 1. An appendix titled "Some Recent Comments on Eighteenth Century Aesthetics" lists selected secondary materials.

136. Elliston, Frederick A., and Jane van Schaik. **Legal Ethics: An Annotated Bibliography and Resource Guide.** Littleton, Colo.: Fred B. Rothman, 1984. 199p.

"This monograph is intended as a reference guide for teachers of professional responsibility and legal ethics, legal scholars and philosophers conducting research on the practice of law" (preface). The field of legal ethics, the authors go on to note, "has come to attract the attention of other academics, notably philosophers working in the emerging discipline of professional ethics," whose interests typically extend beyond formal codes or rules. "Accordingly, the bibliography is much broader in scope than the issues raised by the Model Rules" of the American Bar Association. Part 3, "Related Materials," lists and annotates general books and some articles on ethical theory, philosophical approaches to professional ethics, and philosophy of law.

137. Emmett, Kathleen, and Peter Machamer. **Perception: An Annotated Bibliography.** New York: Garland, 1976. 177p. (Garland Reference Library of the Humanities, vol. 39).

Concentrates on the philosophical literature on perception from the period 1935-1974. Some works from other areas of philosophy and from other disciplines, particularly psychology of perception, are included when, in the compilers' judgment, they "have been or should be important to philosophers interested in perception" (preface). The bibliography is arranged alphabetically by author. A subject index gives access both by concepts and divisions of the field (e.g., awareness, cognitive theories, illusion, intentionality, neurophysiology, realism, primary qualities, sense datum, touch) and by the names of significant figures whose theories are discussed (D. M. Armstrong, J. L. Austin, Ayer, Berkeley, Chisholm, Hume, Locke, Merleau-Ponty, G. E. Moore, H. H. Price, Russell, Ryle, Wittgenstein, and others). Name entries sometimes include works by the individual in question, sometimes not.

Annotations, largely descriptive, are provided for most of the nearly fifteen hundred items listed.

138. Gayley, Charles Mills, and Fred Newton Scott. **A Guide to the Literature of Aesthetics.** Berkeley: Supplement to the Report of the Secretary of the Board of Regents, University of California, 1890. Reprinted, New York: Burt Franklin, 1974. 116p.

Lists primarily nineteenth-century works, mainly books, but also some periodical literature (grouped under the titles of the periodicals). Materials in English, French, and German are included. Many appear also in later bibliographies, but a good number are not readily identifiable otherwise. The only annotations are those which indicate the specific sections of general and collective works that deal with aesthetic issues. Arranged by subject.

139.　Goehlert, Robert, and Clair Herczeg. **Anarchism: A Bibliography.** Monticello, Ill.: Vance Bibliographies, 1982. 122p. (Public Administration Series, Bibliography no. P-902).

　　Covers both the theory and practice of anarchism. Under the term "Philosophy of Anarchism" are sections on works relating anarchistic ideas to ideas on socialism, nonviolence, the state, education, economics, and art. Individual anarchist thinkers covered in separate sections include Bakunin, Godwin, Paul Goodman, Kropotkin, Proudhon, and Stirner.

140.　Goldstein, Doris Mueller. **Bioethics: A Guide to Information Sources.** Detroit: Gale Research, 1982. 366p. (Gale Information Guide Library; Health Affairs Information Guide Series, vol. 8).

　　Among the information sources Goldstein identifies and annotates are organizations, programs, and special library collections; these are collected in part 1. Printed sources (and one computerized database) are distributed between part 2, "General Sources . . .," and part 3, "Topical Sections." The latter includes a good brief bibliography of background works on general ethical theory, a section for general works on bioethics, and sections on the major areas of concern within the broad field of bioethics: abortion, genetic intervention, behavior control, human subjects research, death and dying, and others. The majority of publications listed are from the period 1973-1981, though a special effort was made to identify the most significant pre-1973 writings. All cited items are available at the library of the Center for Bioethics (see entry 370), where the compiler is director of library and information services.

141.　Gothie, Daniel L. **A Selected Bibliography of Applied Ethics in the Professions, 1950-1970: A Working Sourcebok with Annotations and Indexes.** Charlottesville, Va.: University Press of Virginia, 1973. 176p.

　　Includes chapters on ethical issues in the areas of business and management, engineering, government and politics, health sciences, law, science, and social sciences. Most of the books and articles listed are not rigorously "philosophical," but do address issues of philosophical import. The majority of journal articles cited come from professional journals in the fields to which they relate. Annotations are usually too brief and perfunctory to be of any real use.

　　In the area of business and management only, Gothie's work is supplemented by two bibliographies by Donald G. Jones (entries 148 and 149).

142.　**Grundsatzfragen des öffentlichen Lebens: Bibliographie (Darstellung und Kritik), Recht, Gesellschaft, Wirtschaft, Staat / Bases for Social Living: A Critical Bibliography Embracing Law, Society, Economics, and Politics.** Edited by Arthur F. Utz. Vol. 1 (1956-1959), and vol. 2 (1959-1961). Freiburg: Herder, 1960-1962.

　　The title is also given in French and Spanish. Continued as *Bibliographie der Sozialethic* (entry 126).

143. Hammond, William A. **A Bibliography of Aesthetics and of the Philosophy of the Fine Arts from 1900 to 1932.** Rev. ed. New York: Longmans, Green, 1934. Reprinted, New York: Russell & Russell, 1967. 205p.

This selective, not exhaustive, bibliography is dated and largely unannotated, but still valuable for the period covered. Included are books, articles, some doctoral dissertations, and some book reviews. Chapters 1-3 list general treatises and histories; chapters 4-15 cover narrower topics, including individual art forms, problems concerning style and symbolism, and the relation of art to psychology, morality, and religion.

144. Harari, Josué V. **Structuralists and Structuralisms: A Selected Bibliography of French Contemporary Thought (1960-1970).** Ithaca, N.Y.: Diacritics, 1971. 82p.

Structuralism has been an unusually wide-ranging movement. As a method, it has been applied in many disciplines (most famously, perhaps, in anthropology, by Claude Lévi-Strauss). Achieving the status of an ideology, it has challenged other comprehensive philosophies and world views, including Existentialism, Christianity, and Marxism. Harari's selective bibliography organizes the subject chiefly by disciplines (literature, philosophy, anthropology, psychoanalysis, and linguistics and semiotics), without denying the strongly philosophical tenor of the entire movement. The main structuralist thinkers classed specifically as philosophers here are Louis Althusser, Gilles Deleuze, Jaques Derrida, and Michel Foucault.

Harari's work is supplemented by Joan Miller's (entry 160) for the succeeding period.

145. Harlow, Victor E. **A Bibliography and Genetic Study of American Realism.** [n. p.]: Harlow Publishing Co., 1931. Reprint, New York: Kraus, 1970. 132p.

Harlow defines realism as "the philosophic assertion of the most general assumption of all naive experience, to-wit, that the world we experience is real, and independent of our experiencing or knowledge of it" (p. 2). Its origins as an "explicit doctrine" in America are traced to William James. Other major figures include Ralph Barton Perry, Roy Wood Sellars, Arthur Lovejoy, and (under the rubric Critical Realism) George Santayana. Materials are organized by five periods of development, each treated with a short narrative followed by a lengthy bibliography. Writings and writers critical of Realism (in its various forms), e.g., Josiah Royce, are also included.

146. **The Hastings Center's Bibliography of Ethics, Biomedicine, and Professional Responsibility.** Compiled by the staff of the Hastings Center. Frederick, Md.: University Publications of America, 1984. 109p.

This is "both a continuation of and a departure from the previous bibliographies [see entry 128] prepared by The Hastings Center" (preface). Many classic books and articles listed in the earlier volumes are repeated here, but the emphasis is on publications from 1978 through 1982, with a few from 1983. The section titled "Applied and Professional Ethics" is new, and more attention is given to recently prominent issues such as the ethics of neonatal intensive care, the insanity defense, and occupational health hazards. Entries are selectively annotated. There is no subject index, but a detailed subject classification is reflected in the table of contents.

147. Jessop, T. E. **A Bibliography of David Hume and of Scottish Philosophy from Francis Hutcheson to Lord Balfour.** London: Russell & Russell, 1938. Reissued, New York: Russell & Russell, 1966. Reprinted, New York: Garland, 1983. 201p.

See entry 242 regarding the Hume bibliography in part 1. The bibliography on Scottish philosophy is separated in part 2 (pages 75-190). "Scottish" is more than simply a geographical qualifier here; it designates a distinctive philosophical outlook which dominated philosophy in Scotland from Hutcheson (ca. 1725-) to the late nineteenth century. Indicative of this is the deliberate omission of Scottish thinkers during this period (particularly toward the end) who stood outside the tradition, which Jessop characterizes in these terms: "a liberal empiricism with an introspective bias in ethics and aesthetics, widening . . . into a philosophical attitude which, with growing objectivity, has given the major prerogatives to the intimations of experience rather than to the decrees of abstract thinking" (preface). It encompasses the Common Sense school most notably represented by Thomas Reid. Seventy-nine writers are treated individually in this bibliography, which also includes contemporary reviews of the books listed. It should be noted that while Hume deeply influenced many of these philosophers, they were mostly critical of him.

148. Jones, Donald G. **A Bibliography of Business Ethics, 1971-1975.** Charlottesville, Va.: University Press of Virginia, 1977. 207p.

Published under the aegis of the Center for the Study of Applied Ethics at the Colgate Graduate School of Business Administration, University of Virginia, this work updates Gothie's *Selected Bibliography of Applied Ethics in the Professions* (entry 141), with the focus narrowed to business ethics. Few of the roughly two thousand books and articles listed take a distinctly philosophical approach (many present background information or discussion), but they do relate to issues of ethics and values which have philosophical presuppositions and implications. Occasional annotations are provided, but these are generally so brief as to be barely useful.

The bulk of the bibliography's material falls into two major sections characterized by the editors as microethics and macroethics. The former section, "Business Ethics and Functional Areas of Management," deals with specific issues in such areas as accounting, advertising, employee relations, etc., while the latter, "Business and Social Responsibility," deals with issues regarding business aims and practices in relation to the environment, minorities, multinational enterprise, safety and health, etc. Flanking these major divisions are a shorter section for general works and two highly selective sections titled "Theoretical and Applied Ethics" and "Religion and Business Ethics."

149. Jones, Donald G., and Helen Troy. **A Bibliography of Business Ethics, 1976-1980.** Charlottesville, Va.: University Press of Virginia, 1982. 220p.

This work supplements entries 141 and 148. Arrangement remains basically the same as in the 1971-1975 volume, though a few of the specific topical sections have been relabeled or somewhat reorganized, and some new ones have been added (e.g., in the first major division, "Insurance," and "Organizational Life, Values, and Management Behavior"; in the second division, "Bribery and Unusual Foreign Payments," "Whistle Blowing," and "Women in Business"). Sections titled "Codes of Conduct and Self-Regulation" and "Teaching and Training in Business Ethics" have been added near the end.

150. Lachs, John. **Marxist Philosophy: A Bibliographical Guide.** Chapel Hill, N.C.: University of North Carolina Press, 1967. 166p.

Lachs lists, without annotations, 1,557 books, journal and encyclopedia articles, and discussions in general histories of philosophy, in English, French, and German, published up to the end of 1966. His emphasis, however, is on books, especially books in English. He includes some materials which are only obliquely philosophical but do throw light on the underlying philosophical theories—e.g., materials on Soviet educational practice or on the genetics controversies centering around Lysenko. There are thirty-eight chapters, beginning with an introductory comment and a chapter on the classics (works of Marx, Engels, Lenin, Stalin, and Mao). Others cover Marxist themes (Dialectical Materialism, the class struggle); Marxist treatments of specific areas and topics (freedom, Marxist ethics, Marxist aesthetics); Marxist philosophy in specific countries or regions (United States, Soviet Union); and particular types of works (journals of special relevance, bibliographies and reference works). Within chapters, English works are listed first, then French, then German; and within these language groupings, books precede articles. An author index is included.

151. Leming, James S. **Foundations of Moral Education: An Annotated Bibliography.** Westport, Conn.: Greenwood Press, 1983. 325p.

This bibliography focuses on the philosophical and psychological bases for "any examined approach to moral education" (introduction). It covers primarily but not exclusively literature published from the mid-sixties through 1981, some fifteen hundred books, articles, dissertations, and ERIC documents. The philosophical dimension of its subject takes in questions regarding, e.g., the aims of moral education, indoctrination and neutrality, and the relationship of religion to morality generally as well as moral development specifically. It also opens, however, onto the entire domain of moral philosophy. The selectivity mandated here (as in some other areas) is adeptly handled; in fact, Leming's twenty-one pages on ethical theory make an excellent selective, concise, annotated bibliography on recent philosophical ethics. Author and subject indexes are included; the latter is somewhat weak.

152. Leroux, Emmanuel. **Bibliographie mèthodique du pragmatisme: Amèricain, Anglais et Italien.** Paris: Librarie Felix Alcan, 1923. Reprinted, New York: Burt Franklin, 1968. 99p.

Coverage of American Pragmatist writings in this French bibliography is neither remarkable nor any longer of much value. Its usefulness lies rather in its coverage of lesser known Pragmatists in England (notably F. S. C. Schiller) and Italy (e.g., Calderoni, Papini, Vailati), and of critical reaction to Pragmatism in France and elsewhere on the Continent.

153. Lucas, George P., Jr. **The Genesis of Modern Process Thought: A Historical Outline with Bibliography.** Metuchen, N.J.: American Theological Library Association and Scarecrow, 1983. 231p. (ATLA Bibliography Series, no. 7).

Lucas offers a rich and fertile bibliographic resource, though nothing like comprehensive coverage of either Process Philosophy in general or any of its major figures (e.g., Whitehead, Hartshorne). The bibliographic material is subservient to the work's polemic focus: development of a set of inclusive criteria defining Process Philosophy, by means of a survey and analysis of historical antecedents and development. Strictly speaking, in fact, the annotated bibliographic entries are footnotes to six brief essays, albeit they fill 180 or so of the book's 231 pages.

154. Magel, Charles R. **A Bibliography on Animal Rights and Related Matters.** Washington, D.C.: University Press of America, 1981. 602p.

Interest in animal rights as a serious philosophical subject has mushroomed within the last two decades, so far as English-speaking philosophers are concerned (see the evidence in the section "1951-80: Animals and Ethics"). That it is not a new field, however, is clear from the abundance of historical material included in this bibliography (even restricted as it is to Western thought and to materials available in English).

If the ethics of human treatment of animals is the focus, an impressive array of related matters accounts for a majority of entries. Such matters include: philosophical and religious views on the nature of animals; expressions of attitudes toward animals, including literary and artistic; scientific and historical studies of a wide range of uses and treatment of animals alleged by some to violate their rights (meat consumption, animal experimentation, hunting, rodeos, etc.); animal protection and welfare movements, organizations, and laws; suggested alternatives in human treatment of animals. Bibliographic entries number 2,771, and include some general and obliquely related works, with specific relevant portions cited. Arrangement is somewhat complex: by subject, sometimes subdivided chronologically, with separate sections for special formats (government documents, films, periodicals) and non-bibliographic entries (e.g., organizations). Annotations are the exception, not the rule.

Magel's own bias as a fairly radical proponent of animal liberation is undisguised, but materials contrary to his position are by no means slighted.

155. Matczak, Sebastian A. **Philosophy: A Select, Classified Bibliography of Ethics, Economics, Law, Politics, and Sociology.** Louvain: Editions Nauwelaerts; Paris; Béatrice-Nauwelaerts, 1970. 308p. (Philosophical Questions Series, no. 3).

This bibliography is intended to present the more important works relating to philosophical ethics, ethical problems and value issues raised in or by the social science disciplines mentioned in the subtitle, and the philosophical underpinnings of those disciplines. Each area is covered in a separate chapter, which opens with a brief sketch of the most important philosophical problems followed by four to six sections devoted to general studies, studies of particular periods (chronological), materials on special questions, periodicals, and (in some chapters) introductory bibliographies and works relating to particular countries. Entries are not annotated.

That this work has unique value for interdisciplinary research and study is undeniable, but it is less reliable than it should be. Reviewers have commented on the omission of important, even standard works one would expect to find, e.g., some of Hannah Arendt's writings, or works of either Galbraith or Friedman on capitalist economics (cf. *American Reference Books Annual,* 1971, entry 1330; *Review of Metaphysics* 31[September 1977]:121-22). Editions cited are not always standard, and English translations of foreign-language works may be overlooked or ignored.

156. McLean, George F. **An Annotated Bibliography of Philosophy in Catholic Thought, 1900-1964.** New York: Ungar, 1967. 371p. (Philosophy in the 20th Century: Catholic and Christian, vol. 1).

"This comprehensive and annotated bibliography . . . has been compiled as an aid to the professor, student, and general reader. . . . The term 'Catholic thought' is understood as extending to works in or about the tradition of St. Augustine, St. Thomas Aquinas and other Scholastics, as well as to works by or about Catholics of the more recent existential, personalist, or phenomenological orientations" (preface). Part 1 begins with chapters on research instruments and introductory works, followed by eleven chapters "corresponding to the accustomed subject divisions of philosophy courses" (logic, epistemology, cosmology, psychology, etc.). Ethics is covered by two chapters: one on general ethics, the other on special ethics with subsections for legal, medical, sociological, domestic, political, economic, industrial, Marxian, and international ethics. Part 2 consists of four chapters concerned with different schools of Catholic/Christian philosophy: Augustinian, Thomistic, Franciscan, and "Personalist-Existential-Phenomenological."

Each entry, in addition to a descriptive and sometimes critical annotation, includes a code letter or letters indicating level(s) of readership, from A ("readers without a formal introduction to the study of philosophy") to D ("scholars").

157. McLean, George F. **A Bibliography of Christian Philosophy and Contemporary Issues.** New York: Ungar, 1967. 312p. (Philosophy in the 20th Century: Catholic and Christian, vol. 2).

This work is a selective, classified listing of books and articles from 1934 through 1964 concerned with the relationship between philosophy and religion and with issues common to philosophical and religious thought. "Christian" is interpreted in a broad sense for the purpose of this volume, and non-Christian writings which bear on the issues are included. Chapter headings are: (1) "Christian Philosophy"; (2) "Contemporary Philosophies"; (3) "Philosophy and Technology"; (4) "Philosophy of Man and God"; (5) "The Problem of God in a Secular Culture"; (6) "Religious Knowledge and Language"; (7) "Moral Philosophy"; (8) "Teaching Philosophy." English-language materials are emphasized, but coverage is international, with non-English materials following English in any given section. An appendix lists philosophy dissertations presented in United States and Canadian Catholic universities.

Unlike its companion in the two-volume series (entry 156), this bibliography is not annotated and is accordingly less useful, since there is often no clue to the perspective of a cited work on the issue, or even its relevance.

158. Miller, Albert Jay, and Michael James Acri. **Death: A Bibliographical Guide.** Metuchen, N.J.: Scarecrow, 1977. 420p.

Encompasses materials dealing with aspects of death from many perspectives: medical, legal, psychological, sociological, theological, etc., as well as philosophical. Coverage extends from ancient beginnings to roughly 1974. Philosophical materials can be located via the subject index under "philosophy and death," which also refers to related entries including "attitudes toward death among philosophers," "existentialism and death," and various entries beginning with the word "immortality"; and under "ethical problems," which provides cross-references also to "euthanasia" and "right to die."

Robert L. Fulton's *Death, Grief, and Bereavement: A Bibliography, 1845-1975* (New York: Arno Press, 1977, 253p.) is quite similar, but pays somewhat less attention to philosophical material.

159. Miller, Albert Jay. **A Selective Bibliography of Existentialism in Education and Related Topics.** New York: Exposition Press, 1969. 39p.

Except for a few older items included to give some historical perspective, this bibliography lists literature published from 1953 to 1968. Books and articles are separated, but there is no attempt to differentiate or structure the rather surprising miscellany of topics, the relation of some of which to Existentialism is far from clear.

160. Miller, Joan M. **French Structuralism: A Multidisciplinary Bibliography with a Checklist of Sources for Louis Althusser, Roland Barthes, Jaques Derrida, Michel Foucault, Lucien Goldmann, Jaques Lacan and an Update of Works on Claude Lévi-Strauss.** New York: Garland, 1981. 553p. (Garland Reference Library of the Humanities, vol. 160).

Miller's multilingual bibliography, focusing mainly on the period 1968-1978, extends and supplements that by Harari (entry 144), which covered the decade of the sixties. Like Harari's, it treats Structuralism as the multidisciplinary movement it is, while giving due to its pervasively philosophical character. Part 1 lists general and introductory works. Part 2, less restrictive as to dates of coverage, contains reasonably complete bibliographies of works by and on the six representative figures indicated in the subtitle, and a section on Lévi-Strauss designed to supplement a bibliography by C. and F. Lapointe, *Claude Lévi-Strauss and His Critics* (Garland, 1977). Part 3 deals with Structuralism as applied to various disciplines. Besides a thirty-six-page section for philosophy, this also includes a section for Marxism and one titled "Religion/Scripture/Theology" in which philosophical issues figure prominently.

161. Mitcham, Carl, and Robert Mackey. **Bibliography of the Philosophy of Technology.** Chicago: University of Chicago Press, 1973. 205p.

This excellent bibliography, comprehensive and international though not exhaustive, covers a varied literature on "philosophic problems revolving around technology and its meaning to man and society" published from 1925 to 1972. It is organized into five categories: (1) comprehensive philosophical works; (2) ethical and political critiques; (3) religious critiques; (4) metaphysical and epistemological studies, including those concerned with cybernetics and artificial intelligence; and (5) in an appendix, classical documents (mostly from the period prior to 1925) and background materials, including basic histories of technology. Sections 2 and 3 distinguish and segregate works deemed primary and secondary in terms of philosophic content or merit. Arrangement within sections is chronological. Lack of an author index may be a deficiency. Many items have descriptive annotations, and English translations are supplied for non-English titles.

162. Nettlau, Max. **Bibliographie de l'anarchie.** Paris: Bibliothéque des "Temps Nouveaux," no. 8, 1897. Reprinted, New York: Burt Franklin, 1968. 294p.

Compiled by an authority on philosophical anarchism, this "remains the basic bibliography of the early material on the various radical movements of the 19th century ..." (De George, *The Philosopher's Guide*, p. 101). It includes chapters on the "classic" proponents and exponents of anarchism (Proudhon, Bakunin, and Kropotkin) but also on specific variants and movements (e.g., *l'anarchisme-individualiste, le mutuellisme*), including American versions associated with such authors as Josiah Warren, Lysander Spooner, and B. R. Tucker. Most chapters begin with background notes. Annotations, though sometimes extensive, are generally limited to bibliographic matters.

163. Orr, Leonard. **Existentialism and Phenomenology: A Guide for Research.** Troy, N.Y.: Whitston, 1978. 197p.

Orr's bibliography concentrates on works published between 1950 and 1976, with a view to supplementing Douglas's 1950 *Critical Bibliography of Existentialism* (entry 134). Its scope, however, is both broader (it encompasses the wider movement of Existentialism, not just the Paris School) and narrower (it is restricted to works in English). Existentialism is the primary focus, with Phenomenology treated less fully and mainly in its association with Existentialism. Over two thousand books and articles are listed by author. Given this arrangement, the selective subject index is grossly inadequate; it provides a mere seventeen subject headings with forbidding columns of undifferentiated entry numbers (e.g., 139 references under the section titled "Christian Existentialism," 343 under that titled "Heidegger").

164. Oxford University. Oxford Sub-Faculty of Philosophy. **Study Aid Series.** Vols. 1-9. 1975-1981.

This series of selective bibliographies, issued in mimeographed form but more widely distributed than this might suggest, is intended mainly to meet the needs of graduate students. It was conceived, one may guess, to plug some gaps in cumulative bibliographic coverage of specific fields and topics, particularly those emphasized in recent Anglo-American philosophy (some of these have since been filled with more conventional publications). The individual issues are as follows:

1. C. A. B. Peacocke, et al. **A Selective Bibliography of Philosophical Logic.** 3d ed. 1978. 125p.

2. R. Harré and J. Hawthorn. **A Selective Bibliography of Philosophy of Science.** 2d ed. 1977. 69p.

3. P. A. M. Seuren. **A Selective Bibliography of Philosophy of Language.** 1975. 30p.

4. M. Moss and D. Scott, **A Bibliography of Logic Books.** 1975. 106p.

5. R. C. S. Walker. **A Selective Bibliography on Kant.** 2d ed. 1978. 68p.

6. R. C. Lindley and J. M. Shorter. **Philosophy of Mind: A Bibliography.** Part 1: **The Self.** 1977. Part 2: **Philosophy of Action.** 1978. 62p.

7. J. Barnes, et al. **Aristotle: A Bibliography.** Rev. ed. 1981. 88p.

8. W. Newton-Smith. **A Study Guide to the Philosophy of Physics.** Rev. ed. 1979. 49p.

9. J. Baker. **A Select Bibliography of Moral Philosophy.** 1977. 144p.

165. Powell, John P. **Philosophy of Education: A Select Bibliography.** 2d ed. Manchester: Manchester University Press, 1970. 51p.

Powell lists, without annotations, 707 items, divided among twenty-six sections. The four opening sections include books; the remainder, devoted to specific topics such as knowledge, moral education, curriculum, and punishment, focus on journal articles published from 1950 to 1970.

166. Redmond, Walter Bernard. **Bibliography of the Philosophy in the Iberian Colonies of America.** The Hague: Martinus Nijhoff, 1972. 174p. (International Archives of the History of Ideas, 51).

The title's initially curious reference to "the" philosophy is presumably a deliberate reflection of the fact that philosophy in the Spanish and Portuguese colonies meant *Scholastic* philosophy. In fact, the choice of 1810 as the approximate closing date for this bibliography is attributed to the fact that "both the 'pure' and the 'modern' Scholasticism"—two currents distinguished by Redmond in his preface—"tend to be supplemented after 1810 by non-Scholastic philosophies." (A few important later Scholastic works do get registered, however.) Primary materials listed (1,154 items) are mainly "the traditional philosophy (and theology) *cursus* (classroom treatises on logic, physics, psychology, metaphysics, ethics, and the various theology courses) and *conclusiones* (or *theses, asserta,* etc.; lists of opinions defended in scholastic functions), but some other material has also been included (articles in periodicals, 'study plans,' etc.)" (preface). Manuscripts as well as printed works are listed, and many entries indicate locations of manuscripts or printed copies. A separate and much shorter section lists and annotates secondary literature (275 items).

167. Risse, Wilhelm. **Bibliographia Logica.** Hildesheim: Georg Olms, 1965-1979. 4 vols.

No other branch of philosophy presently possesses a bibliography quite so extensive and comprehensive as this one for logic, which is a by-product, as the *Vorwort* (volume 1) explains, of Risse's systematic history of the development of logic, *Die Logik der Neuzeit* (1964-).

Volume 1 (1965, 293p.) lists in chronological arrangement monographs published from 1472 to 1800. Volume 2 (1973, 494p.) does the same for the period 1801-1969. Both volumes cite holding libraries (mainly European but also some American) for most of the works listed. Volume 3 (1979, 412p.) lists articles published both in periodicals and in anthologies, arranged according to a detailed classification system outlined in the front. Volume 4 (1979, 390p.) is a catalog of 3,006 manuscripts, arranged by author if known and by title if not known, with separate sections for medieval and more recent manuscripts. Holding libraries or archives are indicated.

All volumes are thoroughly indexed.

168. Robert, Jean-Dominique. **Philosophie et science: Eléments de bibliographie / Philosophy and Science: Elements of Bibliography.** Paris: Beauchesne, 1968. 384p. (Bibliothèque des archives de philosophie, nouvelle série, 8).

Prior to Blackwell's recently published work (entry 129), Robert's was the closest thing to a full-scale general bibliography of the philosophy of science. Its focus, however, is on the relations between philosophy and science, or as the introduction puts it, "the problems set up both by the distinction between philosophy and sciences and also their necessary connection," rather than on philosophy of science as such. Many works by scientists which bear on these issues are included, among them a number of popular writings addressed to a wide public. Writings in French are probably most numerous, but English runs a very respectable second, with other European languages also well represented.

The majority of entries are grouped under *Travaux catalogués par nom d'auteurs* (works listed by authors' name). They are *coded* to indicate subject matter: e.g., "B" for works relating to biology, "PY" for physics. Sections 3 and 4 are supplements to the main body of the bibliography, covering the years 1965-1966 and 1966-1967.

169. Shields, Allan. **A Bibliography of Bibliographies in Aesthetics.** San Diego: San Diego State University Press, 1974. 79p.

Shields lists bibliographic sources published from 1900 through 1972 (with a scattering of slightly earlier items). Besides a very small number of book-length works, he includes bibliographies and bibliographic essays in journals and collections, and selected (but numerous) works which include some significant bibliographic material, even bibliographic footnotes. Chapters cover works in aesthetics and its history generally and works relating to specific arts, to aesthetic education, and to psychology and art.

170. Steenberghen, Fernand van. **La bibliothèque du philosophe médiéviste.** Louvain: Publicationes Universitaires; Paris: Béatrice-Nauwelaerts, 1974. 540p.

Strictly speaking, this is a collection of descriptive and critical reviews of books relating to medieval philosophy published since 1925. These reviews have been published previously, primarily in the *Revue néoscholastique de philosophie* (1928-1945) and the *Revue philosophique de Louvain* (1946-1973). Works reviewed include monographic studies, bibliographies and other "scholarly instruments," textual editions and translations. While the selection may be to some extent a product of fortuitous factors, it appears that Van Steenberghen, a distinguished historian of medieval philosophy, had occasion to review most of the important works in the field that appeared over the course of his long career. The result is, in effect, a quite comprehensive, extensively annotated bibliography of works that should find a significant place in the library of the philosopher/medievalist, particularly useful for younger scholars needing an orientation to the vast literature.

171. Stein, Gordon. **Freethought in the United Kingdom and the Commonwealth: A Descriptive Bibliography.** Westport, Conn.: Greenwood Press, 1981. 193p.

This work by Stein complements his earlier joint effort with Marshall Brown, *Freethought in the United States* (entry 132). Like the latter, it is not exclusively or even predominantly concerned with philosophic thought, but does present significant philosophical material in a particular context and from a perspective not readily duplicated elsewhere. Four narrative chapters describe the British literature from about 1624 to the present; an alphabetical list of works cited is at the end of each chapter. Appendices cover freethought in Commonwealth countries, library collections on freethought, theses and dissertations, and works in progress.

172. Vasoli, Cesare.**Il pensiero medievale: Orientamenti bibliografici.** Bari: Laterza, 1971. 302p. (Picola biblioteca filosofica Laterze).

A handy, pocket-sized bibliography on medieval thought from "the barbaric age" through Wycliff and Huss, concentrating on philosophy but also encompassing theology, spirituality, and science. Primary arrangement is by major periods, with subsections for specific individuals. One chapter is devoted to *filosofie orientale,* i.e., Byzantine, Arabic, and Jewish philosophies. Materials cited are in many languages, including English, French, German, Latin, and Spanish, but Italian works are most heavily represented. No indexes are provided (the one thing so labeled is really a table of contents).

173. Wainwright, William J. **Philosophy of Religion: An Annotated Bibliography of Twentieth-Century Writings in English.** New York: Garland, 1978. 776p.

Wainwright characterizes his work as "addressed to professional philosophers and graduate students who work in the analytic tradition" and whose focus is philosophical problems rather than "the systems of individual philosophers or the history of philosophical movements" (introduction). The majority of items listed (books, portions of books, and articles) represent the Analytic tradition, but works of "Process philosophers, Neo-Scholastics, Idealists, theologians, historians of religion, psychologists, and so on" are cited when in the compiler's judgment they would (or should) interest Analytic philosophers.

All of the 1,135 entries are annotated. Annotations are typically critical as well as descriptive and sometimes run a full page or more. The eight chapters are: (1) "The Divine Attributes"; (2) "Argument for the Existence of God"; (3) "The Problem of Evil"; (4) "Mysticism and Religious Experience"; (5) "Miracles"; (6) "Faith and Revelation"; (7) "Religious Language"; (8) "The Justification of Religious Belief." An index of authors, editors, and reviewers is provided.

II. COMPUTERIZED DATABASES

174. **BIOETHICSLINE.** Washington, D.C.: Center for Bioethics, Kennedy Institute of Ethics, Georgetown University.

The BIOETHICSLINE database corresponds to the printed *Bibliography of Bioethics* (entry 127) and provides cumulative coverage from 1974 to the present. Its content is compiled by the Center for Bioethics for the National Library of Medicine (NLM), which makes it available to the medical and scholarly community. Online access is provided at many academic, medical, and other special libraries, and is also available to properly authorized individuals and organizations. (For information, contact MEDLARS Management, National Library of Medicine, 8600 Rockville Pike, Bethesda, Md. 20209.) As of 1985, BIOETHICSLINE is not offered by any commercial database vendor.

8

SPECIALIZED BIBLIOGRAPHIES: COUNTRIES, REGIONS, AND SPECIAL CLASSES OF MATERIALS

175. Bechtle, Thomas C., and Mary F. Riley. **Dissertations in Philosophy Accepted at American Universities, 1861-1975.** New York: Garland, 1978. 537p.

Listed are 7,503 dissertations from 120 universities. As a rule, these include only dissertations for degrees earned in departments of philosophy (thus not, for instance, philosophical dissertations done in seminaries). The compilers made an unusual effort, described in the preface, to identify dissertations not reflected in standard sources such as *Dissertation Abstracts* and *Comprehensive Dissertation Index*, notably those completed prior to 1912. Information provided includes, besides author and title, the university, year submitted, and when applicable the *Dissertation Abstracts* number, handy for locating the abstract or for ordering a copy of the dissertation itself from University Microfilms.

Arrangement is by author, not a particularly useful approach unless accompanied with a good subject index. There is a subject index, but not a good one. Too many subject terms, being too broad, have long, undiscriminating strings of references (numbers only). Worse, some dissertations cannot be found where they would reasonably be expected (e.g., one titled "Eros and Philosophy" is absent under the word "eros"; another, on historical objectivity, could not be located under the words "history," "objectivity," or any other likely term).

176. **Bibliografia filosofica italiana,** 1949- . Publisher varies. 1951- .

This annual bibliography, sponsored by the Centro di Studi Filosofici Cristiani di Gallarate, continues a four-volume work covering 1900 through 1950 (entry 190). It differs in its arrangement, however, using a classification scheme that includes both historical periods and branches of philosophy. Initially, the bibliography was published at Milan by C. Marzorati. As of 1978, it was being published at Florence by Leo S. Olschki.

177. **Bibliographie der sowjetischen Philosophie / Bibliography of Soviet Philosophy.** Ed. by J. M. Bochenski, et al. Dordrecht, Netherlands: D. Reidel, 1959-68. Vols. 1-7. (Sovietica: Veröffentlichen des Osteuropa-Instituts, Universität Freiburg/Schweiz).

The seven volumes of this bibliography vary considerably in content. Volume 1 is an index to the major Soviet philosophical journal, *Voprosy filosofii,* for 1947-1956. Volume 2 lists books from 1947-1956 plus books and articles (from a variety of journals) for 1957-1958. Volumes 3, 6, and 7 cover books and articles for, respectively, 1959-1960, 1961-1963, and 1964-1965. Volume 4 is a supplement for 1947-1960 and volume 5 is a cumulative index for 1947-1960. Subject indexes are in English.

From 1967 forward, bibliographic coverage of Soviet philosophy is continued in the journal *Studies in Soviet Thought* (entry 369).

178. **Bibliographie Philosophie,** 1967- . Berlin: Akademie für Gesellschaftswissenschaften bei Z.K. der S.E.D., Institut für Marxistisch-leninistische Philosophie, Zentralstelle für philosophische Information und Dokumentation, 1967- . Vol. 1- .

This East German serial bibliography, published quarterly, is sometimes cited with the words "*mit Autoren und Sach Register*" appended to its title; these words no longer appear on its title page, however. It emphasizes East German publications (books, articles, dissertations, and other literature) but also gives selective attention to Soviet, other East European, and some West German publications. The orientation is overtly Marxist; non-Marxist writings considered important to Marxist thinkers are included, but are segregated from Marxist works within each section of the classified arrangement. Entries are not annotated, but frequently do include descriptors. Each also includes a location (holding library) code. Name and title indexes are included.

179. **A Bibliography of Indian Philosophy.** Madras: Published by the C. P. Ramaswani Aiyar Research Endowment Committee, 1963/68. 2 vols.

The two parts of this bibliography that have been issued list sourcebooks in Sanskrit and, where available, translations in English, relating to: (part 1) the Upanishads, the Bhagavad Gita, the Nyaya, Vaiseshika, Sankhya, Yoga, and Mimamsa systems, and the Vedanta systems comprising Advaita, Visishtadvaita, and Dvaita; (part 2) Navya Naya, Jainism, Buddhism, Saiva Siddhanta, the Vedas, the Dharma Sutras, Sakta Tantra, and works on Bhakti. Projected volumes for recent studies of Indian systems have not materialized, possibly because of the appearance of the bibliography volume of the *Encyclopedia of Indian Philosophies* (entry 198).

180. **Bibliography of Philosophy.** Sainte Ruffine, Moselle, France: Imprimerie Maisonneuve, n.d. 2 vols.

Hiding behind the nondescript title is a bibliography of French philosophical books from 1945 to 1965. It is divided into studies of the history of philosophy (volume 1, 102p.) and original and systematic works of philosophy (volume 2, 80p.). The former are arranged by major periods, from antiquity to the twentieth century; the latter, by individual philosophers, with works about an individual (e.g., Sartre) following those written by him or her. Substantial descriptive and occasionally critical annotations, in English, are particularly valuable. A ten-page introduction by Paul Ricoeur gives a concise overview of French philosophical currents during the period covered.

181. Chan, Wing-tsit. **Chinese Philosophy, 1949-1963: An Annotated Bibliography of Mainland China Publications.** Honolulu: East-West Center Press, 1967. 290p.

This bibliography of Chinese-language works is concerned with studies of traditional Chinese philosophy and modern developments thereof; it does not deal with Chinese Marxist philosophy. Books and articles are in separate sections, each identically arranged by periods, schools, and major philosophers, in roughly chronological order. References are given both in transliteration and in Chinese characters, the former being primary. English translations are provided for titles. Most entries include library locations in the United States, Hong Kong, or Tokyo.

182. Chan, Wing-tsit. **An Outline and Annotated Bibliography of Chinese Philosophy.** Rev. ed. New Haven: Yale Far Eastern Publications, 1969. 220p. (Sinological Series, no. 4).

This work has been largely superseded by Fu and Chan's *Guide to Chinese Philosophy* (entry 183), which adapts some of its material and is aimed at a similar (non-specialist) audience. It remains of value where the later work is not available, and occasionally for differences in the organization of topics and materials. Arrangement is mainly by schools and periods in approximate chronological sequence. A subject index is included.

183. Fu, Charles Wei-hsun, and Wing-tsit Chan. **Guide to Chinese Philosophy.** Boston: G. K. Hall, 1978. 262p. (Asian Philosophies and Religions Resource Guides).

Fu and Chan list and annotate predominantly English-language works for non-specialists who do not have access to primary texts in the original languages. Their first and longest section, "History of Chinese Philosophy," moves from general overviews to specific schools, movements, and periods in approximate chronological sequence, from pre-Confucian and traditional elements through Chinese contemporary Marxism. Sections 2-13 cover specific topics as treated in Chinese philosophies: human nature, ethics, philosophy of religion, epistemology, logic, social and political philosophy, etc. Concluding sections deal with materials on presuppositions and methods (14), comparisons of various philosophies (15), and authoritative texts and their philosophical significance (16).

Included in a series preface are directions for obtaining hard-to-find items listed in this guide in microform or photocopy format from the Institute for the Advanced Study of World Religions (pages xxix-xxx).

184. **Fuentes de la filosofía latinoamericana.** Washington, D.C.: Union Panamericana, 1967. 100p. (Union Panamericana. Bibliografías básicas, 4).

Some eight hundred *fuentes* (sources) on Latin American philosophy are listed in this bibliography, all of them secondary sources; primary sources are outside its scope. "Philosophy is interpreted broadly to include the history of ideas and social and political thought" (introduction). Chapters cover (1) general works, (2) works by country, (3) articles, also subdivided by country, (4) bibliographic sources, and (5) journals. Items listed are mainly in Spanish or Portuguese, but some are in English or other languages. Many entries include descriptive annotations, in Spanish.

185. **Los "fundadores" en la filosofía de América Latina.** Washington, D.C.: Secretaría General, Organización de los Estados Americanos, 1970. 199p. (Union Panamericana. Bibliografías básicas, 7).

Complementing the earlier *Fuentes de la filosofía latinoamericana,* this bibliography covers twenty founders of Latin American philosophy. Born between 1839 and 1893 and active in some cases up to the mid-twentieth century, they constitute a diverse group, united only, the introduction suggests, by "an identity of motivations (the dedication to philosophy) and a community of objectives (the effort to diffuse philosophy and normalize its study)." The more eminent figures among them include Caso and Vasconcelos (Mexico), Deustua (Peru), Farias Brito (Brazil), Ingenieros and Korn (Argentina), Molina (Chile), Varona (Cuba), and Vaz Ferreira (Uruguay). Each thinker is treated with a brief chronology and a bibliography divided into "works by" and "works about." Most items are in Spanish or Portuguese. Annotations are few and brief.

186. Geldsetzer, Lutz. **Bibliography of the International Congresses of Philosophy: Proceedings, 1900-1978 / Bibliographie der internationalen Philosophie Kongresse: Beiträge, 1900-1978.** Munich: K. G. Saur, 1981. 208p.

This is a handy index to the proceedings of sixteen World Philosophical Congresses, from Paris 1900-1903 to Düsseldorf 1978, many of them published in multiple volumes (e.g., twelve volumes for the 1958 Venice Congress). Gives tables of contents and provides collective indexes of authors and subjects.

187. Geldsetzer, Lutz. **In Honorem: Eine Bibliographie philosophischer Festschriften und ihrer Beiträge.** Düsseldorf: Philosophia, 1975. 226p.

Despite the title, not all of the essay collections listed and indexed in this volume are strictly *Festschriften* (intended to honor a particular individual, typically presented on retirement). Notable exceptions include the Library of Living Philosophers series and some volumes in the Boston Studies in the Philosophy of Science (e.g., one on Ernst Mach). It covers, as these examples indicate, English-language as well as German collections, and also some French. It reproduces tables of contents and provides collective author and subject indexes (the latter in German).

188. Holzman, Donald, with Motoyama Yukihiko, et al. **Japanese Religion and Philosophy: A Guide to Japanese Reference and Research Materials.** Ann Arbor, Mich.: University of Michigan Press, 1959. Reprinted, Westport, Conn.: Greenwood Press, 1975. 102p.

This guide is limited to Japanese books (no periodical articles) published since the Meiji era (ca. 1868-). It lists books on all significant religions and philosophical schools, including Shinto, Buddhism, Confucianism, and Christianity (restricted in all cases to Japanese aspects). There is no separation of philosophical materials from religious until the Meiji and post-Meiji periods (entries 826-914), when a distinction between religion and philosophy emerged in Japanese thought under Western influence. Of the earlier schools, the most philosophical is Confucianism (entries 545-695).

189.   Istituto di Studi Filosofici. **Bibliografia filosofica italiana dal 1850 al 1900.** Rome: ABETE, [1969]. 644p.

Similar in coverage and basic arrangement to the previously issued bibliography for 1900-1950 (see entry 190).

190.   Istituto di Studi Filosofici. **Bibliografia filosofica italiana dal 1900 al 1950.** Rome: Edizioni Delfino, 1950-1956. 4 vols.

This comprehensive bibliography of Italian philosophical literature of the first half of this century encompasses primary works by philosophers of the period, secondary studies, editions and reprints of older works, and translations of non-Italian authors. Journal articles are included as well as books. Arrangement is alphabetical by names of individuals, integrating both "works by" and "works about." Volume 4 (U-Z) also includes an extensive section of additions and corrections to volumes 1-3 (A-T), a section for anonymous and pseudonymous works, and an annotated bibliography of Italian journals in philosophy and related fields.

This work was compiled and published under the auspices of the Istituto di Studi Filosofici of the Centro Nazionale di Informazioni Bibliografiche, with collaboration from the Centro di Studi Filosofici Cristiana di Gallarate. See also entries 176 and 189 for coverage of later and earlier periods.

191.   Koehler & Volckmar. **Philosophie und Grenzgebiete, 1945-1964.** Stuttgart: Koehler & Volckmar, 1965. 434p. (Koehler & Volckmar Fachbibliographien).

A bibliography of books and periodicals in philosophy and bordering areas published in Germany or German-speaking countries, especially Switzerland, and some German-language works published elsewhere. Arrangement is by subject classification, with general works (including dictionaries, bibliographies, yearbooks, etc.) gathered in chapter 1, periodicals in chapter 9.

192.   Martínez Gómez, L. **Bibliografía filosófica española e hispanoamericana (1940-1958).** Barcelona: Juan Flors, 1961. 500p. (Libros "Pensamiento"; Serie: Difusion, no. 1).

This 10,166-item bibliography of Spanish and Hispanoamerican philosophy covers not only writings by and about Hispanic philosophers, but also Spanish translations of non-Hispanic authors and writings. It is based chiefly on bibliographies from the quarterly journal *Pensamiento*. The two basic divisions comprise historical materials (chronological arrangement) and systematic materials (with chapters on logic, metaphysics, ethics, etc.). There is an author index.

193. **Obshchestvennye nauki v SSSR. Seria 3: Filosofskie nauki,** 1973- . Moscow: Akademia Nauk SSSR, 1973- .

This bimonthly publication typically provides around fifty "abstracts" (more like reviews, at least in length) of philosophical books published in the Soviet Union and some of its satellites. Though everything else is in Russian, there is an English table of contents. The subject arrangement, dominated by Marxist categories, features major headings such as Dialectical Materialism; scientific atheism; and criticism of modern bourgeois philosophy, reformism and revisionism. More conventional headings (by non-Marxist lights) such as theory of knowledge or methodological problems of social sciences tend to be subsumed under these.

194. Ofori, Patrick E. **Black African Traditional Religions and Philosophy: A Select Bibliographic Survey of the Sources from the Earliest Times to 1974.** Nendeln, Liechtenstein: Kraus-Thomson, 1975. 421p.

The 2,541 items cited in Ofori's bibliography, about half of them annotated, concentrate mainly on African indigenous religions. Philosophy is generally not clearly distinguished, which undoubtedly reflects the nature of African thought. Arrangement is primarily geographical, with sections for broad regions subdivided by countries and sometimes by ethnic groups. A few of these geographical divisions have sections specifically designated for philosophy, in combinations with related concepts such as values or cosmology and with proverbs. There are indexes for authors and for ethnic groups, but not subjects.

195. **Philosophy and History: A Review of German-Language Research Contributions on Philosophy, History, and Cultural Developments.** Vol. 1- . Tübingen: Institute for Scientific Co-operation, 1968- . (German Studies, Section 1).

Issued semi-annually, this publication features substantial reviews (typically a page or more), *in English*, of selected German books, plus a selective bibliography of new books and articles. Philosophy, treated separately from history, takes up a third to half of each issue. Potentially misleading is the practice of listing works under English translations of their titles, in bold face, followed by the original German title in brackets. This should not be construed to mean that the works themselves are available in English translation.

196. Polska Akademie Nauk. Komitet Filozoficzny. **Bibliografia filozofii polskiej.** Warsaw: Państwowe Wydawnictwo Naukowe, 1955-1971. 3 vols.

The three volumes of this bibliography of Polish philosophical writings, which includes writings about non-Polish philosophers, cover the years 1750-1830, 1831-1864, and 1865-1895, respectively. Their arrangement uses a single alphabetical sequence for both authors and individuals who are the subjects of "works about."

197. Poortman, Johannes Jacobus, et al. **Repertorium der nederlandse wijsbegeerte.** Amsterdam: Wereldbibliotheek, 1948. 403p. Supplement I, Amsterdam: Wereldbibliotheek, 1958. 168p. Supplement II, Amsterdam: Buijten en Schipperheijen, 1968. 179p.

This Dutch bibliography and its supplements record two general categories of publication: (1) philosophical works printed in Dutch in the Netherlands or in the Flemish part of Belgium, regardless of the nationality of the author, and thus including translations from other languages; (2) works by Netherlanders in any language and wherever published. There are subject and author listings (the latter restricted to books until supplement II). The base volume covers the period from the Middle Ages to 1947, the supplements, respectively, 1947-1957 and 1958-1967.

198. Potter, Karl H., et al. **Encyclopedia of Indian Philosophies.** Vol. I, **Bibliography.** Rev. ed. Delhi: Motilal Banarsidas, 1983. Princeton: Princeton University Press, 1984. 1023p.

The first edition of this ambitious work, published in 1970 with the title *Bibliography of Indian Philosophies* inaugurated the *Encyclopedia of Indian Philosophies* (see entries 58-59). Though other volumes of the encyclopedia have been slow to appear (two to date), the bibliography has already attained a second edition. The number of authors and works cited, now reportedly in the neighborhood of ten thousand, has been greatly expanded. Among the additions are references to summaries of works in English where such exist. On the other hand, citations of secondary literature written in non-Western languages have been dropped.

Part 1 lists Sanskrit and Tamil texts in chronological order; parts 2 and 3 cover authors and texts of unknown date. All known editions and translations into European languages are cited. If no published versions are known, locations of manuscripts are indicated. Part 4 is devoted to secondary literature in European languages, arranged according to the various philosophic movements and systems. Indexes are by names, titles, and topics.

199. Sandeen, Ernest R., and Frederick Hale. **American Religion and Philosophy: A Guide to Information Sources.** Detroit: Gale, 1978. 377p. (American Studies Information Guide Series, vol. 5; Gale Information Guide Library).

This bibliography "appears in a series of guides to American Studies because religion and philosophy are treated with special attention to their relationship with the rest of American culture," and it combines religion with philosophy because "they grew up as Siamese twins until separated in the late nineteenth century" (preface). Religion, however, gets far more attention than philosophy; there is undeniably more to attend to. The bulk of philosophically oriented material is in chapter 19, "From Pragmatism to Contemporary Philosophy," material on earlier periods and figures (e.g., Edwards, nineteenth-century moral philosophy) being scattered through earlier chapters. General works are in chapter 1. Philosophy since about 1920 is scantily covered, the rationale being that it has become increasingly specialized and has ceased to be distinctively American. Despite its limited aim, this is a useful selective guide to books (and a few journal articles).

200. Sass, Hans-Martin. **Inedita Philosophica. Ein Verzeichnis von Nachlässen deutschsprachinger Philosophen des 19. und 20. Jahrhunderts.** Düsseldorf: Philosophia, 1974. 86 numbered columns [43p.]

This catalog of unpublished papers of nineteenth- and twentieth-century German-speaking philosophers lists primarily manuscripts but also diaries, letters, personal papers, lecture notes, extracts and drafts. Papers of Hannah Arendt, Buber, Hegel, Herder, Jaspers, Mach, Nietzsche, and Schopenhauer are among those included. Gives locations, mainly German libraries and archives, but also some elsewhere, including the Library of Congress (e.g., for Arendt, Friedrich Kapp) and a few other United States locations.

201. Smet, A. J. **Bibliographie de la pensée Africaine: Répertoire et Suppléments I-IV.** Kinshasa-Limete: Faculté de Theologie Catholique, 1972-1975. 285p.

"This bibliography on African thought is in principle limited to studies on the philosophical conceptions of the peoples of Black Africa." Besides publications which are "philosophical in the strict sense of that word," it also lists those "presenting a philosophy in the broad sense of the word, i.e., a more or less elaborated interpretation of African cultural values in a language borrowing from one or the other philosophical system" (introduction). An initial list ("Repertoire") and four supplements are bound together. An analytical table (index) covers the main list plus supplements 1 through 3; a separate table covers supplement 4. Most materials listed are in European languages, including English. No annotations are provided.

202. Voumvlinopoulos, Georges E. **Bibliographie critique de la philosophie grecque depuis la chute de Constantinople a nos jours, 1453-1953.** Athens: [Impr. de l'Institut Français d'Athènes], 1966. 236p.

Philosophers of "modern" Greece—spanning a five-hundred-year period beginning with the fall of Constantinople in 1453—are arranged in chronological sequence. Perhaps five or six hundred in number, they are obscure for the most part. Their names are given in both Roman and modern Greek alphabets. Literature cited includes "works by" and "works about." Annotations, headings, and other non-bibliographic information are in French. A historical introduction and overview is provided on pages 5-22.

9

SPECIALIZED BIBLIOGRAPHIES: BIBLIOGRAPHIES ON INDIVIDUALS

ARISTOTLE

203. Barnes, Jonathan, et al. **Aristotle: A Bibliography.** Rev. ed. Oxford: Sub-Faculty of Philosophy, 1981. 88p. (Study Aid Series, no. 7).

In the absence of a more comprehensive and more widely available work, this very selective bibliography in the Oxford Study Aid series (see entry 164) merits mention here. "Designed primarily to suit the interests of English-speaking philosophers" (preface), it includes chapters on Aristotle's logic, metaphysics, philosophy of science, psychology, ethics, and politics, and on the *Poetics.*

AUGUSTINE, SAINT

204. Andresen, Carl. **Bibliografia Augustiniana.** 2d rev. ed. Darmstadt: Wissenschaftliche Buchgesellschaft, 1973. 317p.

Includes works by Augustine and about him, the latter mainly from the middle third of this century. Uses a classified arrangement (see classification table on pages 1-5) and is thoroughly indexed by authors, subjects, personal names (as subjects or in titles), and references to specific Augustinian works, Biblical texts, and classical authors. Also has a chronological list of Augustine's writings. The preface is in Latin and German.

205. Bavel, Tarsicius J. van, with F. Van der Zande. **Répertoire bibliographique de Saint Augustin, 1950-1960.** The Hague: Martinus Nijhoff, 1963. 991p. (Instrumenta Patristica, III).

Though covering a mere decade of Augustinian scholarship, this has an astonishing 5,502 entries, of which perhaps a third are cross-references. It offers the advantage, for those who read French, of substantial annotations, and uses a system of asterisks to rate items according to level of readership and/or importance. The book has a classified arrangement, supplemented by a subject index.

206. Institut des Études Augustiniennes. Paris. **Fichier augustinien / Augustine Bibliography.** Boston: G. K. Hall, 1972. 4 vols. Microfilm ed.: 8 reels. **Premier supplément / First Supplement.** Boston: G. K. Hall, 1981. 516p.

Base volumes reproduce some 63,000 typewritten cards compiled by the Institut, established in 1943 as a center for Augustinian studies and bibliography. Access is by author (volumes 1-2) and by subject (volumes 3-4), the latter via a classified arrangement. Works by as well as about Augustine are listed. Some thirteen thousand additional cards, covering works published between 1971 and 1978, are represented in the supplement.

The microfilm version of the base set is on 35mm film at 15X reduction.

207. Miethe, Terry L. **Augustinian Bibliography, 1970-1980, with Essays on the Fundamentals of Augustinian Scholarship.** Westport, Conn.: Greenwood Press, 1982. 218p.

Intended to supplement several older bibliographies, notably Andresen's (entry 204) and the *Fichier augustinien* (entry 206), Miethe's work takes in pre-1970 items if they were omitted from the earlier works. Included, for instance, are some 140 dissertations from the 1890s to 1970. Arrangement is by broad subjects, including sections for items relating to specific works by Augustine. Entries are unannotated. The four essays appended to the bibliography are misleadingly titled and of negligible value.

BERGSON, HENRI

208. Gunter, P. A. Y. **Henri Bergson: A Bibliography.** Bowling Green, Ohio: Philosophy Documentation Center, Bowling Green State University, 1974. 457p. (Bibliographies of Famous Philosophers).

Lists chronologically 472 works by Bergson, and by author 3,919 works about Bergson. Brief uncritical annotations are provided for nearly all of the former and some of the latter. Separate subject indexes, both very broad, cover the two sections. "Works About" includes some but not all dissertations.

BERKELEY, GEORGE

209. Jessop, Thomas Edmond. **A Bibliography of George Berkeley, with an Inventory of Berkeley's Manuscript Remains by A. A. Luce.** 2d ed., revised and enlarged. The Hague: Martinus Nijhoff, 1973. 155p. (International Archives of the History of Ideas, 66).

Aims to list Berkeley's own writings exhaustively, and writings on Berkeley adequately if somewhat less than exhaustively. For the former, editions and translations are listed, with detailed bibliographic descriptions and annotations (though not so full as those of Keynes; see entry 210). Writings on Berkeley are divided by subject areas, with those relating to his philosophy subdivided by countries (English-language, French-language, German-language, Italy, others). The inventory of manuscript remains and letters (part 3) is by their locations.

The first edition of this work was published by Oxford University Press in 1934.

210. Keynes, Geoffrey. **A Bibliography of George Berkeley, Bishop of Cloyne: His Works and His Critics in the Eighteenth Century.** Oxford: Clarendon Press; Pittsburgh: University of Pittsburgh Press, 1976. 285p. (The Soho Bibliographies, XVIII).

Compiled by a collector of Berkeleyana, this catalog of early editions of Berkeley and his critics provides meticulous descriptions and annotations concerned with bibliographic and physical details and publishing history.

BUBER, MARTIN

211. Cohn, Margot, and Rafael Buber. **Martin Buber; Eine Bibliographie seiner Schriften, 1897-1978 / Martin Buber: A Bibliography of His Writings, 1897-1978.** Jerusalem: Magnes Press, Hebrew University; Munich: K. G. Saur, 1980. 160p.

The title is also in Hebrew, as is the foreword. A chronological listing of Buber's voluminous writings, including editions and translations: about fifteen hundred items. Notes and comments are in English, "except where Hebrew items are concerned" (foreword). Indexes are provided for titles, titles in Hebrew, themes, and languages.

Supersedes Moshe Catanne's *Bibliography of Martin Buber's Works (1897-1957)* (Jerusalem: Bialik Institute, 1958).

212. Moonan, Willard. **Martin Buber and His Critics: An Annotated Bibliography of Writings in English through 1978.** New York: Garland, 1981. 240p. (Garland Reference Library of the Humanities, vol. 161).

Writings by and about Buber are listed in separate sections, each arranged chronologically. Excellent descriptive annotations are provided for most "writings about." The latter are also indexed by author and subject, while "writings by" are indexed by title and translator. A commendable feature is a list of bibliographic sources consulted.

BURKE, EDMUND

213. Gandy, Clara I., and Peter J. Stanlis. **Edmund Burke: A Bibliography of Secondary Studies to 1982.** New York: Garland, 1983. 357p.

Chapters especially relevant for study of the philosophical aspects of Burke's thought and activity are chapter 4 on his aesthetic theory, chapter 5 on his political thought, and chapter 6 on his ideas on economics, society, and religion. Each chapter is introduced by a brief overview. Many entries are annotated, sometimes at considerable length.

CAMUS, ALBERT

214. Fitch, Brian T., and Peter C. Hoy. **Albert Camus: Essai de bibliographie des études en langue française consacrées à Albert Camus (1937-1970).** 3d ed. Paris: Minard, 1972. Unpaged. (Calepins de bibliographie, no. 1).

Includes writings on Camus in French, arranged chronologically. Indexed by author and, in the case of reviews of Camus's books, by title of the publication in which the review appeared.

215. Hoy, Peter C. **Camus in English: An Annotated Bibliography of Albert Camus's Contributions to English and American Periodicals and Newspapers (1945-1968).** 2d ed., revised and enlarged. Paris: Minard, 1971. Unpaged.

Materials listed in this slim bibliography are primarily literary and political statements, and include articles, excerpts from books, and interviews. First edition was a finely printed and illustrated limited edition of 250 numbered copies (Wymondham, England: Brewhouse Press, 1968, 29p.).

216. Roeming, Robert F. **Camus: A Bibliography.** Madison, Wis.: University of Wisconsin Press, 1968. 298p.

Has 3,432 unannotated entries, listing editions and translations of Camus's writings and works about Camus in all languages, arranged by author. Much of the material is literary or political. Has index of authors by language, a chronological index, and index of journals in which articles are published, but lacks any subject approach. Computer printout is clear but somewhat hard to scan.

CROCE, BENEDETTO

217. Borsari, Silvano. **L'opera di Benedetto Croce.** Naples: Istituto italiano per gli studi storici, 1964. 619p.

Croce's works are here listed by year of publication from 1882 through 1962, a total of 4,530 items, including reviews, prefaces, edited books, etc. Translations are listed separately (items 4531-4659). Annotations are limited to bibliographic matters. There is a combined name and title index.

218. Cione, Edmondo. **Bibliografia Crociana.** [Rome]: Fratelli Bocca, 1965. 481p. (Biblioteca di scienze moderne, 155).

Parts 1-4, which list works by Croce, are largely superseded by Borsari (entry 217). Part 5 lists, chronologically, about 1,250 writings on Croce through 1954, and includes brief annotations. While the majority of items are in Italian, there are also many in English, French, German, and other languages.

DESCARTES, RENÉ

219. Sebba, Gregor. **Bibliographia Cartesiana: A Critical Guide to the Descartes Literature, 1800-1960.** The Hague: Martinus Nijhoff, 1964. 510p. (International Archives of the History of Ideas, 5).

Lists about three thousand books and articles in numerous languages. Features two parts: (1) "Introduction to Descartes Studies": 562 of the most significant works, including bibliographical, biographical, introductory, and general studies; and (2) an alphabetical bibliography, including items listed in part 1. Part 1 is fully annotated, with annotations often evaluative; part 2 is more selectively annotated. Two subject indexes are provided: classified ("systematic") and alphabetical ("analytic").

DEWEY, JOHN

220. Boydston, Jo Ann, ed. **Guide to the Works of John Dewey.** Carbondale, Ill.: Southern Illinois University Press; London: Feffer & Simons, 1970. 396p.

Intended for use either as a complement to Dewey's *Collected Works* or as an independent resource, this guide comprises twelve essays by noted scholars surveying areas of Dewey's thought (psychology, ethics, theory of art, philosophy of religion, education and schooling, etc.). All but one (an essay titled "Dewey's Lectures and Influence in China") are followed by a checklist of his writings in that area, including unpublished writings, transcripts, etc., as well as published writings. A detailed subject and title index is provided.

221. Boydston, Jo Ann, and Robert L. Andresen. **John Dewey: A Checklist of Translations, 1900-1967.** Carbondale, Ill.: Southern Illinois University Press; London: Feffer & Simons, 1969. 123p.

The main section lists alphabetically sixty-seven books and articles by Dewey, including collections of his writings, each followed by a list of translations by language. Separate sections list materials originally published in languages other than English: some (in French) subsequently translated into English, others (in Japanese and Chinese) not. A chronological list of translations is included in the introductory material.

222. Boydston, Jo Ann, and Kathleen Poulos. **Checklist of Writings about John Dewey, 1887-1977.** 2d ed. Carbondale, Ill.: Southern Illinois University Press; London: Feffer & Simons, 1978. 476p.

Lists in separate sections (1) published works, including encyclopedia articles and (selectively) newspaper and magazine articles; (2) unpublished works (dissertations and theses); (3) reviews of Dewey's works; and (4) reviews of books about Dewey. More than three hundred items that are new or newly discovered since the first edition (*Checklist of Writings about John Dewey, 1887-1973*; Carbondale and London, 1974) are not integrated but are listed separately in a supplement (pages 295-350). Author index consolidates old and new materials, title indexes do not. There is no subject index.

223. Thomas, Milton Halsey. **John Dewey: A Centennial Bibliography.** Chicago: University of Chicago Press, 1962. 370p.

Writings of Dewey, 1882 through 1960, are listed chronologically on pages 1-153, and include books, articles, reviews, published letters to editors, etc. Reprintings and translations are listed under the entry for the original edition. Entries for books include tables of contents. Writings about Dewey, including dissertations, are listed by author on pages 155-293. Reviews of books about Dewey are also listed here, but reviews of books by him are in the first part (in each case under the entry for the work reviewed). The second part is largely superseded by the Boydston and Poulos *Checklist* (entry 222), but Thomas's excellent, detailed subject index (integrated with author/title index) has no counterpart in the later work.

DILTHEY, WILHELM

224. Herrmann, Ulrich. **Bibliographie Wilhelm Dilthey: Quellen und Literatur.** Weinheim: Julius Beltz, 1969. 237p.

Works by Dilthey are listed primarily in chronological sequence, with separate sections for collected works, translations, reviews, letters and diaries. Works about Dilthey – books, articles, dissertations, reviews – are arranged in sixteen subject sections. An author index is provided.

DUNS SCOTUS, JOHN

225. Schäfer, Odulfus. **Bibliografia de Vita, Operibus, et Doctrina Iohannis Duns Scoti.** Rome: Orbis Catholicus-Herder, 1955. 233p.

Nineteenth- and twentieth-century writings on Duns Scotus up to 1952 are arranged by author. There are a subject index ("Index analyticus") and a name index for coauthors, editors, and other contributors, and for cross-references to problematic Latin, French, and Spanish names. The introduction is in Latin.

EDWARDS, JONATHAN

226. Johnson, Thomas Herbert. **The Printed Writings of Jonathan Edwards, 1703-1758.** Princeton: Princeton University Press, 1940. Reprinted, New York: Burt Franklin, 1970. 136p.

This standard bibliography of Edwards's works is arranged chronologically according to the first edition of each item, and includes detailed bibliographic descriptions for all the early editions. Entries include holding library codes. Index of titles includes numerous cross-references.

227. Lesser, M. X. **Jonathan Edwards: A Reference Guide.** Boston: G. K. Hall, 1981. 421p. (Reference Guides in Literature).

This is primarily an annotated bibliography of writings about Edwards, arranged chronologically from 1729 through 1978. A chronology of works *by* Edwards (without bibliographic particulars) precedes the introduction, which is a fifty-two-page bibliographic essay and overview of Edwards scholarship and interpretation. Index combines author, title, and subject entries, but subject entries are grouped together under Edwards's name.

228. Manspeaker, Nancy. **Jonathan Edwards: Bibliographical Synopses.** Lewiston, N.Y.: Edwin Mellen Press, 1981. 278p. (Studies in American Religion, vol. 3).

Includes a listing of Edwards's published works and a comprehensive though not exhaustive bibliography of books, chapters of books, articles, and dissertations about him, from his own time up to the present. "Most entries are annotated, though some are not and others are summarized so briefly as to make the comments of little value" (*Choice* 19[Dec. 1981]:490).

ENGELS, FRIEDRICH

229. Eubanks, Cecil L. **Karl Marx and Friedrich Engels: An Analytical Bibliography.** New York: Garland, 1984. 299p. (Garland Reference Library of Social Science, vol. 100).

Individual and collected works by Engels are listed on pages 16-23. Secondary studies which focus specifically on Engels can be identified through the indexes of books, articles, and dissertations. See also entry 261.

230. Rubel, Maximilien. **Bibliographie des oeuvres de Karl Marx. Avec en appendice un répertoire des oeuvres de Friedrich Engels.** Paris: Marcel Rivière, 1956. 273p. **Supplement,** 1960. 79p.

See entry 262. The Engels appendix, on pages 239-58, lists 151 works by Engels in chronological sequence.

FĀRĀBI, ABU-NASR MUHAMMAD AL-

231. Rescher, Nicholas. **Al-Fārābi: An Annotated Bibliography.** Pittsburgh: University of Pittsburgh Press, 1962. 54p.

Al-Fārābi (ca. 870-950) "must be numbered among the five or six greatest philosophers of Islam" (introduction) and is also celebrated as a commentator on Aristotle. He influenced both Jewish and Scholastic philosophy in the Middle Ages. Rescher provides a comprehensive inventory of printed materials, including editions and translations of Al-Fārābi's works, arranged by author, editor, or translator, followed by classified listings of Al-Fārābi's works and of secondary studies. Though many items are in Arabic, Rescher aptly comments on the striking "indication of the very substantial amount of material available in Western languages" (introduction).

FICHTE, JOHANN GOTTLIEB

232. Baumgartner, Hans Michael, and Wilhelm G. Jacobs. **J. G. Fichte-Bibliographie.** Stuttgart: Friedrich Frommann, 1968. 346p.

Lists works by Fichte, including editions and translations, an   ᵏs about him, overwhelmingly in German but also in English and other langague   'erage from

1791 through 1967. The arrangement is classified, with personal name index and title-keyword index.

FOUCAULT, MICHEL

233. Clark, Michael. **Michel Foucault: An Annotated Bibliography: Tool Kit for a New Age.** New York: Garland, 1983. 608p. (Garland Bibliographies of Modern Critics and Critical Schools, vol. 4; Garland Reference Library of the Humanities, vol. 350).

Attempts to be "totally comprehensive for works by and about Foucault in French and English" (preface). Extensively annotated, it provides lengthy summaries for the major books of this leading French Structuralist, and short summaries even (in many cases) for brief reviews. A section on background works selectively includes books and essays that are not primarily about Foucault but do mention him. Indexes for authors, book titles, article titles, and topics are included.

GILSON, ETIENNE HENRI

234. McGrath, Margaret. **Etienne Gilson: A Bibliography / Une bibliographie.** Toronto: Pontifical Institute of Mediaeval Studies, 1982. 124p.

Lists 935 items by Gilson, an important Neo-Thomist philosopher in his own right as well as a major historian of philosophy. Includes works edited, prefaces, and book reviews. Also lists 260 items about Gilson, including five theses. Includes name and subject indexes.

HEGEL, GEORG WILHELM FRIEDRICH

235. Steinhauer, Kurt. **Hegel Bibliography: Background Material on the International Reception of Hegel within the Context of the History of Philosophy / Hegel Bibliographie: Materialen zur Geschichte der internationalen Hegel-Rezeption und zur Philosophie-Geschichte.** Munich: K. G. Saur, 1980. 894p.

Part 1 lists Hegel's works, including editions of complete and selected works, single editions, and correspondence. Part 2 is a bibliography of secondary sources, arranged chronologically (by decades) from 1802 to 1975. Offers unusually comprehensive international coverage (including, for example, Japanese works). There are an index of authors, editors, and translators, and a subject index of German keywords.

HEIDEGGER, MARTIN

236. Sass, Hans-Martin. **Martin Heidegger: Bibliography and Glossary.** Bowling Green, Ohio: Philosophy Documentation Center, Bowling Green State University, 1982. 513p. (Bibliographies of Famous Philosophers).

Works by Heidegger are listed by year of first publication, with later editions and translations following the original edition. This is followed by a listing of translations by language. Works about Heidegger (about fifty-three hundred items) are listed by author, except for a separate chapter listing papers and addresses presented at

Heidegger conferences. There is a subject index, but it is in German only, and is less discriminating than it might be, resulting sometimes in long lists of reference numbers. Other indexes include names (as subjects), editors and translators, titles of Heidegger's works, and reviews of his works.

This compilation by Sass largely supersedes his earlier *Heidegger-Bibliographie* (Meisenheim am Glan: Anton Hain, 1968) and a supplement, *Materialen zur Heidegger-Bibliographie, 1917-1972* (Meisenheim am Glan: Anton Hain, 1975). However, differences in arrangement—e.g., a chronological listing of the literature about Heidegger—may occasionally warrant reference to the earlier volumes.

For a note on the glossary (not in the earlier works), see entry 87.

HERDER, JOHANN GOTTFRIED

237. Günther, Gottfried, Siegfried Seifert, and Albina A. Volgina. **Herder-Bibliographie**. Berlin: Aufbau, 1978. 644p.

This is an international bibliography. Part 1 lists primary literature, with special sections for collected works, letters, and translations (by language). Part 2 covers secondary literature, organized under a variety of thematic headings and subheadings. Some descriptive, though minimal, annotations are provided.

HOBBES, THOMAS

238. Hinnant, Charles H. **Thomas Hobbes: A Reference Guide.** Boston: G. K. Hall, 1980. 275p. (A Reference Guide in Literature).

Lists (in a single sequence) works about Hobbes as well as editions of works by Hobbes, from 1679 through 1976. Writings about Hobbes are annotated with brief descriptive annotations. A chronological list of Hobbes's writings is included in the introductory material. There is an index of names and subjects, with subject entries gathered under Hobbes's name.

239. · Macdonald, Hugh, and Mary Hargreaves. **Thomas Hobbes: A Bibliography.** London: Bibliographical Society, 1952. 84p.

This is a descriptive bibliography of early editions of Hobbes, listing 109 items. Includes notes on circumstances of authorship and publishing history.

240. Sacksteder, William. **Hobbes Studies (1879-1979): A Bibliography.** Bowling Green, Ohio: Philosophy Documentation Center, Bowling Green State University, 1982. 194p. (Bibliographies of Famous Philosophers).

Dates of coverage indicated in the title represent the second and third centennials of Hobbes's death in 1679. Editions and translations of Hobbes's works, including some which saw their first publication after 1879, are listed in sections 1-3 and in section 7 (the latter a listing by editor and translator). Secondary literature is listed according to format (books, chapters of books, journal articles, etc.) in sections 4-6 and 8.

HUME, DAVID

241. Hall, Roland. **Fifty Years of Hume Scholarship: A Bibliographical Guide.** Edinburgh: Edinburgh University Press, 1978. 150p.

Based partly on an earlier, privately published *Hume Bibliography, from 1930* (York: Roland Hall, 1971, 80p.), and carries forward the work by Jessop (entry 242). It covers the years 1925 to 1976, but also includes a list of the main writings on Hume, from 1900 to 1924 (pages 17-26). Books, articles, and dissertations are listed by year of appearance. There are indexes for authors, for languages other than English, and for subjects (fairly detailed). The essay "The Development of Hume Scholarship," pages 1-14, is noteworthy.

242. Jessop, Thomas Edmond. **A Bibliography of David Hume and of Scottish Philosophy.** London: Russell & Russell, 1938. Reissued, New York: Russell & Russell, 1966. Reprinted, New York: Garland, 1983. 201p.

See entry 147. "Of Hume's works every edition that appeared in his lifetime has, I believe, been catalogued here, and probably almost all of the subsequent editions whether in English or in translation. The list of writings about him is incomplete . . . , but it is full enough to give a proportioned view of the range, geographical as well as chronological, of the interest he excited" (preface).

HUSSERL, EDMUND

243. Lapointe, Francois. **Edmund Husserl and His Critics: An International Bibliography (1894-1979), Preceded by a Bibliography of Husserl's Writings.** Bowling Green, Ohio: Philosophy Documentation Center, Bowling Green State University, 1980. 351p. (Bibliographies of Famous Philosophers).

Part 1, devoted to Husserl's writings, includes sections on the Husserl archives and the *Husserliana*, published conversations, correspondence, and editorial work. Part 2, devoted to works about Husserl, employs some divisions by subject (general discussions, studies and reviews of individual works, proper names, and subject descriptors) combined with some divisions by format (books and reviews, dissertations); there is some cross-listing, but no apparent consistency. The appendix lists 266 addenda.

JAMES, WILLIAM

244. Perry, Ralph Barton. **Annotated Bibliography of the Writings of William James.** New York: Longmans, Green, 1920. Reprinted, North Salem, N.H.: Verbeke, 1968. Reprinted, Folcroft, Pa.: Folcroft Library Editions, 1973. Reprinted, Dubuque, Iowa: William C. Brown, n.d. 69p.

"In view of the fact that much of James's most important thought appeared in the form of essays and reviews, often under a title which gave no clue to the contents, some such guide as this is indispensable . . ." (prefatory note). Barton provides a chronological list with brief summaries of subject matter or thesis for nearly every item cited, as well as tables of contents for books and collections of essays.

245. Skrupskelis, Ignas K. **William James: A Reference Guide.** Boston: G. K. Hall, 1977. 250p. (Reference Guides in Literature).

Books and shorter writings about James in English are listed by year, from 1868 through 1974, and briefly summarized. Separate sections list selected writings in other languages, American dissertations, and some of James's "Spirit Writings" (works alleged to have been transmitted after death through spiritualistic mediums). There is an integrated author, title, and subject index.

JASPERS, KARL

246. Gefken, Gisela, and Karl Kunert. **Karl Jaspers: Eine Bibliographie. Band 1. Die Primärbibliographie.** Oldenburg: n.p., 1978. (Reproduced from manuscript).

This is a chronological bibliography of Jaspers's works (469 items) from 1909 to 1977. Translations and reprintings (not separately numbered) are listed under entry for the original edition. A ninety-two-page introductory essay on Existential philosophy precedes the bibliography.

KANT, IMMANUEL

247. Adickes, Erich. **German Kantian Bibliography.** Boston: Ginn and Ginn, 1893-1896. Reprinted, Würzburg: A. Liebing, 1966? Reprinted, New York: Burt Franklin, 1970. 623p.

A "Bibliography of writings by and on Kant which have appeared in Germany up to the end of 1887" (preface), this work is arranged chronologically; exceptions and subtleties are explained in the preface. Adickes offers descriptive and critical comment for most items. A valuable resource on the first century of development of and reaction to Kantian philosophy. Name and subject indexes are provided.

248. Walker, R. C. S. **A Selective Bibliography on Kant.** 2d ed. Oxford: Sub-Faculty of Philosophy, 1978. 68p. (Study Aid Series, vol. 5).

This slender volume in the series issued by the Oxford Sub-Faculty of Philosophy (see entry 164) warrants special mention due to the lack (as of this writing) of any major current Kantian bibliography. If Kant's exceptional importance in the history of philosophy makes such a lacuna surprising, it also suggests a possible explanation: the sheer volume of Kantian studies confronting any would-be bibliographer is prohibitive. Walker's highly selective compilation, which aspires to be "of some use to graduate students," includes a section on works by Kant and their English translations, and eight sections on writings about Kant, five of them devoted to studies of specific major works. Unconventional but useful features are two lists titled "Compulsory reading" and "Slightly less than compulsory reading."

KIERKEGAARD, SØREN AABYE

249. Himmelstrup, Jens, with Kjeld Birket-Smith. **Søren Kierkegaard: International Bibliography / International Bibliografi.** Copenhagen: Nyt Nordisk Forlag, Arnold Busck, 1962. 221p.

Covers the period from 1835 to about 1955 (the centennial of Kierkegaard's death), with more haphazard coverage to as late as 1960. Both of the main divisions—editions of Kierkegaard's works and literature about Kierkegaard—are arranged according to language. Arrangement within language sections is chronological in part 1, by author in part 2. Represented, in addition to the Scandinavian languages and the major languages of Western Europe, are Russian, other East European languages, Greek, Hebrew, and Japanese, though the preface warns that coverage for some of these is inevitably sketchy. Title page, preface, table of contents, and most headings are in Danish and English; subject index terms are in Danish only.

Himmelstrup's work was supplemented by Aage Jorgensen, *Søren Kierkegaard-litteratur 1961-1970: En Forelobig Bibliografi* (Maarslet, Denmark: Aage Jorgensen, 1971, 99p.).

250. Lapointe, Francois H. **Søren Kierkegaard and His Critics: An International Bibliography of Criticism.** Westport, Conn.: Greenwood Press, 1980. 430p.

Part 1, works by Kierkegaard, includes translations and groups materials by language. Part 2, works about Kierkegaard, employs a mixed arrangement by formats (books and reviews, dissertations) and subjects, including a chapter arranged by proper names. The bibliography encompasses publications through 1979, is selectively annotated, and includes an index of authors and editors.

KINDI, ABU-YUSUF YA'QUB IBN ISHAQ AL-

251. Rescher, Nicholas. **Al-Kindī: An Annotated Bibliography.** Pittsburgh: University of Pittsburgh Press, 1964. 55p.

This work is similar in content and arrangement to Rescher's earlier work on Al-Fārābi (entry 231). The first major Arabic-writing philosopher, Al-Kindī (ca. 805-870) "made a great contribution to the establishment of Greek learning in the orbit of Islam" (introduction).

LEIBNIZ, GOTTFRIED WILHELM

252. Müller, Kurt, and Albert Heinekamp. **Leibniz-Bibliographie: Die Literatur über Leibniz bis 1980.** 2d rev. ed. Frankfurt am Main: Vittorio Klostermann, 1982. 742p.

Lists writings on Leibniz's work, thought, and influence in classified subject arrangement. Coverage extends from Leibniz's lifetime to 1980. Effort has been made to make bibliographic descriptions, particularly of the early literature, as complete as possible. Annotations are limited to bibliographic matters. Author and subject indexes are provided.

253. Ravier, Emile. **Bibliographie des oeuvres de Leibniz.** Paris: Libraire Félix Alcan, 1937. Reprinted, Hildesheim: Georg Olms, 1966. 704p.

Restricted to works by Leibniz, a vast body of writings with often complex publication histories. Sections cover, for example, books and articles published by Leibniz; anonymous reviews published by him; works written by him and published in his lifetime by others; and works published posthumously (listed by century of publication). An appendix lists the contents of major collections of Leibniz writings, including collections of his voluminous letters. Annotations, limited largely to bibliographic matters, are in French.

LOCKE, JOHN

254. Christopherson, Halfdan Olans. **A Bibliographical Introduction to the Study of John Locke.** Oslo: Norske Videnskaps Akademi, 1930. Reprinted, New York: Burt Franklin, 1968. 134p.

This extended bibliographic essay treats Locke's writings in relation to their historical context and the development of Locke's thought, and discusses secondary works from 1704 to 1928 by thematic categories (e.g., writings relating to Locke's *Essay,* to his educational thought, to his political and economic writings). An author index is included.

255. Hall, Roland, and Roger Woolhouse. **80 Years of Locke Scholarship: A Bibliographic Guide.** Edinburgh: Edinburgh University Press, 1983. 215p.

Materials on Locke from 1900 to 1980 are listed by year, and within each year by author. Indexes afford access by author, language, and subject. There are no annotations.

256. Yolton, Jean S., and John W. Yolton. **John Locke: A Reference Guide.** Boston: G. K. Hall, 1985. 294p. (A Reference Guide to Literature).

This is a list with descriptive, generally non-critical annotations of more than eighteen hundred secondary works from 1689 to 1982, by year of publication. Indexes for names (of authors and of persons mentioned in annotations) and subjects are provided. (Source: *Choice* 22[July/August 1985]:1622).

LOVEJOY, ARTHUR ONCKEN

257. Wilson, Daniel J. **Arthur O. Lovejoy: An Annotated Bibliography.** New York: Garland, 1982. 211p. (Garland Bibliographies of Modern Critics and Critical Schools, vol. 2; Garland Reference Library of the Humanities, vol. 344).

Best known as a historian of ideas, Lovejoy also made contributions (though less influential) to important debates in American philosophy. Both aspects of his career, and other activities (e.g., his role in organizing the AAUP), are encompassed by this bibliography, which lists and amply annotates some 315 publications by Lovejoy and some 225 secondary sources.

LUKÁCS, GEORG (GYORGY)

258. Lapointe, Francois H. **Georg Lukács and His Critics: An International Bibliography with Annotations (1910-1982)**. Westport, Conn.: Greenwood Press, 1983. 403p.

Lists only materials *about* Lukács, a Hungarian Marxist philosopher and literary critic with a considerable reputation even outside East European Marxist circles. Divisions cover (1) books and reviews; (2) dissertations and theses; (3) essays and articles; and (4) items arranged by proper names (relating Lukács to other thinkers). Parts 1 and 3 are divided according to language. Many of the twenty-one hundred entries are annotated, often at length, with some of the annotations lifted from other sources such as *Dissertation Abstracts International*.

MARCEL, GABRIEL

259. Lapointe, Francois H., and Claire C. Lapointe. **Gabriel Marcel and His Critics: An International Bibliography (1928-1976)**. New York: Garland, 1977. 287p. (Garland Reference Library of the Humanities, vol. 57).

Lists, without annotations, 3,001 items through early 1976, including works by and works about Marcel. Covers Marcel's activity as a dramatist and literary critic as well as his more strictly philosophical work. Combines certain divisions by format (books, dissertations, articles) with divisions arranged by proper names and subjects. There is an index of authors and editors.

MARITAIN, JACQUES AND RAÏSSA

260. Gallagher, Donald A., and Idella Gallagher. **The Achievement of Jacques and Raïssa Maritain: A Bibliography, 1906-1961**. Garden City, N.Y.: Doubleday, 1962. 256p.

This is an extremely comprehensive if not exhaustive international bibliography of books, booklets, parts of books, articles, prefaces, forewords, introductions, and translations. Lists hundreds of items by and about Jacques Maritain, the leading Thomist philosopher of this century, and scores of items by and about his wife Raïssa, who is less famous but also a well-published author of philosophical, theological, and literary works. A thirty-page introduction and a chronology of the Maritains' lives precede the bibliography. A subject index is included.

MARX, KARL

261. Eubanks, Cecil L. **Karl Marx and Friedrich Engels: An Analytical Bibliography**. 2d ed. New York: Garland, 1984. 299p. (Garland Reference Library of Social Science, vol. 100).

A forty-two-page introduction provides an overview of Marx's and Engels's most important writings, the Marx-Engels relationship, biographies, and the major interpreters. The bibliography itself, which is not annotated, lists individual and collected works by Marx and Engels, and, in separate sections, books, articles, and doctoral dissertations about them. Separate subject indexes also cover each of these types of material.

262. Rubel, Maximilien. **Bibliographie des oeuvres de Karl Marx, avec en appendice un répertoire des oeuvres de Friedrich Engels.** Paris: Marcel Rivière, 1956. 273p. **Supplement,** 1960. 79p.

This catalog of Marx's extensive output (some 885 items, plus a handful of dubious works), arranged in approximate chronological sequence, includes references to collected editions, notably the *Marx-Engels Gesamtausgabe* (1927-1935). Annotations, in French, are concerned chiefly with bibliographic details and publication history, but occasionally comment on a work's content or significance.

MERLEAU-PONTY, MAURICE

263. Lapointe, Francois, and Claire C. Lapointe. **Maurice Merleau-Ponty and His Critics: An International Bibliography (1942-1976); Preceded by a Bibliography of Merleau-Ponty's Writings.** New York: Garland, 1976. 169p. (Garland Reference Library of the Humanities, vol. 51).

Works by Merleau-Ponty are arranged in five sections: monographs and reviews thereof; dissertations; studies of individual works of Merleau Ponty; studies relating him to other thinkers; and items arranged by subject. Cross-references make this otherwise cumbersome division workable, though they are not always adequate. As to coverage, the closing date should more accurately be given as 1975; even at that, there are some significant gaps in coverage of articles and dissertations from 1973 to 1975.

MILL, JOHN STUART

264. Laine, Michael. **Bibliography of Works on John Stuart Mill.** Toronto: University of Toronto Press, 1982. 173p.

This international bibliography, listing 1,971 items in many languages, is arranged by author, with a subject index (somewhat unsatisfactory in its use of broad subject terms with long series of reference numbers) and a separate index for names as subjects. Appendices list verse, cartoons, and portraits and other representations.

265. MacMinn, N., J. R. Hainds, and J. M. McCrimmon. **Bibliography of the Published Writings of John Stuart Mill.** Evanston, Ill.: Northwestern University Press, 1945. 101p. (Northwestern Studies in the Humanities, 12).

Edited from Mill's own manuscript, with corrections and notes. Reportedly "not quite complete" (*Encyclopedia of Philosophy,* vol. 5, p. 322).

MONTESQUIEU, BARON DE

266. Cabeen, David Clark. **Montesquieu: A Bibliography.** New York: New York Public Library, 1947. 87p.

"Has 650-odd titles by and about M., most of them evaluated and located at New York Public Library, Columbia, or occasionally other important libraries. The *Bibliography* has an 8-page index, including reasonably complete subject lists" (Cabeen, ed., *Critical Bibliography of French Literature* [1951], vol. 4, p. 157).

NIETZSCHE, FRIEDRICH

267. Reichert, Herbert William, and Karl Schlechta. **International Nietzsche Bibliography.** Rev. and expanded edition. Chapel Hill: University of North Carolina Press, 1968. 162p. (University of North Carolina Studies in Comparative Literature, 45).

The first edition (1960) of this full though selective bibliography included 3,973 items in twenty-four languages, grouped by language. The revised edition adds 566 items which are grouped together rather than merged with the original entries. A subject index has been added. Some entries are briefly annotated.

PASCAL, BLAISE

268. Maire, Albert. **Bibliographie générale des oeuvres de Pascal.** Paris: L. Giraud-Badin, 1925-1927. 5 vols.

Many secondary works are included in this bibliography along with exhaustive listings of editions, reprintings, and translations of Pascal's writings. Individual volumes are devoted to specific writings or groups of writings; e.g., volume 4 deals with Pascal's most important philosophical work, the *Pensées*.

PEIRCE, CHARLES SANDERS

269. **A Comprehensive Bibliography and Index of the Published Works of Charles Sanders Peirce with a Bibliography of Secondary Studies.** Ed. by Ketner, Kloesel, Ransdell, Fisch, and Hardwick. Greenwich, Conn.: Johnson Associates, 1977. 337p.

Part 1 is an index to the microfiche collection *Charles Sanders Peirce: Complete Published Works, Including Selected Secondary Materials,* published by Johnson Associates. Like the collection itself, the index is organized chronologically. Fiche numbers are indicated, and works by and about Peirce are distinguished by the letters "P" (Peirce) and "O" (others). Under an extremely broad definition of published works (indicated in the preface), Peirce's output is more enormous than usually thought, and far exceeds what is included in his *Collected Papers.* Part 2 is a supplementary bibliography of secondary works, arranged by author. It repeats the "O" items from part 1 but also includes many works not part of the microfiche collection.

270. Robin, Richard S. **Annotated Catalogue of the Papers of Charles S. Peirce.** [n.p.]: University of Massachusetts Press, 1967. 268p.

This is a catalog of and guide to the Peirce papers in the Houghton Library at Harvard. Part 1 lists manuscripts, arranged by subject; part 2 lists correspondence.

PLATO

271. McKirahan, Richard D., Jr. **Plato and Socrates: A Comprehensive Bibliography, 1958-1973.** New York: Garland, 1978. 592p. (Garland Reference Library of the Humanities, vol. 78).

Continues the coverage provided for 1950-1957 by H. F. Cherniss's bibliographies published in the German annual *Lustrum*. Lists over forty-six hundred items, not counting book reviews, in more than thirty languages. The subject arrangement is facilitated by numerous cross-references and a number of special indexes imbedded within the subject sections. Sections devoted to individual Platonic dialogues include subdivisions for texts and translations, studies, and textual criticism. There are no annotations. An author index is provided.

See also entry 284.

272. Ritter, Constantin. **Bibliographies on Plato, 1912-1930.** New York: Garland, 1980. 909p. (in various pagings). (Ancient Philosophy: Editions, Commentaries, Critical Works).

Reprints bibliographic essays in German originally published in *Jahresberichte über die Fortschritt des klassischen Altertumswissenschaft,* published at Leipzig by O. R. Reisland, 1912-1930. Each essay bears the title "Berichte über die in den letzten Jahrzehnten über Platon erschienenen Arbeiten" [Information on works about Plato that have appeared in the last decade].

273. Skemp, J. B. **Plato.** Oxford: Clarendon Press, 1976. 63p. (Greece and Rome: New Surveys in the Classics, no. 10).

Features concise bibliographic essays surveying various aspects of Platonic scholarship: recent editions of Plato's works, textual scholarship, Plato's relationship to Socrates and the Sophists, key ideas and dimensions of his thought (the forms, theory of knowledge, ethics, physics, etc.), and "The Latest Phase: The Unwritten Doctrines" (chapter 10).

RAWLS, JOHN

274. Wellbank, J. H., Dennis Snook, and David T. Mason. **John Rawls and His Critics: An Annotated Bibliography.** New York: Garland, 1982. 683p. (Garland Reference Library of the Humanities, vol. 303).

Rawls's own writings are modest in number (about two dozen are listed, among them only one book), but not in significance, as more than twenty-five hundred secondary works included in this bibliography attest. Most of these deal with Rawls's seminal work, *A Theory of Justice.* Annotations are often extensive. Arrangement is by author, with indexes for second authors, titles, reviews (including reviews of related works), and subjects or "concepts."

ROUSSEAU, JEAN-JACQUES

275. Dufour, Théophile. **Recherches bibliographiques sur les oeuvres imprimées de J.-J. Rousseau.** Paris: L. Giraud-Badin, 1925. 2 vols. Reprinted, New York: Burt Franklin, 1971. 2 vols. in 1.

"Indispensable research tool. In addition to descriptions of printed editions of R.'s works, this work is particularly important because it lists R. manuscripts at Library of Neuchatel. Also lists books belonging to R." (Cabeen, ed., *Critical Bibliography of French Literature* [1951], vol. 4, p. 209).

276. Sénelier, Jean. **Bibliographie générale des oeuvres de J.-J. Rousseau.** Paris: Encyclopedie Francaise, 1949. Reprinted, New York: Burt Franklin, 19??. 282p.

"Elaborate and indispensable bibliography. Corrects and complements Dufour [entry 275] and extends research to date of publication. Chronological presentation. . . . Description and location of MSS. Dissemination of R.'s writings by countries" (Cabeen, ed., *Critical Bibliography of French Literature* [1951], vol. 4, p. 251).

RUSSELL, BERTRAND ARTHUR WILLIAM

277. Martin, Werner. **Bertrand Russell: A Bibliography of His Writings, 1895-1976 / Eine Bibliographie seiner Schriften, 1895-1976.** Munich: K. G. Saur; Hamden, Conn.: Linnett Books, 1981. 332p.

A chronological bibliography of Russell's vast output, with commentaries in both English and German supplied for major works. An appendix includes a chronological index of main works, an index of translations by language, a very short (four-page) bibliography of secondary works, title index, and list of sources.

SANTAYANA, GEORGE

278. Saatkamp, Herman J., Jr., and John Jones. **George Santayana: A Bibliographical Checklist, 1880-1980.** Bowling Green, Ohio: Philosophy Documentation Center, Bowling Green State University, 1982. 286p. (Bibliographies of Famous Philosophers).

Primary sources, arranged chronologically, begin with Santayana's student efforts at the Boston Latin School and at Harvard — including even his drawings for the *Harvard Lampoon* — and also include reprintings, in full or in part, of his many books and articles. Entries for books include tables of contents. Manuscript collections are listed separately. Sections for works about Santayana cover books, articles, reviews (of books by and books about him), and dissertations. Author, title, and subject indexes are provided.

SARTRE, JEAN-PAUL

279. Belkind, Allen. **Jean-Paul Sartre: Sartre and Existentialism in English: A Bibliographical Guide.** Kent, Ohio: Kent State University Press, 1970. 234p. (The Serif Series: Bibliographies and Checklists, no. 10).

Part 1 lists English translations of Sartre's works, including philosophical and literary works, film scripts, magazine articles, prefaces and introductions to books by others, and interviews. Parts 2 through 6 list writings in English about Sartre, including books, pamphlets, and dissertations (annotated), periodical articles (minimally annotated), and reviews. Appendix gives list of sources. There is an index of authors, editors, and translators.

280. Contat, Michel, and Michel Rybalka. **Les Écrits de Sartre: Chronologie, bibliographie commentée.** Paris: Gallimard, 1970. 788p. English edition (revised): **The Writings of Jean-Paul Sartre.** Volume 1, **A Bibliographical Life.** Transl. by Richard C. McCleary. Evanston, Ill.: Northwestern University Press, 1974. 654p. (Northwestern University Studies in Phenomenology and Existential Philosophy).

Includes a detailed chronology of Sartre's writing and publishing activities, plus a profusely annotated bibliography of his published works, also in chronological sequence. An appendix lists films scripted by Sartre or based on his writings. A second appendix, in the French edition only, reproduces some "rediscovered texts." Included are indexes of titles, names/subjects, and (in the French edition only) periodicals in which Sartre published.

The English edition includes revisions and updating to spring 1973, and integrates "a concise bibliography of Sartre's translations into English" (p. xix).

281. Lapointe, Francois H., and Claire Lapointe. **Jean-Paul Sartre and His Critics: An International Bibliography (1938-1980).** 2d ed., revised and annotated. Bowling Green, Ohio: Philosophy Documentation Center, Bowling Green State University, 1981. 697p. (Bibliographies of Famous Philosophers).

Contains 10,908 numbered entries, grouped partly according to format (books and reviews thereof; dissertations), partly according to subject (studies of individual works; names; topics). Arrangement within each group is by language: English, French, and others. Annotations, added since the first edition (same publisher, 1975), are frequent for books and general essays or articles, sporadic for other categories (none are given for dissertations).

SCHOPENHAUER, ARTHUR

282. Hübscher, Arthur. **Schopenhauer-Bibliographie.** Stuttgart: Frommann-Holzboog, 1981. 331p.

Lists works by Schopenhauer, including translations, and works about him. Of 2,395 items, the vast majority are in German, some in other European languages, relatively few in English. An index of names is provided.

SCHWEITZER, ALBERT

283. Griffith, Nancy Snell, and Laura Person. **Albert Schweitzer: An International Bibliography.** Boston: G. K. Hall, 1981. 600p.

Covers the many facets of Schweitzer's life and thought, and includes writings in many languages as well as some non-print materials. Works by Schweitzer are annotated, works about him infrequently. Chapter 6 deals specifically with Schweitzer's philosophical work, including his concept of "reverence for life," but some material of philosophical interest may also be found in the sections "Theology and Religion" and "Albert Schweitzer and World Peace."

SOCRATES

284. McKirahan, Richard D., Jr. **Plato and Socrates: A Comprehensive Bibliography, 1958-1973.** New York: Garland, 1978. 592p. (Garland Reference Library of the Humanities, vol. 78).

Materials concerned with Socrates as a historical figure, and not simply as a character in Plato's dialogues, are listed in a forty-five-page section near the end of this book. See also entry 271.

SPINOZA, BENEDICT (BARUCH)

285. Oko, Adolph S. **The Spinoza Bibliography.** Boston: G. K. Hall, 1964. 700p.

This work, published under the auspices of the Columbia University Libraries, reproduces catalog cards for about seven thousand items, accumulated by Oko over many years and in many cases bearing his annotations. Coverage is to 1942, with few entries dated later than 1940. Arrangement is according to a subject classification outlined in the front; inconveniently, headings are shown only at the beginning of each section and not repeated on each page. For each item, one location (only) is indicated, with preference given to Columbia, home of the Oko-Gebhardt collection of Spinoziana, and after that to Hebrew Union College, where Oko built up an extensive Spinoza library.

286. Wetlesen, Jon. **A Spinoza Bibliography, 1940-1970.** 2d rev. ed. Oslo: Universitetsforlaget, 1971. 47p.

The title page states that this second edition is "arranged as a supplementary volume to A. S. Oko's *Spinoza Bibliography*" (see above). An earlier version (*A Spinoza Bibliography, Particularly on the Period 1940-1967*; Oslo: Universitetsforlaget, 1968, 88p.) also included on a selective basis material covered by Oko, but in this edition Wetlesen has "omitted almost every reference to works published before 1940" (preface).

TEILHARD DE CHARDIN, PIERRE

287. McCarthy, Joseph M. **Pierre Teilhard de Chardin: A Comprehensive Bibliography.** New York: Garland, 1981. 438p. (Garland Reference Library of the Humanities, vol. 158).

Lists, without annotations, 621 works by Teilhard de Chardin, and 4,317 works about him. The former are arranged chronologically, except for collaborative works (collected at the end, by name of first coauthor). "Works about," arranged by author, include principally items in French, German, and English, and some in other languages, with English translations of non-English titles supplied where not obvious. A subject index is included.

THOMAS AQUINAS, SAINT

288. Bourke, Vernon J. **Thomistic Bibliography, 1920-1940.** St. Louis: The Modern Schoolman, 1945. (Supplement to vol. XXI). 312p.

Has 6,667 numbered and unannotated entries, arranged in an analytical subject scheme adapted with minor modifications from Mandonnet and Destrez, whose work (entry 289) is carried forward here. Like its predecessor, and also like its successor for the subsequent period (entry 290), this work functions to some extent, but not fully, as a bibliography for Thomism as a school of thought, as well as for St. Thomas as an individual (in any case a tenuous distinction, since Thomistic philosophy typically makes constant reference to St. Thomas and his writings). An index of proper names includes both authors and persons mentioned in titles.

289. Mandonnet, P., and J. Destrez. **Bibliographie thomiste.** Le Saulchoir, Kain, Belgium: Revue des sciences philosophiques et théologiques, 1921. (Bibliothéque thomiste, no. 1). 2d ed. Paris: Librairie Philosophique J. Vrin, 1960. 121p.

A list of 2,219 items, published up to 1920, classified under five major categories: (1) life and personality of St. Thomas; (2) works of St. Thomas; (3) philosophical doctrines; (4) theological doctrines; and (5) doctrinal and historical relations. See also entry 289.

The second edition is basically a reprinting, with a new introduction.

290. Miethe, Terry L., and Vernon J. Bourke. **Thomistic Bibliography, 1940-1978.** Westport, Conn.: Greenwood Press, 1980. 318p.

This latest Thomistic bibliography is arranged much like its predecessors, entries 288 and 289, and has 4,097 entries. It has no annotations, but the introduction includes some discussion of new research tools and of recent developments in Thomistic scholarship. See also entry 288.

TILLICH, PAUL

291. Crossman, Richard C. **Paul Tillich: A Comprehensive Bibliography and Keyword Index of Primary and Secondary Writings in English.** Metuchen, N.J.: American Theological Library Association and Scarecrow Press, 1983. 181p. (ATLA Bibliography Series, no. 9).

Though considered primarily a theologian, Tillich was arguably the most philosophical of modern theologians, and unquestionably one who has drawn an unusual amount of attention from philosophical quarters. Crossman's bibliography covers English-language books, articles, dissertations, and (more selectively) book reviews through roughly 1981, concerned with any aspect of Tillich's thought (and in a few cases with his personal life). Separate keyword indexes are provided for subject terms and personal names; the former suffers somewhat from a lack of discrimination common with this mode of indexing.

VICO, GIAMBATTISTA

292. Crease, Robert. **Vico in English: A Bibliography of Writings by and about Giambattista Vico (1668-1744).** Atlantic Highlands, N.J.: Published for the Institute for Vico Studies by Humanities Press, 1978. 48p. (Vichian Studies, 1).

This slim, unannotated bibliography includes English translations of Vico, and books, chapters of books, articles, dissertations, and reviews on Vico in English through early 1978. A seventeen-page section on works which discuss or mention Vico carries comprehensiveness to an extreme by including some works with only the barest mention of him. Ironically, at least two more substantial items (a Yale dissertation and a *Philological Quarterly* article, both from 1976) were missed.

VOLTAIRE, FRANÇOIS–MARIE AROUET DE

293. Bengesco, Georges. **Voltaire: Bibliographie de ses oeuvres.** Paris: Emile Perrin, 1882-1885. Reprinted, Nendeln, Liechtenstein: Kraus Reprint, 1967. 4 vols.

This catalog of Voltaire's prodigious output and numerous editions thereof includes a list of more than ten thousand letters in the Moland edition of Voltaire's collected works (Paris, 1877-1885) plus some others. Because Bengesco spreads his materials over a wide variety of rubrics, making it difficult to locate specific titles, an index, *Table de la bibliographie de Voltaire par Bengesco,* compiled by Jean Malcolm, was published, though much later (Geneva: Institut et Musée Voltaire, 1953, 127p.).

WHITEHEAD, ALFRED NORTH

294. Woodbridge, Barry A. **Alfred North Whitehead: A Primary-Secondary Bibliography.** Bowling Green, Ohio: Philosophy Documentation Center, Bowling Green State University, 1977. 405p. (Bibliographies of Famous Philosophers).

Lists all of Whitehead's known writings (some newly discovered) and attempts to include all secondary materials through June 1976 "which might be of even negligible value to those studying Whitehead or the application of his thought . . ." (introduction). It is not actually quite as complete as this suggests, but it does have over eighteen hundred entries, not counting reviews (included selectively, and listed under the works with which they deal). Annotations, generally non-critical, are provided for works that lent themselves to brief summaries. There is a subject index.

WITTGENSTEIN, LUDWIG JOSEF JOHANN

295. Borgis, Ilona. **Index zu Wittgensteins "Tractatus logico-philosophicus" und Wittgenstein-Bibliographie.** Freiburg im Breisgau: Karl Alber, 1968. 113p.

This work's bibliography (approximately half of the book) is international in scope and includes works by Wittgenstein (mainly notebooks, lectures, etc.) and works about him (books, dissertations, and articles). See also entry 309.

296. Lapointe, Francois H. **Ludwig Wittgenstein: A Comprehensive Bibliography.** Westport, Conn.: Greenwood Press, 1980. 297p.

Covers both works by and about Wittgenstein, with the latter distributed among six chapters: (1) books, and reviews thereof (with lists of contents for anthologies); (2) dissertations; (3) studies of individual works by Wittgenstein; (4) general discussions; (5) studies relating Wittgenstein to other thinkers; and (6) studies listed under more than two hundred subject descriptors. Many items are listed in more than one chapter. The book's coverage is international, through 1979.

10

DIRECTORIES AND BIOGRAPHICAL SOURCES

297. **Directory of American Philosophers, 1984-85.** 12th ed. Ed. by Archie J. Bahm in cooperation with Richard H. Lineback. Bowling Green, Ohio: Philosophy Documentation Center, Bowling Green State University, 1984. 406p.

New editions of this directory have been published every two years since the first edition of 1962/1963. The bulk of this issue, as of previous ones, is a directory of United States college and university philosophy departments arranged first by states and then alphabetically by institutions. Information provided includes address, phone number, and a list of faculty members. Additional sections cover graduate assistantships, research centers and institutes, societies, journals, and publishers. A separate section of the *Directory* covers Canada in similar fashion. Indexes (covering United States and Canadian sections together) include names of philosophers, with their addresses; institutions; centers and institutes; societies; journals; and publishers. A brief statistical section is included at the back.

298. **Directory of Women in Philosophy.** Ed. by Caroline Whitbeck with Deanna Barousse. Bowling Green, Ohio: Philosophy Documentation Center, Bowling Green State University, 1981. 38p.

This is an alphabetical list of women in academic philosophy in the United States and Canada, and of a few working abroad. In addition to institutional address and telephone number, it gives information about degrees held, fields of specialization, position, dissertation and/or publications (up to six). Indexed by state and country and by fields of specialization.

Earlier editions, under Whitbeck's name alone, were dated 1976-1977 and 1979-1980.

299. **International Directory of Philosophy and Philosophers / Répertoire internationale de la philosophie et de philosophes.** Ed. by Gilbert Varet and Paul Kurtz. New York: Humanities Press, 1965. 235p.

As a directory, this first edition has been superseded by four subsequent editions (see the fifth edition, entry 300). The later ones, however, do not include the survey articles on philosophical activity and trends in individual countries that may give this original edition some continuing usefulness. Particularly good examples are the articles on South Africa and the USSR. An article is not provided for every country covered by the directory (e.g., Australia, Austria, Bolivia, Indonesia, Turkey), but there are articles for many of them, even some whose place in the philosophical world has not been particularly prominent (e.g., El Salvador, Finland, Portugal, Venezuela, Yugoslavia). The articles are in English, French, or (less often) Spanish.

300. **International Directory of Philosophy and Philosophers, 1982-85.** 5th ed. Ed. by Ramona Cormier, Paul Kurtz, Richard H. Lineback, and Gilbert Varet. Bowling Green, Ohio: Philosophy Documentation Center, Bowling Green State University, 1982. 287p.

A companion work to entry 297, this directory excludes the United States and Canada. The categories of information included are similar, but arrangement is somewhat different. Aside from international organizations, all information is presented by country. Five categories of information are generally included: university and college philosophy departments; institutes and research centers; associations and societies; journals; and publishers. Information supplied for departments (or faculties) of philosophy includes address, names of faculty members with their rank and fields of specialization, enrollments, types of degrees offered and number of such degrees awarded in the last five years, plus some other data. Consult the preface for other details of coverage and arrangement. Indexes are provided for each of the five categories, and there is also one for individual philosophers.

Content and editors of previous editions have varied. See especially entry 299 (first edition).

301. Kiernan, Thomas P. **Who's Who in the History of Philosophy.** New York: Philosophical Library, 1965; Vision Press, 1966. 185p.

Aiming to serve as a "quick, concise and easily accessible source of reference," this volume goes somewhat beyond the typical "Who's Who" format to present, along with dates and important events in the philosophers' lives, "a concise exposition or representation of the principal points" in their philosophy (preface). The user may take as fair warning the author's acknowledgment of the difficulty and near-presumptuousness of this aim. Included by Kiernan are the major and secondary figures in the history of philosophy one would expect to find, but also some who are more obscure and not often represented in the standard philosophical dictionaries and encyclopedias. Examples include Mary Whiton Calkins (American Idealist), Callicles (known through Plato's *Gorgias*), and Ptah-Hotep (Egyptian, "often considered the first philosopher in history"). The typical entry is five to twenty lines in length, but major figures such as Aristotle and Kant may be allotted two pages or more.

302. Lange, Erhard, and Dietrich Alexander, eds. **Philosophenlexikon.** Berlin: Dietz, 1982. West Berlin: Das europäische Buch, 1982. 975p.

This East German "dictionary of philosophers" is strongly colored by its Marxist-Leninist perspective. It spans the entire history of Western philosophy, but its special strength is its coverage of Marxist and socialist thinkers, including figures little known outside the orbit of Soviet and East European Marxism. The longest articles are on Marx, Engels, and Lenin, but there are none on Stalin and Mao. Similarly symptomatic of the vicissitudes of Marxist intellectual life is the sarcastic characterization of Ernst Bloch as a "bourgeois philosopher who understood himself as a Marxist."

303. Menchaca, José A. **Diccionario bio-bibliográfico de filósofos.** Bilbao: El Mensajero del Corazon de Jesus & Universidad de Deusto, 1965- .

Only a small portion of this ambitious work has appeared so far: fasciculo 1o., names beginning with "A" (1965) and fasciculos 2o. and 3o., names beginning with "B" (1969). Whether it is still in progress is uncertain. Many obscure figures are included in the volumes published to date. Each entry includes a chronology of important dates, a source for bibliography (often one of the major philosophical bibliographies or encyclopedias, or even a general encyclopedia such as the *Britannica*), and lists of works by and selected studies about the individual.

304. Runes, Dagobert D., ed., with Lester E. Dennon and Ralph B. Winn, assoc. eds. **Who's Who in Philosophy.** Vol. 1: **Anglo-American Philosophers.** New York: Philosophical Library, 1942. Reprinted, New York: Greenwood Press, 1969. 293p.

Typical of the "Who's Who" genre (though no direct relation to any standard work such as *Who's Who in America*), this work provides lots of biographical data but no description of an individual's thought or other narrative information. The data normally include date and place of birth, degrees (where and when), title of dissertation, positions held, publications (articles and books), awards and honors, and professional memberships. The philosophers included, over five hundred of them, were all living at the time of publication and include, besides Americans and Britons, émigrés from other countries. Though of course quite out-of-date, this volume may still come in handy occasionally for the numerous minor figures included in it, or in the case of more prominent individuals, for information not provided elsewhere.

The reprint edition contains no revisions whatsoever. A projected second volume covering other countries was never issued.

305. Thomas, Henry. **Biographical Encyclopedia of Philosophy.** Garden City, N.Y.: Doubleday, 1965. 273p.

"In this book," states Thomas in his introduction, "I have presented the lives and the thoughts of the outstanding philosophers—some four hundred in all—who have offered the healing of wisdom in the epidemic of man's inhumanity to man." The orientation suggested by those words definitely governed the selection of thinkers included in this encyclopedia. Philosophers known primarily as logicians, or for highly technical contributions, tend to be omitted (e.g., Ayer, Carnap, Frege, Mach, Ryle) or deemphasized (Wittgenstein gets twelve lines). Many borderline figures, on the other hand, are included: Einstein, Havelock Ellis, George Fox, Anatole France, Goethe, Gregory I, Oliver Wendell Holmes, Johan Huizinga, Jeremiah, Walt Whitman, and John Wycliff. Eastern thinkers come in for attention as well as Western. Thomas is fond of biographical details, colorful descriptions, and anecdotes, especially to reveal a thinker's human side (see, e.g., the articles on Abelard, Dewey, Gregory I, and Locke). As might be expected, the expositions of an individual's ideas are at a popular level.

306. Ziegenfuss, Werner. **Philosophen-Lexikon: Handwörterbuch der Philosophie nach Personen.** Berlin: Walter de Gruyter, 1949. 2 vols.

Ziegenfuss's work may best be labeled biobibliographical; even very short entries on minor figures include bibliographies of principal works by them (designated *Schriften*) and selected works about them (designated *Literatur*). Short entries, in fact, predominate; often just one, two, or three lines (apart from the bibliographies), they typically include the most basic biographical data and a brief indication of the individual's significance. Longer articles on more important figures provide greater depth and detail: Hume gets five pages, Plato ten, Kant thirty-four. German thinkers get more entries and often more space than others, relative to their importance; but this "bias" is neither surprising nor necessarily censurable. Some critics have noted with disapproval the inclusion of, or the amount of space devoted to, individuals whose significance was more political than intrinsic (the five pages on race theorist Houston Stewart Chamberlain being perhaps the most egregious example). This is interesting in light of the work's history (to which Ziegenfuss alludes in his *Vorwort*). A substantial part (A through J) had already been published, in six fascicles, before World War II (1936-1937), but the remainder was suppressed for political reasons. The work was finally published as a whole after the war, largely in its original form: the biographical material received only minor updating, while bibliographies were brought up to 1945 for German publications, 1939 for non-German.

This *Philosophen-Lexikon* was planned to supplant an earlier one by Rudolf Eisler (Berlin: Mittler, 1912). It covers all periods and countries, but deliberately emphasizes philosophy since Hegel, and especially that of the twentieth century.

11

CONCORDANCES AND INDEXES TO INDIVIDUAL PHILOSOPHERS

307. Ast, Friedrich. **Lexicon Platonicum sive Vocum Platonicarum Index.** Leipzig: Weidmann, 1835-1838. 3 vols. Reprinted, Bonn: Habelt, 1956. 3 vols. in 2. Reprinted, New York: Burt Franklin, 1969. 3 vols.

A Greek-Latin lexicon to Plato's terminology is combined with a keyword index in this work. "The classical dictionary for Plato's original text" (Koren, *Research in Philosophy,* p. 98). Brandwood, however, in his newer *Word Index to Plato* (entry 310), avers that the *Lexicon Platonicum* "has long been recognized as an inadequate aid to the study of Plato" (p. ix).

308. Bonitz, Hermann. **Index Aristotelicus.** Vol. 5 of **Aristotelis Opera,** ed. by I. Bekker. Berlin: Reimer, 1870. Reprinted separately, Graz: Akademische Druck- und Verlagsanstalt, 1955. Reprinted separately, Berlin: Walter de Gruyter, 1961. 878p.

This is a complete concordance of the Bekker edition of Aristotle's Greek text. "An invaluable index of Greek words" (*Encyclopedia of Philosophy*, vol. 1, p. 162).

309. Borgis, Ilona. **Index zu Wittgensteins "Tractatus logico-philosophicus" und Wittgenstein-Bibliographie.** Freiburg im Breisgau: Karl Alber, 1968. 113p.

A word index to the German text of Wittgenstein's *Tractatus,* a landmark of twentieth-century philosophy (see entry 321 for an index to the English translation). Reference is given to the numbered propositions which constitute the structure of the text, quoting those that are most significant while citing others by number only. See also entry 295.

310. Brandwood, Leonard. **A Word Index to Plato.** Leeds, England: W. S. Maney, 1976. 1003p.

Brandwood's index, a product of computer technology and fifteen years of dogged labor, some of it described as "depressing drudgery," provides complete references to all Greek words occurring in the Platonic corpus, "except for the definite article *kai,* . . . the latter included only in certain mechanically identifiable combinations with other conjunctions or particles" (introduction). It is based on the Oxford Classical Text edition edited by John Burnet (Oxford, 1899-1907), but can be used with others since its references use the standard page, section, and line numbers of the Stephanus edition. References are grouped by dialogue, ordered according to a broadly chronological scheme. Footnotes comment on problematic words and sometimes give bibliographic references. An index of quotations is appended at the back.

311. Cahné, Pierre-Alain. **Index du Discours de la Méthode de René Descartes.** Rome: Edizioni dell' Ateneo, 1977. 90p. (Lessico intellettuale europeo, XII; Corpus Cartesianum, 2).

The original French text of Descartes's little classic is subjected to an exhaustive analysis designed, seemingly, more for linguistic than for philosophical study. Besides a concordance of all significant words, there is a list of those not so significant (*mots outils,* mainly articles and prepositions) giving number of occurrences, plus a hierarchical index of words in order of frequency of occurrence. Page references are to the standard Adam-Tannery edition, using, somewhat confusingly, what looks like a four-digit number to represent separate page and line numbers (e.g., 2827 = page 28, line 27).

312. Deferrari, Roy Joseph, and Sister M. Inviolata Barry. **A Complete Index of the "Summa Theologica" of St. Thomas Aquinas.** Washington, D.C.: Catholic University of America Press, 1956. 386p.

This index is based on the Leonine edition of the *Summa* (Rome, 1888-1908) and on certain passages from the Vives edition (Paris, 1871-1880) that are not included in the former. "Since this Index has been prepared for those interested in the content of St. Thomas' thinking rather than in his literary style, no attempt has been made to separate individual words into their inflectional forms as is the usual procedure in making an *index verborum.* . . . Likewise, words of no philosophical significance, such as *et, cum,* and *qui,* are omitted" (foreword). References are to standard divisions of the text, mainly numbered parts, questions, and articles.

313. Feick, Hildegard. **Index zu Heideggers "Sein und Zeit."** 2d rev. ed. Tübingen: Max Niemeyer, 1968. 132p.

An index to key terms in the German original of *Being and Time,* giving not merely locations but in most cases quotations showing the context of their use, and also citing occurrences in *other* works of Heidegger. The second edition updates the first (published in 1961) by incorporating references to works of Heidegger's later years. A *Seiten-Konkordanz,* in back, cross-references works which have been published in several different editions.

314. **Index Thomisticus: Sancti Thomae Aquinatis Operum Omnium Indices et Concordantiae.** Roberto Busa, S. J., editor-in-chief. [n.p.]: Frommann-Holzboog, 1974- .

"This is a reference tool of such grandiose proportions that it cannot be ignored" (Miethe & Bourke, *Thomistic Bibliography, 1940-1978,* p. xiii). Indeed, the *Index Thomisticus* takes the prize for the most voluminous reference work to be recorded here. It comprises three sections plus a supplement. Section 1, *Indices,* in ten volumes, contains indexes of distribution, summaries of the dictionary, and indexes of frequency. Sections 2 and 3 comprise the *Concordantiae*: complete concordances for, respectively, all of Aquinas's works, in thirty-one volumes, and for additions by other authors that are included in older editions of the *Opera Omnia,* in eight volumes. Miethe and Bourke question the wisdom of including the latter, "since they represent neither the thought nor the language of Saint Thomas" (*op. cit.,* p. xiv). The supplement, *S. Thomae Aquinatis Opera Omnia,* is a printing of the complete Latin works in seven volumes. A small guide in Latin and English, *Clavis Indicis Thomistici* (Frommann-Holzboog, 1979, 47p.) was issued when the set was still incomplete; a larger introductory volume to the entire *Index* reportedly was to be published last.

The *Index Thomisticus* has been hailed as "of incomparable importance to Thomistic research" (*New Scholasticism* 50 [1976]:237-49). Miethe and Bourke, on the other hand, express reservations, fearing the potential for error in the computerized compilation (they cite an example) and suggesting that while "without doubt [it] has some utility for students of medieval Latin usage . . . the very size of the *Index* renders it cumbersome for the investigation of Saint Thomas' thought" (*op. cit.,* p. xiv).

315. Kaal, Hans, and Alastair McKinnon. **Concordance to Wittgenstein's Philosophische Untersuchungen.** Leiden: E. J. Brill, 1975. 596p.

This is a word index to all significant words in the German text of Wittgenstein's *Philosophical Investigations* (third edition), which even in the British and American editions is printed side-by-side with the English translation. Short, often fragmentary quotations show the context for each occurrence of a word; locations are identified by both page and line numbers. A brief *Vorwort,* by the publisher, is in German, but there is an introduction in English.

316.   Martin, Gottfried, et al. **Allgemeiner Kantindex zu Kants gesammelten Schriften.** Vols. 16/17, 20. Berlin: Walter de Gruyter, 1967, 1969.

The *Allgemeiner Kantindex* aspired to be a comprehensive index to the Kantian corpus based on the so-called *Akademie*-edition of the *Gesammelte Schriften* (*GS*). Its intended scope is explained in the *Vorwort* to volumes 16-17, the first to appear of many projected volumes (a precise number was not announced). Publication goal for the entire series was 1994, but a recent inquiry (summer 1985) produced the information that publication of any future volumes is uncertain, due in part to the death in 1972 of the editor-in-chief, Gottfried Martin. It may be noted, too, that the *GS* itself is not yet complete. To date, only volumes 16-17 and 20 of the *Allgemeiner Kantindex* have been published. The former contain an index of word frequencies in works published by Kant himself (as distinguished from those published posthumously), comprising the first nine volumes of the *GS*. Volume 20 is an index of personal names for volumes 1-23 of the *GS,* comprising published works, letters, and manuscripts. Other planned volumes were to provide location indexes to all significant words in the *GS,* indexes of word frequencies in writings not published by Kant himself, personal name and source indexes, and finally, a subject index for the entire *GS.* As a provisional measure, a separate subject index for the *Critique of Pure Reason* only has been issued (see entry 317), though this is not formally part of the *Allgemeiner Kantindex.*

317.   Martin, Gottfried, and Dieter-Jürgen Löwisch. **Sachindex zu Kants "Kritik der reinen Vernunft."** Berlin: Walter de Gruyter, 1967. 351p.

An alphabetical subject index to the German text of Kant's *Critique of Pure Reason* as published in the *Akademie*-edition of his *Gesammelte Schriften.* References give page numbers plus line numbers of relevant passages.

Though it bears a close relationship to the project of the *Allgemeiner Kantindex,* which was headed by Martin (see entry 316), this volume is not actually part of that series.

318.   McKinnon, Alastair. **The Kierkegaard Indices.** Leiden: E. J. Brill, 1970-1975. 4 vols.

Preparation of these *Indices,* sophisticated research tools "designed to encourage and assist serious scholarly study of Kierkegaard's published works" (introduction, volume 2), was accomplished by extensive use of the formidable power of computers (even at what now seems a fairly crude stage of their development). The result might well intimidate anyone short of a true Kierkegaard specialist, but for the latter these may be indispensable timesavers. Titles and content of the four volumes are as follows:

I.   **Kierkegaard in Translation / en traduction / in Übersetzung** (1970, 133p.). Correlates the page numbers of both the third and second Danish editions of the collected works with those of "the best and most widely available English, French and German translations."

II.   **Fundamental polyglot konkordanz til Kierkegaards Samlede Vaerker** (1971, 1137p.). This is a concordance of 586 of the most fundamental terms in Kierkegaard's writings, set in context, with reference to their occurrences in the Danish third and second editions and the corresponding pages and lines of the English, French, and German translations.

III. **Index verborum til Kierkegaards Samlede Vaerker** (1973, 1322p.). Indexes every word in Kierkegaard's writings except those included in volume 2 plus certain common articles and prepositions. Provides page and line locations in the Danish third edition only (but these may be correlated with other editions via the tables in volume 1).

IV. **A Computational Analysis of Kierkegaard's Samlede Vaerker** (1975, 1088p.). Presents the various lexical properties of the Kierkegaard corpus with the use of rank and frequency lists and a number of summary tables and graphs.

319. Oehler, Richard. **Nietzsche-Register: Alphabetisch-systematische Übersicht über Friedrich Nietzsches Gedankenwelt.** Stuttgart: Alfred Kröner Verlag, 1965. 533p. (Kröners Taschenausgabe, vol. 170).

In his *Vorwort,* Oehler plausibly suggests that an aid to subject access is more essential for Nietzsche than for most other thinkers, due to the predominantly aphoristic form of his writings. This *Register* is an index to the main concepts and names in Nietzsche's works, keyed to the edition of the German text published as volumes 70 through 83 of Kröners Taschenausgabe. It references the most significant passages, not merely citing volume and page numbers but also quoting fragments of the text in which the terms are embedded.

320. Organ, Troy Wilson. **An Index to Aristotle in English Translation.** Princeton: Princeton University Press, 1949. Reprinted, New York: Gordian Press, 1966. 181p.

This is a detailed topical index to Aristotle's works based on the eleven-volume English translation edited by W. D. Ross and J. A. Smith (Oxford University Press, 1908-1931). The page numbers cited are those of the Bekker edition of the Greek text (issued by the Berlin Academy, 1831-1870), which are referenced in the margins of the Oxford translations and also in many other English editions of Aristotle's works.

321. Plochmann, George Kimball, and Jack B. Lawson. **Terms in Their Propositional Context in Wittgenstein's "Tractatus": An Index.** Carbondale, Ill.: Southern Illinois University Press, 1962. 229p.

In contrast to the *Tractatus* index by Borgis (entry 309), this is an index to the English translation, not the German original. Unlike Borgis, too, it provides a contextual quote for each reference, not just the most significant occurrences. Also includes a German-English wordlist, a list of logical symbols, and a selective bibliography covering materials dealing with the *Tractatus* only.

12

MISCELLANEOUS OTHER REFERENCE WORKS

322. Boydston, Jo Ann. **John Dewey's Personal and Professional Library: A Checklist.** Carbondale, Ill.: Southern Illinois University Press, 1982. 119p.

"Compiled at the Center for Dewey Studies, this bibliography is the most complete list of books in Dewey's personal library and in the libraries of his immediate family. All entries are annotated to include author inscriptions, notes and marginalia by Dewey, and other information necessary to trace the development of, and influence on, Dewey's thought" (*Harvard Educational Review* 53[February 1983]:103).

323. **Great Books of the Western World.** Vols. II and III: **The Great Ideas: A Syntopicon.** Mortimer Adler, editor-in-chief. Chicago: Encyclopedia Britannica, 1952. 2 vols.

The *Syntopicon* serves as a thematic guide and index to the 443 classics collected in the *Great Books of the Western World* (54 volumes), among which philosophical and philosophically significant works easily make up a majority. Its utility, however, need not be limited to its use with the *Great Books* set, which, admirable as it is, has its drawbacks (it often does not offer the best available texts or translations, and it lacks either scholarly apparatus or aids for the general reader struggling with archaic language or arcane concepts). In many cases, it is possible to use the *Syntopicon* with other editions of the works represented in the set, though this may require varying degrees of diligence and ingenuity.

Each of the *Syntopicon*'s 102 chapters is devoted to a fundamental term or concept (beauty, democracy, God, infinity, one and many, science, virtue and vice, wisdom, etc.) and consists of five parts: (1) an introduction in the form of a survey essay; (2) an outline of topics; (3) references to relevant texts, arranged according to the outline of topics; (4) cross-references to related concepts and topics; and (5) additional readings, referring to works not included in the *Great Books*. An inventory of terms at the end of the second volume lists narrower subject terms (from "a priori" to "zoology") and directs one to the relevant chapters on broader concepts.

324. **Great Treasury of Western Thought: A Compendium of Important Statements on Man and His Institutions by the Great Thinkers in Western History.** Ed. by Mortimer J. Adler and Charles Van Doren. New York: R. R. Bowker, 1977. 1771p.

The great thinkers in Western history included in this superb compilation of quotations are not all philosophers, at least in any rigorous sense. Nonetheless, philosophers and philosophic writing are more than generously represented. The quotations are organized into twenty chapters on major themes: love, mind, ethics, politics, liberty and equality, art and aesthetics, nature and the cosmos, religion, and others. These are further divided into a total of 127 sections for more specific topics. Examples of these sections include "Moral Freedom" (under ethics); "Progress, Regress, and Cycles in History" (under history); "Time" (under nature and the cosmos). The quotations, arranged chronologically within these sections, are typically longer than those in other collections of quotations, "running to more than 100 words on the average" (preface) and often much longer. Indexing is very thorough; besides an author index, there is a subject and proper name index with over 50,000 entries.

That one of the editors (Adler) is prominently associated with the *Great Books of the Western World* is not incidental. The preface alludes to the foundation of the present work in "that collection of the most worthwhile books to be read" and its innovative index, the *Syntopicon* (see entry 323). But while it stands in the *Great Books* tradition, the *Great Treasury* is by no means limited to writers and writings included in the *Great Books*; "almost twice as many writers are included," notes the preface. In any case, it is a work that stands by itself and has a value all its own.

325. Harrison, John, and Peter Laslett. **The Library of John Locke.** 2d ed. Oxford: Clarendon Press, 1971. 313p.

This work is an aid to the study of intellectual influences on Locke or of the intellectual climate and currents of his time. It includes an essay by Laslett titled "John Locke and His Books" and a catalog of his personal library (pages 67-267). The book is illustrated.

326. Hinske, Norbert, and Wilhelm Weischedel. **Kant-Seitenkonkordanz.** Darmstadt: Wissenschaftliche Buchgesellschaft, 1970. 299p.

Published as a supplementary volume of the Wissenschaftliche Buchgesellschaft edition of Kant's complete works, also known as the Weischedel edition. "It offers a thorough juxtaposition of all existing complete editions," including the original editions, Rosenkranz, Hartenstein 1 and 2, Kirchmann, the *Akademie*-edition (Preussische Akademie der Wissenschaften), Vorlander, Cassirer, and Weischedel. For each of Kant's works, it lists the volume and/or page numbers in each edition, followed by a detailed table matching page numbers in the original edition with those in the other editions. For the *Critique of Pure Reason*, it provides separate tables for the "A" and "B" editions. Foreword in German and English.

327. Hogrebe, Wolfram, Rudolf Kamp, and Gert König. **Periodica philosophica: eine internationale Bibliografie philosophischer Zeitschriften von den Anfängen bis zur Gegenwart.** Düsseldorf: Philosophia, 1972. 728 columns.

This is an international listing of some five thousand journals, both extant and defunct, in the field of philosophy broadly defined (broadly enough to include borderline journals in religion, psychology, general humanistic studies, etc.). Data provided typically include country and dates of publication, first and (if applicable) last issue numbers, sponsoring organization(s), and previous and subsequent titles. A special section, labeled *Kettenregister* ("chain index"), diagrams complex series of title changes, splits, mergers, etc. There is also a classified subject index (*Bereichsregister*) and a country index (*Länderregister*).

328. Jasenas, Michael. **A History of the Bibliography of Philosophy.** Hildesheim: Georg Olms, 1973. 188p.

An extended bibliographic essay which describes and discusses philosophical bibliographies, from a pioneering work by Frisius in 1592 through the major serial bibliographies being published as of 1960, this book focuses on works that aimed at comprehensive coverage of the field of philosophy. In addition to describing content and arrangement, Jasenas dwells extensively on historical details concerning the compilation and publication of such bibliographies, and the influences at work upon the bibliographers.

Jasenas divides the history of philosophical bibliography into five major phases: Rennaissance, modern, German *Aufklärung,* post-Kantian, and twentieth century. Appendices contain lists of bibliographies included, arranged chronologically and alphabetically; a list of other bibliographies, *not* discussed by Jasenas; and, somewhat anomalously, a "short-title list of major philosophical works discussed in standard histories of philosophy."

329. Magill, Frank N., ed., with Ian P. McGreal, assoc. ed. **Masterpieces of World Philosophy in Summary Form.** New York: Harper, 1961. 1166p. New York: Salem Press, 1961. 2 vols.

Two hundred philosophical classics are summarized in the manner of the *Masterplots* series and many similar works with which Magill's name is associated. On this particular project, twenty collaborators are listed, among them several prominent and well-respected scholars (e.g., Richard Popkin, Roy Wood Sellars, Frederick Sontag). The selection of works covered, if not beyond debate, is judicious, and the summaries are generally well done. Arrangement is chronological, from the fragments of Anaximander (sixth century B.C.) to Wittgenstein's *Philosophical Investigations* (1953). An alphabetical list of titles is at the front, author index at the back. A glossary of philosophical terms (pages xix-xxxii) can be helpful, though definitions are brief.

A much-expanded version of this work appeared in 1982 under a new title (see entry 330).

330. Magill, Frank N., with Ian P. McGreal, assoc. ed. **World Philosophy: Essay-Reviews of 225 Major Works.** Englewood Cliffs, N.J.: Salem Press, 1982. 5 vols.

This work incorporates all of the material in *Masterpieces of World Philosophy in Summary Form* (see entry 329). The older material is augmented, however, by new material of three kinds:

(1) Twenty-five additional summaries of works not covered in the earlier volume. Some are older works previously excluded (e.g., Clive Bell's *Art,* Hegel's *Phenomenology of Spirit,* the *I Ching*), others are recent works of exceptional importance or prominence (Quine's *Word and Object,* Rawls's *Theory of Justice*).

(2) Summary reviews of at least two works of pertinent literature, i.e., secondary sources, relating to each of the primary texts summarized. For Plato's *Republic,* for instance, there are summaries, each nearly two pages in length, of a book and an article dealing with some important aspects of the *Republic.*

(3) Short bibliographies of additional recommended readings. In the case of the aforementioned example, Plato's *Republic,* four additional works are recommended, including Levinson's *In Defense of Plato* and Popper's *Open Society and Its Enemies.*

One somewhat odd result of the strictly chronological arrangement employed in this set, as in its predecessor, is the juxtaposition of Western and non-Western works. The placement of Confucius between Anaximander and Heraclitus may be chronologically sound, but has little meaning in view of the absolute geographical and cultural gap separating the Chinese philosopher from his Greek contemporaries.

The five volumes cover the following periods: (1) sixth to third centuries B.C.; (2) third century B.C. to A.D. 1713; (3) 1726-1896; (4) 1896-1932; (5) 1932-1971.

331. Maison des Sciences de l'Homme, Paris. Service d'Echange d'Informations Scientifiques. **Liste mondiale des périodiques spéciales en philosophie / World List of Specialized Periodicals in Philosophy.** Paris: Mouton, 1967. 124p. (Publications série C: Catalogues et inventaires).

In this work philosophical journals are listed by country and indexed by subject, by publishing bodies, and by titles. Each entry in the main list includes, besides bibliographic and publishing data, a concise characterization indicating the typical length and number of articles per issue, regular features such as reviews, subject content, and noteworthy features or characteristics. Like its title, the list is bilingual (French and English) throughout, the subject index not excepted.

332. Moulton, Janice M. **Guidebook for Publishing Philosophy.** Rev. and updated ed. Newark, Del.: American Philosophical Association, 1977. 151p.

"The purpose of the *Guidebook* is to provide, in a single source, helpful information for those who want to make public their work in philosophy"—more specifically, "information about publishing, presenting, and circulating unsolicited work." This information ranges from general advice on the practices and protocols of book and journal publishing, to specific information on over sixty journals and nineteen publishers (with addresses, manuscript requirements, and subject matter covered or likely to be considered), to opportunities for presenting papers at philosophical conferences. The *Guidebook* is intended primarily for United States and Canadian philosophers. While somewhat out of date by this time, it is still useful.

333. **The Plato Manuscripts: A New Index.** Prepared by the Plato Microfilm Project of the Yale University Library under the Direction of Robert L. Brumbaugh and Rulon Wells. New Haven: Yale University Press, 1968. 163p.

A catalog of microfilms of "extant pre-1500 manuscripts containing Plato's works in whole or in part," this work consists of two indexes, one arranged by holding library, and the other by title of Platonic dialogue. A short bibliography (nineteen items) of textually oriented works is included on page 163.

334. Ruben, Douglas H. **Philosophy Journals and Serials: An Analytical Guide.** Westport, Conn.: Greenwood Press, 1985. 147p. (Annotated Bibliograhies of Serials: A Subject Approach, no. 2).

Unlike other serials lists included in this chapter (cf. entries 327, 331, and 336), Ruben's is limited to English-language serials. It lists, however, over three hundred titles. Entries include full annotations with exceptionally detailed information about publishers, prices, circulation, manuscript selection, acceptance rates, coverage in indexes and abstracts, and target audiences, and also evaluative comments on strengths and weaknesses. Arrangement is alphabetical by title, with subject and geographical indexes.

335. Runes, Dagobert D., comp. **Treasury of Philosophy.** New York: Philosophical Library, 1955. Reprinted as **Treasury of World Philosophy.** Paterson, N.J.: Littlefield, Adams, 1959. 1280p.

Runes's *Treasury* is a compendium of representative selections, a few paragraphs to several pages in length, from about 375 philosophers and others whose writings resonate with philosophical import. Arrangement is alphabetical by authors' names. That each figure is represented by a single excerpt exposing (usually) only one aspect of his or her thought is rather limiting. And the compiler's particular choices no doubt reflect, in many cases, his personal predilections. Yet in general the excerpts do at least typify their authors' thought.

Preceding each selected passage is a brief biographical sketch with comments on the individual's contributions and significance. These, too, tend to reflect somewhat personal tastes and evaluations, but can be useful for the popular audience for whom this work seems designed.

336. U.S. Library of Congress. General Reference and Bibliography Division. **Philosophical Periodicals: An Annotated World List.** Comp. by David Baumgardt. Washington, D.C.: Government Printing Office, 1952. 89p.

This list was "designed to give some basic information on the variegated philosophical interests of periodicals being issued currently [i.e., ca. 1952] in some 71 political areas" (introduction). In the case of countries with extensive general magazine and journal publishing, inclusion is limited to professional publications. "In the case of political areas, however, whose literary production is more limited, the non-formal philosophical press has been liberally taken into account." This feature, together with some of the brief notes characterizing scope or emphasis, give this dated work some residual value. A total of 489 titles is listed.

337. Valdés, Mario J., and Maria Elena de Valdés. **An Unamuno Source Book: A Catalogue of Readings and Acquisitions with an Introductory Essay on Unamuno's Dialectical Enquiry.** [Toronto and Buffalo, N.Y.]: University of Toronto Press, 1973. 305p.

This specialized work is designed to aid the scholar interested in influences on the thought of the important Hispanic thinker Miguel de Unamuno y Jugo. "The bulk of the work consists of a complete register of the 5,700 volumes at Salamanca [Unamuno's home], including titles discovered in Unamuno's personal catalog (1900-1917) but now missing from the collection. Systematic perusal of the *Obras completas* (Vergara edition) provided further references to books, newspapers, and journals that Unamuno read or to which he contributed material and that are not in the Salamanca collection. These are listed in two appendices, with references to the *Obras completas.* Bibliographic entries are complete, and most are annotated with symbols indicating significant aspects of each title" (*American Reference Books Annual,* 1974, entry 1195).

13

CORE JOURNALS

338. **American Philosophical Quarterly,** 1964- . Bowling Green, Ohio: Philosophy Documentation Center, Bowling Green State University. Quarterly.

Apart from lists of books received, the *APQ* publishes five to ten articles per issue, mostly but not exclusively written by American contributors and mostly but not exclusively oriented toward Analytical philosophy. Surveys of recent work in specific areas of philosophy are a periodic feature. The April issue carries selected papers presented at the American Philosophical Association Pacific Division Conference.

339. **Analysis,** 1933-1940, 1947- . Oxford: Basil Blackwell. Quarterly.

As its title connotes, *Analysis* serves philosophers of an Analytical bent; it was founded by a group of philosophers heavily influenced by Wittgenstein, Russell, and G. E. Moore. As a matter of policy it publishes only short contributions, some of them less than a page long. Many of these are brief exchanges between prominent and sometimes not-so-prominent philosophers, primarily British and American.

340. **Archiv für Geschichte der Philosophie,** 1888-1932, 1959- . Berlin: Walter de Gruyter. 3/yr.

A primary vehicle for European scholarship in the history of philosophy, the *Archiv* also has American and British coeditors, and a fair proportion of its articles (though few of its book reviews) are in English. Other articles are in German and French.

341. **British Journal for the Philosophy of Science,** 1950- . Aberdeen, Scotland: Aberdeen University Press. Quarterly.

This is the official journal of the British Society for the Philosophy of Science, an eminent institution whose stated purpose is "to study the logic, the method and the philosophy of science as well as those of the various special sciences, including the social sciences." It carries articles, short discussions, substantial book reviews, lists of recent publications, brief announcements, and (in alternate issues) abstracts from two other leading journals in the field, *Philosophy of Science* and *Synthese*.

342. **British Journal of Aesthetics,** 1960- . Oxford: Oxford University Press. Quarterly.

The official organ of the British Society of Aesthetics, this journal publishes articles concerned with "theoretical study of the arts (both fine and practical) and related types of experience from a philosophical, psychological, scientific, historical, critical or educational viewpoint." In keeping with this broad definition, it draws contributions from a diversity of disciplines and perspectives, though a substantial proportion are by philosophers. The journal carries book reviews, lists of books and journal issues received, and brief announcements.

343. **Diogenes,** 1953- . Florence: Casalini Libri. Quarterly.

Diogenes is sponsored by the International Council for Philosophy and Humanistic Studies, affiliated with UNESCO. It is published in parallel English, French, and Spanish editions; annual anthologies are issued in Arabic, Hindi, Japanese, and Portuguese. Not a technical philosophical journal, but aimed at a general readership, *Diogenes* deals with a diversity of issues in a variety of humanities disciplines. While many of its articles are philosophical only in a broad sense, and some not at all, it does afford substantial coverage of philosophical thought from a broad and intentionally international range of perspectives.

344. **Ethics: An International Journal of Social, Political and Legal Philosophy,** 1890- . Chicago: University of Chicago Press. Quarterly.

This is the foremost journal covering ethical theory (generally though not always staying somewhat close to practical concerns) and the areas indicated by its subtitle. It is not quite so international as the subtitle may suggest; Anglo-American contributors and concerns dominate, though it inclines less sharply toward Analytical philosophy than most other front-rank American journals. Some of its contributors are not professional philosophers, and many of the articles are of potential interest to social scientists, those concerned with public policy, and the educated general reader. About one-third of each issue is devoted to book reviews and book notes.

345. **History and Theory: Studies in the Philosophy of History,** 1960- . Middletown, Conn.: Wesleyan University Press. 3/yr.

For serious work in philosophy of history, *History and Theory* is the standard journal. Interdisciplinary in nature, some of its articles address methodological and conceptual problems of historiography that are tangential to philosophy. It is of interest to many historians and social scientists as well as philosophers. Short monographic studies and periodic bibliographies of the field (the latter particularly important) are published as an annual *Beiheft* (supplement).

346. **International Journal for Philosophy of Religion.** 1970- . The Hague: Martinus Nijhoff. Quarterly.

Sponsored by the Society for Philosophy of Religion, this journal features articles and book reviews offering philosophical insights, theories, and arguments on a broad spectrum of issues relating to religion. It is the leading journal devoted to philosophy of religion, and is widely indexed (e.g., in the *Humanities Index* and several religion indexes). It is not, however, as indispensable for coverage of its field as most other specialized journals listed in this chapter are for theirs, since many of the important debates in philosophy of religion are carried on in general philosophical journals.

347. **International Philosophical Quarterly,** 1961- . Bronx, New York: Fordham University. Quarterly.

"Founded to provide an international forum in English for the interchange of basic philosophical ideas between the Americas and Europe and between East and West," the *IPQ* is coedited by the philosophy faculties of Fordham University and the Belgian Facultes Universitaires Notre Dame de la Paix. "Its primary orientation is to encourage vital contemporary expression—creative, critical, and historical—in the intercultural tradition of theistic, spiritualist, and personalist humanism, but without further restriction of school within these broad perspectives." Within that framework it offers articles on a wide range of subjects, including some concerned with non-Western philosophy. A somewhat regular "Contemporary Currents" section surveys recent literature on a particular problem, movement, or philosopher. Book reviews, shorter book notices, and lists of books received also appear regularly.

348. **Journal of Aesthetics and Art Criticism,** 1941- . Greenvale, N.Y.: American Society for Aesthetics, [C. W. Post Center, Long Island University]. Quarterly.

Sponsored by the American Society for Aesthetics, this journal publishes "studies of the arts and related types of experience from a philosophic, scientific, or other theoretical standpoint, including those of psychology, sociology, anthropology, visual arts history, art criticism, and education." A typical issue has ten or so scholarly articles and a dozen or more book reviews of varying length. The annual "Selective Current Bibliography for Aesthetics and Related Fields" has been an important feature since 1945. The journal carries notes and news, especially regarding the society, whose membership list it also publishes annually.

349. **Journal of Medicine and Philosophy,** 1976- . Dordrecht, Netherlands: D. Reidel. Quarterly.

In the fast-maturing field of medical ethics, the *Journal of Medicine and Philosophy* is the most concentratedly philosophical (the more widely circulated *Hastings Center Report,* while excellent, tends to focus more on other aspects of bioethical issues: sociological, psychological, legal, economic, etc.). *JMP* boasts an impressive array of affiliations: "established under the auspices of the Society for Health and Human Values"; "sponsored by the Center for Ethics, Medicine and Public

Issues, a joint project of Baylor College of Medicine, the Institute of Religion, and Rice University, with the cooperation of the Kennedy Institute of Ethics, Georgetown University." Most but not all issues center on particular themes, announced in advance. One to three book reviews appear in some issues.

350. **Journal of Philosophy,** 1904- . New York: Journal of Philosophy, [Columbia University]. Monthly.

A well-established journal with a distinguished history, the *Journal of Philosophy* tends to be more technical and its articles less generally accessible now than in former years. It remains, however, one of the most widely circulated philosophical journals. While varying considerably in content, it emphasizes the concerns of Anglo-American philosophy, particularly with logical and linguistic analysis. It regularly carries book reviews, some of article length, lists of new books, and announcements and news items. The October and November issues publish the program and selected papers for the Eastern Division Conference of the American Philosophical Association.

351. **Journal of Symbolic Logic,** 1936- . Providence, R.I.: Association for Symbolic Logic. Quarterly.

Though specialized and technical, the *Journal of Symbolic Logic* is among the most important philosophical journals and enjoys a higher circulation than most others listed in this chapter. It publishes original technical papers, expository articles, and, less frequently, historical studies and philosophical articles relating to or using symbolic logic. Contributors may be from anywhere in the world. Among the useful features for those working in this field are reviews of important articles as well as books, abstracts of conference papers and articles in other journals, and notices and membership lists of the sponsoring organization.

352. **Journal of the History of Ideas,** 1940- . Philadelphia: Temple University. Quarterly.

Broader in scope than the history of philosophy, this distinguished journal "devoted to cultural and intellectual history" is nonetheless extremely valuable for the history of philosophy generally and also for cross-disciplinary or borderline fields such as aesthetics and political philosophy. A typical issue carries six to eight articles plus some shorter notes, a single lengthy review article, and a list of books received.

353. **Journal of the History of Philosophy,** 1963- . St. Louis: Journal of the History of Philosophy, [Washington University]. Quarterly.

This standard journal for work in the history of Western philosophy has an international contributorship. It publishes articles, discussions, and notes, many substantial book reviews, some shorter book notes, and lists of books received. The vast majority of articles and reviews are in English, an occasional few in other major Western languages.

354. **Mind: A Quarterly Review of Philosophy**, 1876- . Oxford: Basil Blackwell. Quarterly.

One of the oldest philosophical journals extant, and one of the most influential, *Mind* has long represented the mainstream of Anglo-American and particularly British philosophy. Articles and discussions on philosophy of language, philosophical psychology, and ethical theory are especially common. It carries a good number of book reviews and notices of books received. The membership list of its sponsoring body, the Mind Association, is published annually.

355. **The Monist: An International Quarterly Journal of General Philosophical Inquiry**, 1890-1936, 1962- . LaSalle, Ill.: Hegeler Institute. Quarterly.

The subtitle of this journal more adequately reflects its present content than its title, which hearkens back to the philosophical position of its founder, Paul Carus. Since its revival after a twenty-five year hiatus, it has featured individual issues devoted to specific topics, announced in advance. In addition to the articles, some of which are contributed by invitation, it publishes abstracts of new books and lists books received. "Not a groundbreaking journal, perhaps, but the topical approach, and the reliability of its contributions make it very useful for undergraduates" (Farber, *Classified List of Periodicals for the College Library*, 5th ed., 1972, p. 335).

356. **New Scholasticism**, 1927- . Washington, D.C.: American Catholic Philosophical Association, Catholic University of America. Quarterly.

The journal of the American Catholic Philosophical Association, *New Scholasticism* usually carries, as the chronicles of that organization's secretary, several pages of news and notices: ACPA meetings; other meetings and conferences; new series, periodicals, bibliographies, critical editions, and translations; special collections; funded research and scholarship opportunities; and teaching appointments. Its articles, which as the title indicates generally represent Neo-Scholastic thought, include both historical studies and substantive philosophical argument. Book reviews and lists of books received are also published.

357. **Philosophical Quarterly**, 1950- . Oxford: Basil Blackwell. Quarterly.

Published for the Scots Philosophical Club and St. Andrews University, *PQ* is not restricted to Scottish contributors, though they are mainly British. Analytical in orientation, it is not limited in scope, but seems to favor articles on metaphysics, ethics, logic, philosophy of language, and history of philosophy. It gives "special attention to surveys of philosophical literature and to book reviews." About twenty reviews are published in each issue.

358. **Philosophical Review**, 1892- . Ithaca, N.Y.: Sage School of Philosophy, Cornell University. Quarterly.

The *Philosophical Review* has grown into a prestigious journal representing Analytical philosophy, general in scope but tending to emphasize epistemology and metaphysics. It carries book reviews, typically ten or twelve per issue, and lengthy lists of books received.

359. **Philosophical Studies: An International Journal for Philosophy in the Analytic Tradition**, 1950- . Dordrecht, Netherlands: D. Reidel. Bimonthly (frequency varies somewhat).

The orientation of this journal is clearly identified in its subtitle. It serves especially as a vehicle for "quick publication . . . emphasizing the rapid exchange of notes and criticism" (publisher's catalog). Contributed (sometimes invited) articles are expected to "contain rigorous argumentation and precise analysis of key concepts," and while ranging over most areas of philosophy, tend to concentrate on issues in logic and linguistic theory. Articles generally presuppose some background, though they are supposed to be "intelligible to philosophers whose expertise lies outside the subject matter of the article." Lists of books received are published in most issues, but no reviews.

360. **Philosophy**, 1925- . Cambridge: Cambridge University Press. Quarterly.

The official journal of the Royal Institute of Philosophy, *Philosophy* aims "to promote the study of philosophy in all its branches." Contributors are expected, states its editorial policy, "to avoid needless technicality." The journal carries articles by American as well as British and Commonwealth authors, and while its content is mostly representative of Anglo-American philosophy, it is "not committed to any school or method." Book reviews, booknotes (often lengthy discussions), and lists of books received are regular features. The institute's Lecture Series are published annually as supplements to the journal.

361. **Philosophy and Phenomenological Research**, 1940- . Providence, R.I.: Brown University. Quarterly.

This is the official journal of the International Phenomenological Society. Rooted in the European Phenomenological movement and particularly attentive to Phenomenological method and concerns, it is nonetheless open to other points of view and has always offered great diversity in its articles. It carries book reviews, lists of recent publications, and professional notes and news.

362. **Philosophy and Public Affairs**, 1971- . Princeton: Princeton University Press. Quarterly.

Launched in the politically turbulent early seventies, *Philosophy and Public Affairs* is founded on the conviction that philosophical examination and discussion can contribute to the clarification and resolution of substantive political, social, legal, and economic issues. Most contributors are philosophers, but avoidance of technical language along with its subject matter makes this one of the more promising journals for general readership. It includes articles only.

363. **Philosophy East and West**, 1951- . Honolulu: University Press of Hawaii. Quarterly.

The broadly conceived aim of this journal of Asian and comparative thought is to publish "specialized articles in Asian philosophy and articles which seek to illuminate, in a comparative manner, the distinctive characteristics of the various philosophical traditions in the East and West," and also "articles which exhibit the relevance of philosophy for the art, literature, science, and social practice of Asian civilizations, and those original contributions to philosophy which work from an intercultural basis." It is the foremost English-language journal for the study of Eastern philosophies. Besides articles and discussions, it includes book reviews, lists of books received, brief listings of articles from other periodicals, and notes and news.

364. **Philosophy of Science,** 1934- . Lansing, Mich.: Philosophy of Science Association [Michigan State University]. Quarterly.

A historically important journal in its field, this is the official organ of the Philosophy of Science Association, whose membership is listed in the first issue of each volume. Articles generally presuppose some background and are often quite technical. Responses to earlier articles are not uncommon. Generally, there are four to six book reviews per issue.

365. **Philosophy Today,** 1957- . Celina, Ohio: Messenger Press, Society of the Precious Blood. Quarterly.

Though not in the front rank of philosophical journals and somewhat uneven in quality, *Philosophy Today* is useful for the amount of attention it devotes to Continental philosophy, ignored or neglected by most of the standard American and British journals. Some of its articles are translations from French and German journals. While it is "directed to the interests of scholars and teachers within the Christian tradition," this defines its primary (but hardly exclusive) target audience, not the subject matter and the philosophers it takes into its purview.

366. **Review of Metaphysics,** 1947- . Washington, D.C.: Philosophy Education Society [Catholic University of America]. Quarterly.

The *Review* is a highly regarded journal, broad in scope though emphasizing metaphysical topics, and open to a diversity of philosophical viewpoints. It is also known for a variety of useful features in addition to standard articles and critical discussions: summaries and comments for books received; abstracts of articles in leading English-language journals; announcements; and annual lists (in the September issue) of doctoral dissertations, numbers of faculty in graduate philosophy departments, visiting faculty from abroad, and American faculty visiting abroad.

367. **Revue internationale de philosophie,** 1938-1939, 1948- . Brussels: Michael Meyer. Quarterly.

The *Revue internationale* publishes articles in English, French, German, Italian, and Spanish. Each issue is devoted to a single topic, sometimes an individual philosopher, and often includes an extensive bibliography. It also carries news and announcements, book reviews, lists of books received, and contents of other journals. It is useful as a representative of European philosophy.

368. **Revue philosophique de Louvain,** 1894- . Louvain: Institut superieur de Philosophie, Université Catholique de Louvain. 3/yr.

Because of its extensive book review and *Chronique* sections – the latter including obituaries and announcements of new journals, bibliographies, and other reference works, meetings and conferences, lecture series and colloquia, awards and prizes—the *Revue philosophique,* like the *Revue internationale* (entry 367), is very helpful for those who wish to keep in touch with European philosophy. Originally titled *Revue néo-scholastique,* it continues to reflect a Neo-Scholastic orientation in many of its articles; but in other respects, including its book listing and reviewing efforts, it strives for broad as well as international coverage. The language is predominantly French, but articles in English appear occasionally and summaries in English (printed at the ends of articles) are standard.

369. **Studies in Soviet Thought,** 1961- . Dordrecht, Netherlands: D. Reidel. 8/yr. (somewhat irregular).

For anyone interested in philosophical thought and developments in the Soviet Union and, to some extent, other Soviet-bloc countries, *Studies in Soviet Thought* is an important vehicle. It is presently sponsored by the Institute of East-European Studies, University of Fribourg, Switzerland; the Center for East Europe and Russia at Boston College; and the Seminar for Political Theory and Philosophy at the University of Munich. Each issue has four or five articles and discussions, mostly in English but sometimes in French or German, and a half dozen or so book reviews. Periodic bibliographies carry forward the *Bibliographie der sowjetischen Philosophie,* discontinued as a separate publication after 1968 (see entry 177). It should be borne in mind that this is a journal *about,* not *of,* Soviet philosophy. (A sampling of articles from Soviet journals, in translation, is published in the quarterly *Soviet Studies in Philosophy*, 1962- , White Plains, N.Y.: M. E. Sharpe. The same publisher also issues *Chinese Studies in Philosophy,* 1967- , similar in concept.)

14

PRINCIPAL RESEARCH CENTERS, PROFESSIONAL ASSOCIATIONS, AND OTHER PHILOSOPHICAL ORGANIZATIONS

I. RESEARCH CENTERS, COUNCILS, AND INSTITUTES

370. **Center for Bioethics, Kennedy Institute of Ethics.** Founded 1971. Dr. Edmund Pellegrino, director. Georgetown University, Washington, D.C. 20057. (202) 625-2371. Library, (202) 625-2383.

Most prominent among the ongoing projects of the Center for Bioethics is the preparation of the annual *Bibliography of Bioethics* (entry 127) and the corresponding computerized database, BIOETHICSLINE (entry 174). Other regular publications include a monthly current awareness service, *New Titles in Bioethics* (1975-), and *Scope Notes.* Additional publications result periodically from the center's research and service activities; the *Encyclopedia of Bioethics* (entry 57) is a major past effort. Doris Goldstein's 1982 *Bioethics: A Guide to Information Sources* (entry 140) is based on holdings of the center's extensive library. An Intensive Bioethics course is sponsored annually.

371. **Center for Dewey Studies.** Founded 1961. Jo Ann Boydston, director. Southern Illinois University, 807 South Oakland, Carbondale, Ill. 62901. (618) 453-2629.

The center has been engaged in publishing a collected edition of John Dewey's works, various bibliographies, and other tools to aid research on Dewey (cf. entries 220, 221, 222, and 322). More generally, it promotes Dewey scholarship by collecting resources, answering scholars' inquiries, and sponsoring research fellowships and essay contests.

372. **Center for Philosophic Exchange.** Founded 1969. Jack Glickman, director. Department of Philosophy, State University of New York at Brockport, Brockport, N.Y. 14420. (716) 395-2420.

The Center for Philosophic Exchange sponsors public lectures and seminars on a variety of topics, produces and lends videotapes thereof, and publishes papers in its *Annual Proceedings*.

373. **Center for Philosophy and History of Science (CPHS).** Founded 1971. Boston University, 111 Cummington Street, Boston, Mass. 02215. (617) 353-2604.

The CPHS organizes and sponsors research in the philosophy and history of science carried on by faculty members of Boston University and by visiting research associates. It also holds weekly colloquia and one or two research conferences per year. Research results and papers presented at its conferences are widely disseminated in professional journals and books, including the series Boston Studies in Philosophy of Science.

374. **Center for Philosophy and Public Policy (CPPP).** Founded 1976. Henry Shue, director. University of Maryland, College Park, Md. 20742. (301) 454-4103.

The CPPP is an educational and research center concerned with conceptual and ethical aspects of public policy. It sponsors working groups of philosophers, policymakers, and others to study specific issues and problems; develops model curricula and other educational materials; offers experimental courses; and conducts workshops and debates. A quarterly newsletter, *QQ: Report from the Center for Philosophy and Public Policy,* makes its research accessible to a non-academic audience. CPPP activities have also resulted in the publication of monographs on topics as diverse as governmental responsibility in life and death choices, lawyers' roles and ethics, reverse discrimination, energy and the future, and income support.

375. **Center for Philosophy of Science (CPS).** Founded 1960. Nicholas Rescher, director. 615 Thackeray Hall, University of Pittsgurgh, Pa. 15260. (412) 624-1050.

The CPS conducts research in the philosophy and history of science through a sizeable body of resident scholars affiliated with the sponsoring university and through a smaller number of visiting scholars. It issues two monograph series: the Pittsburgh Series in Philosophy and History of Science (California Press) and the CPS Series in Philosophy and History of Science (University Press of America). In addition, it sponsors annual lecture series and conferences and periodic workshops. Closely associated with the CPS are the Archives of Scientific Philosophy in the Twentieth Century, part of the University of Pittsburgh's Hillman Library.

376. **Center for Process Studies.** Founded 1974. John B. Cobb, executive director. 1325 North College, Claremont, Calif. 91711. (714) 626-3521, ext. 224.

The center's mission is to promote interest in and discussion of Process philosophy, particularly as represented by Alfred North Whitehead and Charles Hartshorne. It has over four hundred dues-paying members, many affiliated with regional groups. It holds conferences, seminars, and lectures; sponsors visiting scholars; publishes the journal *Process Studies* (1971- , quarterly) and a quarterly newsletter; and maintains a comprehensive library on Whitehead and Hartshorne and, more selectively, other Process thinkers.

377. **Center for the Study of Ethics in the Professions (CSEP).** Founded 1976. Mark S. Frankel, director. ITT Center, Illinois Institute of Technology, Chicago, Ill. 60616. (312) 567-3017.

The center conducts and promotes scholarship, education, and service programs dealing with ethical and social issues affecting such professions as engineering, architecture, science, business, and law. It maintains an extensive research library, open to the public, of books, journals, unpublished materials, court decisions, and codes of ethics, as well as a referral bank of groups concerned with applied ethics or professional education. Inquiries by phone or mail are accepted. The center publishes *Perspectives on the Professions* (quarterly) and sponsors other activities eventuating in publications (see, e.g., entry 136).

378. **Council for Philosophical Studies.** Founded 1965. Alan R. Mabe, executive secretary. 203 Dodd Hall, Florida State University, Tallahassee, Fla. 32308. (904) 644-1483.

The Council for Philosophical Studies sponsors a wide range of programs "for the advancement of teaching and research in philosophy." Best known to many American philosophy teachers are its Summer Institutes, which are held throughout the country and bring participants (who receive financial support from the council) in contact with leading scholars in specific fields. It also supports and arranges for visits by leading philosophers to "isolated campuses," directs placement of foreign scholars in American institutions, directs a community college philosophical consultants' program, maintains a speakers' bureau, sponsors competitions, conducts research programs, and issues publications and educational resources related to its programs. Membership on the council is limited and by election.

379. **Hastings Center.** Founded 1969. Dr. Daniel Callahan, director. 360 Broadway, Hastings-on-Hudson, N.Y. 10706. (914) 478-0500.

The Hastings Center is a non-profit research and educational organization concerned with ethical issues in medicine, biology, and social sciences. Its former official name, Institute of Society, Ethics, and the Life Sciences, has recently been dropped in favor of its more familiar "nickname." The center publishes a bimonthly journal, *The Hastings Center Report* (1971-); *IRB: A Review of Human Subjects*

Research (1979- , 10/yr.); and formerly regular but now sporadic bibliographies (see entries 128 and 146). It also conducts and sponsors research, workshops, conferences, and consultation activities.

380. **Husserl-Archiv.** Founded 1938. Kardinaal Mercierplein 2, B-3000, Louvain, Belgium.

In addition to serving as the depository for Edmund Husserl's manuscripts, correspondence, and private library, the Husserl-Archiv conducts a wide range of activities to promote philosophical research in Phenomenology and the dissemination of its results. It publishes two important series: *Husserliana,* which includes a critical edition of Husserl's collected works as well as other documents and studies; and *Phaenomenologica,* concerned with Phenomenology in general, including thinkers other than Husserl. The Archiv also organizes international conferences, acts as an information clearinghouse and coordinating center for Phenomenological scholarship, and maintains an extensive library.

381. **Institut International de Philosophie / International Institute of Philosophy.** Founded 1937. 173 Boulevard Saint-Germain, Paris VI, France.

The institute fosters international contact and cooperation by helping to organize international meetings and promoting exchanges of philosophy professors. It compiles the *Bibliographie de la philosophie* (entry 99), cooperates in publishing the *Répertoire bibliographique de la philosophie* (entry 107), and occasionally issues other publications. Membership is restricted and by election.

382. **Institute for Advancement of Philosophy for Children (IAPC).** Founded 1974. Matthew Lipman, director. Montclair State College, Upper Montclair, N.J. 07043. (201) 893-4277.

The IAPC seeks to assist and advance efforts to teach children to think independently, logically, and ethically. Activities aimed toward this end include educational experiments, in-service education for teachers, development of curricular materials, sponsorship of internships and fellowships, and publication of *Thinking: The Journal of Philosophy for Children* (1979- , quarterly) and a bimonthly *Philosophy for Children Newsletter.* Affiliated with the IAPC are the International Council for Elementary and Secondary School Philosophy and the Center for the Improvement of Reasoning in Early Childhood.

383. **National Council for Critical Analysis.** Founded 1968. Pasqual S. Schievella, director. P.O. Box 137, Port Jefferson, N.Y. 11777. (516) 928-6745.

The council seeks to encourage philosophical dialogue outside traditional academic circles and to promote the introduction of philosophy on all levels of education, including precollege. It publishes the *Journal of Critical Analysis* (1969- , quarterly) and the *Journal of Pre-College Philosophy* (1975- , quarterly). Members include about five hundred professionals in education and philosophy.

384. **Philosophy Documentation Center.** Founded 1966. Richard H. Lineback, director. Bowling Green State University, Bowling Green, Ohio 43403. (419) 372-2419.

Since its inception nearly twenty years ago, the Philosophy Documentation Center has grown rapidly both in stature and in the range of its activities revolving around "the collection, storage, and dissemination of bibliographic and other types of information in philosophy." Chief among its activities are the compilation of *The Philosopher's Index* (entry 101), publishing the printed version, and supplying data for the computer-searchable database to DIALOG (entry 108). As a valuable adjunct to this service, the library of its home institution, Bowling Green State University, is able to supply through its Interlibrary Loan Department most of the journal articles and books cited in the *Philosopher's Index*; to keep the demand manageable, however, the library requests that one first try to locate items in other libraries. The PDC also publishes both the *Directory of American Philosophers* (entry 297) and the *International Directory of Philosophy and Philosophers* (entry 300); the series Bibliographies of Famous Philosophers (see, e.g., entries 208, 236, 240, 243, 278, 281, and 294); and three journals which it cosponsors: *American Philosophical Quarterly* (entry 338), *History of Philosophy Quarterly,* and *Teaching Philosophy*. It cosponsors and operates the *Philosophy Research Archives* (see entry 101), acts as the U.S. National Center for the *Bibliographie de la philosophie* (entry 99), typesets philosophical journals, and sells mailing lists of United States and Canadian philosophers.

385. **Royal Institute of Philosophy.** Founded 1925. 14 Gordon Square, London 4C1H OAG, England.

The Royal Institute, whose purpose is "to promote the study of philosophy in all its branches," has about a thousand members, sponsors an annual lecture series, and holds biennial conferences. The lectures are published as supplements to the institute's important journal, *Philosophy* (entry 360), the conference papers in the *Conference Proceedings.*

386. **S.I.U. Translation Center.** Founded 1967. George W. Linden, director. Southern Illinois University at Edwardsville, Edwardsville, Ill. 62026.

The Translation Center gathers information on philosophical translations in progress or recently completed, in order to forestall duplication of effort. Translators are urged to report their projects. Information is published regularly in the back of the *Philosopher's Index* (entry 101). Direct inquiries are also invited.

387. **Social Philosophy and Policy Center.** Founded 1981. Fred D. Miller, Jr., executive director. Bowling Green State University, Bowling Green, Ohio 43403. (419) 378-2706.

This relatively new center seeks "to promote the examination of public policy issues from a philosophical perspective." Main activities include sponsorship of scholarly conferences involving philosophers and political scientists; support of research fellows; maintenance of a library; and publication of a journal, *Social Philosophy and Policy* (1983- , biannual), and a monograph series, Studies in Social Philosophy and Policy.

388. **World Institute for Advanced Phenomenological Research and Learning.** Founded 1975. Anna-Teresa Tymieniecka, president. 348 Payson Road, Belmont, Mass. 02178. (617) 489-3696.

The institute (occasionally referred to as the World Phenomenological Institute) conducts a wide range of programs and activities to promote and consolidate Phenomenological philosophy, particularly of an interdisciplinary character concerned with "the human being and the human condition." Its mission is carried out in part by an academic and administrative staff at the institute, and in part by three affiliated societies: (1) the International Husserl and Phenomenological Research Society, (2) the International Society for Phenomenology and Literature, and (3) the International Society for Phenomenology and the Human Condition. Research seminars are conducted frequently, including an annual seminar in Cambridge, Massachusetts, known as the Boston Forum for the Interdisciplinary Philosophy of the Human Being. Proceedings of the Boston Forum and other institute-sponsored research are published in *Analecta Husserliana: The Yearbook of Phenomenological Research* (1971- , Dordrecht, Netherlands: D. Reidel). Other publishing efforts include the *Phenomenology Information Bulletin: A Review of Phenomenological Ideas and Trends* (1976-), and a series, The Phenomenology of Man and of the Human Condition.

II. PROFESSIONAL ASSOCIATIONS AND SOCIETIES

389. **Allgemeine Gesellschaft für Philosophie in Deutschland.** Founded 1948. [Address changes annually with change of officers.]

The principal association of professional philosophers in West Germany, the Allgemeine Gesellschaft holds regular meetings and conferences and publishes two journals: *Allgemeine Zeitschrift für Philosophie* (1976- , 3/yr.) and *Zeitschrift für philosophische Forschung* (1947- , quarterly).

390. **American Catholic Philosophical Association (ACPA).** Founded 1926. Catholic University of America, Washington, D.C. 20064. (202) 635-5518.

With some sixteen hundred members, the ACPA is the second largest philosophical association in the United States. It holds an annual national meeting and quarterly regional meetings, bestows awards for service to the profession, operates a placement service, and has committees on research, publication, college teaching, and other concerns. It publishes an important journal, *New Scholasticism* (entry 356), and *Proceedings of the ACPA*.

391. **American Philosophical Association (APA).** Founded 1900. David A. Hoekema, executive secretary. University of Delaware, Newark, Del. 19711. (302) 451-1112.

Numbering some sixty-five hundred members in 1985, the APA is the major United States association, gathering under its wings professional philosophers of every stripe and shade. It comprises three regional divisions—Eastern, Western, and Pacific—each with its own president and executive committee and each holding an annual conference (usually in late December, March, and April, respectively). There is no strict demarcation of divisional lines, and it is not uncommon for members of one division to attend and even to present papers at other divisions' conferences. National affairs and coordination are handled by a board of officers and executive secretary, with the help of divisional presidents and representatives and the chairs of five standing national committees. The *Proceedings and Addresses of the APA* (5/yr., subscription available to non-members) contains the programs and presidential addresses of the divisional meetings, news of the association, information on grants and fellowships, items on teaching philosophy, a philosophical calendar, and other announcements. Other publications include *Jobs in Philosophy*, listing available positions, and newsletters on philosophy and law, philosophy and medicine, and teaching philosophy.

A large number of smaller organizations hold meetings in conjunction with the regional APA conferences, and are listed in the conference programs.

392. **American Society for Aesthetics.** C. W. Post Center, Long Island University, Greenvale, N.Y. 11548. (516) 299-2341.

This association of some eight hundred philosophers and non-philosophers "interested in the study of the arts from a philosophic, scientific, historical, critical, or educational point of view" publishes the *Journal of Aesthetics and Art Criticism* (entry 348) and a newsletter, holds annual meetings, and in other ways promotes research, discussion, and publication in aesthetics.

393. **American Society for Political and Legal Philosophy (ASPLP).** Founded 1955. Martin P. Golding, secretary/treasurer, Department of Philosophy, Duke University, Durham, N.C. 27708. (919) 648-3838.

The ASPLP's purpose is to encourage "interdisciplinary exploration, treatment and discussion of those issues of political and legal philosophy that are of common interest" to the social sciences, law, and philosophy. It publishes an annual, *Nomos* (1958-). Membership is by nomination and election. Annual conferences are coordinated with meetings, in rotation, of the American Philosophical Association Eastern Division, American Political Science Association, and Association of American Law Schools.

394. **Aristotelian Society.** Founded 1880. 31 W. Heath Drive, London NW11 7QG.

One of the oldest philosophical bodies in existence, the Aristotelian Society is not devoted to Aristotelianism but is one of Britain's principal general interest philosophical associations. It holds meetings every two weeks and an annual joint session with the Mind Association (entry 409). It publishes *Proceedings of the Aristotelian Society* (1887- , annual) and supplementary volumes.

395. **Association for Symbolic Logic.** Founded 1936. Department of Mathematics, 1409 W. Green Street, University of Illinois, Urbana, Ill. 61801. (217) 333-3350.

The association promotes research and critical studies on formal or mathematical logic and related fields, and publishes the *Journal of Symbolic Logic* (entry 351). Many of its approximately fourteen hundred members are mathematicians. Annual meetings are usually held in conjunction with alternate meetings of the American Mathematical Society and the American Philosophical Association Eastern Division.

396. **Australasian Association of Philosophy.** Founded 1923. Department of Philosophy, La Trobe University, Bundoora, Melbourne, Vic. 3083, Australia.

The association has some four hundred members, mostly professors of philosophy, throughout Australia and New Zealand. The "-asian" in its name and in the title of its journal, the *Australasian Journal of Philosophy* (1923- , quarterly), does not signify any special interest in oriental philosophy; the orientation of the membership and of the journal is predominantly Analytical. (Contributors to the journal need not be members of the association, and often include British and American philosophers.)

397. **Bertrand Russell Society.** Founded 1974. 3802 N. Kenneth Ave., Chicago, Ill. 60641. (312) 286-0676.

The society, which had some three hundred members in 1985, seeks to further understanding of Russell's work and to promote ideas and causes he believed in. In addition to holding meetings, it presents an annual award, supports doctoral research with an annual grant, maintains a library, and publishes the *Russell Society News*. Members also receive *Russell,* a semiannual publication of the Russell Archives, McMaster University, Hamilton, Ontario, Canada.

398. **British Society for the Philosophy of Science.** Founded 1960. Honorable secretary. Philosophy Department, London School of Economics, Houghton Street, London WC2A 2AE.

The society publishes the *British Journal for the Philosophy of Science* (entry 341) and holds monthly meetings and an annual conference.

399. **British Society of Aesthetics.** Founded 1960. Department of Philosophy, Birkbeck College, Malet Street, London WC1.

The society publishes the *British Journal of Aesthetics* (entry 342) and promotes study, research, and discussion in the field of aesthetics. It holds an annual conference and periodic colloquia.

400. **Canadian Philosophical Association / Association Canadienne de Philosophie.** Founded 1957. Simard Hall, University of Ottawa, Ottawa K1N 6N5. (613) 238-2601.

True to its bilingual name, this eight-hundred-or-so-member association embraces both English-speaking and French-speaking philosophers and publishes a bilingual journal, *Dialogue* (1962- , quarterly). It holds an annual meeting. Membership is open to faculty and students at institutions of higher learing, associate membership to others interested in its objectives.

401. **Conference of Philosophical Societies.** Founded 1977. Richard T. De George, chair. c/o Department of Philosophy, University of Kansas, Lawrence, Kans. 66045. (913) 864-3976.

The conference serves as a coordinating body for joint action, dissemination of information, and discussion of common concerns for American philosophical societies (forty-seven as of 1984). It issues a *Philosophical Calendar* (bimonthly) and meets annually at the American Philosophical Association Eastern Division conference.

402. **Hegel Society of America.** Founded 1969. Department of Philosophy, Villanova University, Villanova, Pa. 19085.

Aiming to promote the study of Hegel's philosophy, its context and influence, and also to promote original philosophic thought in the spirit of Hegel, the society holds biennial meetings and symposia, publishes their proceedings, and acts as a clearinghouse for information about Hegel scholarship through its journal, *The Owl of Minerva* (1969- , quarterly).

403. **International Association for Philosophy of Law and Social Philosophy.** Founded 1909. c/o Institute of Sociology, Parkweg 12, Ch-4051, Basel, Switzerland. **American Section (AMINTAPHIL).** Founded 1963. Rex Martin. Department of Philosophy, University of Kansas, Lawrence, Kans. 66045. (913) 864-3976.

This international organization of about two thousand members promotes research in and discussion of philosophy of law and social philosophy through its quarterly publication, *Archiv für Rechts- und Sozial-philosophie / Archives for Philosophy of Law and Social Philosophy* (1907- , quarterly), and through world congresses held every two years. The American Section holds its own plenary conferences every eighteen to twenty-four months and issues a newsletter and occasional other publications. Membership requires scholarly qualifications and is subject to approval by two members of the executive board.

404. **International Federation of Philosophical Societies / Fédération Internationales des Sociétés de Philosophie (FISP).** Founded 1948. Evandro Agazzi, secretary-general. Seminaire de Philosophie, Université de Fribourg, CH-1700 Fribourg, Switzerland.

The FISP organizes the quinquennial International Congress of Philosophy, the proceedings of which it publishes, and also promotes other international activities. Among several publishing efforts, it cosponsors publication of the *Bibliographie de la philosophie* (entry 99) and *Chroniques de la philosophie* (every ten years). It has approximately one hundred member societies worldwide, and is in turn one of twelve international humanities organizations federated to the International Council for Philosophy and Humanistic Studies (ICPHS), organized under the auspices of UNESCO.

405. **International Society for Neoplatonic Studies.** Founded 1973. R. Baine Harris, executive director. Department of Philosophy, Old Dominion University, Norfolk, Va. 23508. (804) 440-3861.

The society has some five hundred members in the United States and abroad, including philosophers, classicists, historians, and religious and literary scholars. It publishes an annual newsletter, *Neoplatonic Studies*, and sponsors a book series, Studies in Neoplatonism: Ancient and Modern.

406. **International Society for the Study of Medieval Philosophy / Société internationale pour l'Etude de la Philosophie Médiévale (SIEPM).** Founded 1958. c/o Institut supérieur de Philosophie, Collège Thomas More, SH2, Chemin d' Aristote 1, 1348 Louvain-la-Neuve, Belgium.

The society, which claims members in forty-six countries, promotes study of medieval thought and international collaboration in this field by, among other activities, organizing international congresses every five years and publishing the annual *Bulletin de philosophie médiévale* (1954-).

407. **International Union of the History and Philosophy of Science; Division of Logic, Methodology and Philosophy of Science.** Founded 1956. 12 Rue Colbert, Paris II, France.

Among its many activities, this body organizes periodic international congresses devoted to the areas indicated by its name, and cosponsors the *Journal of Symbolic Logic* (entry 351). It is one of two divisions of the IUHPS, the other being concerned with the history of science.

408. **Metaphysical Society of America.** Founded 1950. Mark Jordan, secretary-treasurer. P.O. Box 903, Notre Dame, Ind. 46556. (219) 239-7172.

The stated purpose of the six-to-seven-hundred-member society is "to turn the attention of the philosophical community from more limited objectives to concern with the ultimate questions of philosophy, which are questions about the nature of reality." It promulgates no particular answers to such questions. A national meeting is held annually. New members must be sponsored by two current members.

409. **Mind Association.** Founded 1900. 108 Cowley Road, Oxford OX4 1JF, England.

Main activities of the Mind Association are to publish its prestigious journal, *Mind* (entry 354), and to organize an annual joint conference with the Aristotelian Society (see entry 394).

410. **Phi Sigma Tau.** Founded 1955. Lee C. Rice, national executive secretary. Department of Philosophy, Marquette University, Milwaukee, Wis. 53223. (414) 224-6857.

A national college honor society in philosophy reporting 120 chapters and over fifteen thousand members in 1985, Phi Sigma Tau seeks to promote interest and study in philosophy among students at accredited institutions. Its semiannual journal, *Dialogue* (1956-), publishes papers by graduate and undergraduate students. A newsletter also appears twice a year.

411. **Philosophy of Education Society.** Founded 1941. Emily E. Robertson, 128 Huntington Hall, Syracuse University, Syracuse, N.Y. 13210. (315) 432-3343.

The society's roughly 650 members include many professors of education and others in the field of education, as well as professional philosophers. It cosponsors the leading journal dealing with philosophical issues of education, *Educational Theory* (1950- , quarterly) and publishes an annual *Proceedings*. Annual national meetings are held in the spring.

412. **Philosophy of Science Association.** 18 Morrill Hall, Department of Philosophy, Michigan State University, East Lansing, Mich. 48824. (517) 353-9392.

The association, which has about one thousand members, endeavors "to further studies and free discussion from diverse standpoints in the field of philosophy of science." Principal activities include biennial national meetings and publications of the journal *Philosophy of Science* (entry 364), a newsletter, proceedings of the biennial meetings, and *Current Research in Philosophy of Science*.

413. **Société Française de Philosophie.** Founded 1901. 12 Rue Colbert, 75002 Paris, France.

The society publishes the leading French philosophical journal, *Revue de métaphysique et de morale* (1893- , quarterly), as well as the *Bulletin de la Société Française de Philosophie* (1901- , quarterly). Historical projects have included sponsorship of (and members' contributions to) Lalande's *Vocabulaire technique et critique de la philosophie* (see entry 31) and organization of international congresses on Descartes and on Bergson.

414. **Society for Ancient Greek Philosophy.** Department of Philosophy, State University of New York at Binghamton, Binghamton, N.Y. 13901. (607) 798-2886.

The society, which has some five hundred members, seeks to further the study of ancient philosophical texts and to promote coordination between philosophers and classical scholars. It holds meetings in conjunction with the American Philological Association as well as with the American Philosophical Association divisions. It has published two volumes of *Essays in Ancient Greek Philosophy* (SUNY Press, 1971 and 1983).

415. **Society for Asian and Comparative Philosophy.** Founded 1968. Department of Philosophy and Religion, Northland College, Ashland, Wis. 54806.

To serve scholars in the areas of Asian and comparative philosophy, the society sponsors workshops and research conferences, issues a newsletter, and sponsors the journal *Philosophy East and West* (entry 363) as well as a monograph series. It reported some three hundred members in 1985.

416. **Society for Phenomenology and Existential Philosophy.** Founded 1961. Department of Philosophy, State University of New York at Stony Brook, Stony Brook, N.Y. 11794. (516) 246-6561.

The society seeks to further interest in Phenomenology, Existentialism, and other Continental philosophies, and to promote Phenomenological studies in human or behavioral sciences. Its more than nine hundred members include professors of psychology, psychiatry, literature, the arts, and social sciences, as well as philosophers. It sponsors a series, Selected Studies in Phenomenological and Existential Philosophy, volumes of which have been published by Nijhoff and the SUNY Press every two or three years. The society holds an annual meeting in the fall.

417. **Society for the Advancement of American Philosophy.** Founded 1972. Fairfield University, Fairfield, Conn. 06430. (203) 255-5411.

The society aims to promote research and original creative works in American philosophy, primarily by serving as a forum for the exchange of information. It has some five hundred members. It holds an annual meeting, as well as regional meetings concurrently with the American Philosophical Association divisions.

418. **Society for the Philosophical Study of Marxism.** Founded 1962. 1426 Merritt Drive, El Cajon, Calif. 92020. (714) 447-1641.

Formerly the Society for the Philosophical Study of Dialectical Materialism, this organization aims "to provide interested philosophers of all viewpoints with opportunities to clarify issues and treat problems pertaining to Marxism." It issues a newsletter and has published some monographs. Meetings are with the American Philosophical Association divisions and one national meeting every four years.

419. **Society for Women in Philosophy.** Founded 1971. [Addresses of divisional officers change annually.]

The society holds meetings in conjunction with the American Philosophical Association divisional conferences, publishes a semiannual newsletter, and distributes a directory of women philosophers available for employment. Divisions (as of 1985) include Eastern, Midwest, Southwest, and Pacific.

420. **Society of Christian Philosophers.** Founded 1978. Department of Philosophy, Calvin College, Grand Rapids, Mich. 49506. (616) 957-6412 or 957-6488.

The society promotes fellowship among Christian philosophers and philosophical discussion of issues that arise from their Christian commitment. Its journal, *Faith and Philosophy* (1984- , quarterly), welcomes submissions on issues related to Christian faith "from those who do as well as those who do not share its Christian commitment." Meetings are held in conjunction with the American Philosophical Association divisional conferences and the American Catholic Philosophical Association conference; additional regional gatherings occur throughout the year.

421. **World Union of Catholic Philosophical Societies (WUCPS).** Founded 1948. Rev. George F. McLean, secretary-general. School of Philosophy, Catholic University of America, Washington, D.C. 20064. (202) 635-5636.

A coordinating body of Catholic philosophical societies in many countries, the WUCPS also conducts seminars and has sponsored a project on the mediation of values to social life, involving regional studies and reports on present-day values of the cultures of Africa, Latin America, India, and North America-Europe. Meetings of the WUCPS are held annually, a general assembly every five years.

AUTHOR/TITLE INDEX

Numbers in this index refer to entries, not pages. The letter "n" following an entry number indicates that the author or title is mentioned in the annotation.

SUBJECT INDEX

Numbers in this index normally refer to entries, not pages. Page references to topics discussed in the introduction (chapter 1) are preceded by the letters "p." or "pp." The letter "n" following an entry number indicates that the relevant item is mentioned in the annotation.